Infants,
Toddlers, and
Caregivers

Infants, Toddlers, and Caregivers

Janet Gonzalez-Mena
Napa Valley College

Dianne Widmeyer Eyer
Cañada College,
Redwood City

Mayfield Publishing Company
Mountain View, California

To Magda Gerber

Library of Congress Cataloging-in-Publication Data
Gonzalez-Mena, Janet.
  Infants, toddlers, and caregivers.

  Bibliography: p.
  Includes index.
  1. Child care—United States. 2. Child development—
United States. 3. Education, Preschool—United States—
Activity programs. I. Eyer, Dianne Widmeyer. II. Title.
HQ778.7.U6G66 1989   362.7'12   88–13715
ISBN 0–87484–879–2

Manufactured in the United States of America

10 9 8 7 6

Mayfield Publishing Company®
1240 Villa Street
Mountain View, California 94041

Sponsoring editor, Franklin C. Graham; production editor, Sondra Glider; manuscript
editor, Sylvia Stein; text and cover designer, Victoria Vandeventer; illustrations, Melissa Leith
Ash-Askins; cover photographer, Elizabeth Crews. The text was set in 10/12 New Baskerville
Roman by BookMasters and printed on 50# Finch Opaque by Malloy Lithographing, Inc.

Infants, Toddlers, and Caregivers is a revised edition of *Infancy and Caregiving*. © 1980 by
Mayfield Publishing Company.

Contents

Part 3   Focus on the Program   161

Preface

This book can be used for training caregivers in infant-toddler centers, teachers in day care or preschool programs that include two year olds, and family day care providers who serve infants and toddlers. It can also be used for parent education.

The people who will find it useful include community college and four-year college teachers, public health nurses, social workers, counselors, parent educators, high school child development teachers and others who deal with caregivers. Program directors and training coordinators will find it valuable as a guide for training staff.

The philosophy of caregiving that is spelled out in the ten principles in the first chapters and that underlies the rest of the book comes from Magda Gerber and Tom Forrest, M.D., who co-directed the Demonstration Infant Program in Palo Alto, California, from 1972 to 1977. Magda Gerber is still teaching the philosophy in her present program, Resources for Infant Educarers, based in Los Angeles, California. The original philosophy upon which Magda Gerber has built and which this book reflects was conceived by Emmi Pikler, M.D., in Hungary, and is well known in parts of Europe.

The content of this book is deeply imbedded in research, but that research has not been cited to the point of exhaustion. Since this book is designed to be both practical and easily understood, theory and research are explained mostly in terms of practical application. It has been said that education should consist of the "what" and the "so what." The facts, information, theory, and concepts are the "what." The importance of these is the "so what." We have tried very hard to include the "so what" throughout the book. It is not enough for caregivers to have knowledge; they must know what to do with it. This book makes very clear that knowing how to act is as important as having a head full of information. In fact, too much information can get in the way of action, creating a condition known as "analysis paralysis." For that reason this book has been carefully designed to present information in a way that averts that condition. Nothing is worse for infants and toddlers than a caregiver whose education has made it difficult for him or her to take action.

This book is organized in such a way that the information that makes it unique comes right away in Part 1. The emphasis is on the caregiver's actions and relationships and how they make up the curriculum in infant-toddler programs, both center based and in family day care.

Part 2 presents basic child development information along with the curriculum implications of that information (the "what" and the "so what"). This part, too, reflects the basic philosophy found throughout.

Part 3 looks at additional infant-toddler day care components—environments and adult relationships. These are examined from a programmatic point of view in both center and family day care settings.

The appendix includes an Environmental Chart which combines the information from all three parts into one concise but comprehensive chart designed for practical use in program design and implementation. The chart tells you what to do when and with what, based on infants' and toddlers' specific stage-related developmental needs.

Also included in the appendix is a checklist for determining quality in infant-toddler programs.

Throughout the book the readers are asked to think back to the past or asked how they would feel under certain circumstances. The purpose of these questions is to help readers reflect on their own experience in order to gain understanding and perspective as well as to find their own ways of doing things. We want readers not only to gain in knowledge as well as application of that knowledge, but also to truly understand little children. Above all we want them to feel confidence in their ability to relate to very young children in whole and healthy ways. The goal is that each reader, in his or her own individual way, become the best caregiver possible.

As co-authors faced with the problem of how to make our two voices speak as one to the reader, we use the first person singular (I) throughout the text.

Introduction

When we first began writing about infants and toddlers in the mid 1970s, child care outside the home in this country generally started at the age of three. The idea of infant-toddler care (except for in-home care and family day care) was new to America. No one knew if it was here to stay. The ghosts of yesteryear's orphan babies, ruined by institutionalization, hovered over the child care field and led many to question whether infants and toddlers belong in day care at all.

Things have changed. The children graduating from the early infant-toddler centers have proved that these can be good places for young children to spend their first years. The key is *quality*. And quality is what this book is about.

Another change has been the dramatic increase in the *demand* for out-of-home care for our youngest citizens. While research was still deciding that it's okay to care for infants and toddlers in groups, mothers were marching off to work in greater numbers than ever before, and these numbers continue to grow. Finding quality care for their infants is a major concern of these parents. Although many infant and infant-toddler programs have come into being in recent years, they haven't kept pace with the ever growing demand. Family day care has not been able to meet the need either. Waiting lists testify to the huge number of children not being served—children of all ages, but especially infants and toddlers. As we move into the 1990s, child care is commanding increased attention as our society asks who will care for our children while a majority of mothers work outside the home.

One of us, Janet Gonzalez-Mena, became concerned with this question in the mid 1970s when she discovered Magda Gerber and the world of infant care while working at Cañada College. She became an intern in Gerber's program, the Demonstration Infant Program (co-directed by Tom Forrest, M.D.), where she learned the philosophy on which this book is based.

A few years later she became even more concerned with this question while directing a family day-care program for Family Service Agency in San Mateo County. Her job there was to oversee a network of family day-care homes, some of which served infants and toddlers. As the need for infant-toddler care grew, she helped open an infant center that served children from birth to two years of age, applying the philosophy she learned from Gerber and Forrest. It was during this period that the two of us wrote *Infancy and Caregiving*, which the present book—*Infants, Toddlers, and Caregivers*— now replaces.

Infancy and Caregiving focused on infants and younger toddlers. For a few years there existed a gap as infant programs came into being, serving mostly children from a few months to two years. They provided beginning child care. But when the child reached two, parents were faced with the fact that "preschools," as many child care programs were called, only took children who were two years, nine months old. They also usually required that children be toilet trained. This gap in care left parents with a dilemma. The two to three year old didn't seem to fit anyone's program, except of course for the family day-care providers, who have been, and still are, the backbone of the child care system in this country.

The gap has been closed now, and it's no longer next to impossible to find care for the two to three year old. Infant programs have expanded upward to include toddlers of this age range. And programs for preschoolers have expanded downward to include the two year old. Therefore this book concerns itself with an age range of birth to three years.

In this book the youngest children—those from newborn to walking—are called infants. The children who are walking (from about a year old) to two years are called young toddlers. The children from two to three are called older toddlers. Children from three to five are called preschoolers.

Although this book will surely be of value to parents, it speaks directly to caregivers—those who plan to or already care for children under three outside of the child's home. These adults may be beginning students in child care and development classes, or they may be family day-care providers or infant-toddler center workers. Some may be toddler teachers in preschool programs.

What to call the adults in this book was a concern. Adults in the teacher/caregiver role go by different titles, depending on where they work.

Napa Valley College, where Gonzalez-Mena now teaches, has a Child Care
Lab School where all the adults are called "teachers," regardless of the age of
the children they work with. Magda Gerber coined the term "educarers,"
which she uses to call the people she trains to work with children under
three. We decided to call the adults in this book "caregivers" to simplify
matters and to emphasize the importance of "caring" in programs for the
youngest children. The caregiver role incorporates that of teacher, educator,
child rearer, and surrogate parent.

As infant and toddler programs increased in number, many directors and caregivers struggled with what it means to "educate" a child under
three. In planning programs for the very young, questions of curriculum
came up. To define education and to answer these curriculum questions,
some looked to school-type models. But infants and toddlers don't thrive in
school settings like they do in warm, rich environments modeled after
homes. And they don't learn best from school-like activities, especially those
that are teacher directed and group oriented. The prime times for infants
and toddlers to learn are during one-to-one interactions between an adult
and a child, that is, during caregiving times. So to the uninitiated, very little
that occurs during the day in an infant center, or even a toddler program,
looks educational. One of the purposes of this book is to help people better
articulate to the uninitiated how infant-toddler care is much more than just
custodial care, but is truly educational as well.

As in *Infancy and Caregiving,* respect is the foundation of the philosophy on which this book is built. Is respect different from kindness and
warmth? The answer is yes. What does it mean to "respect" infants and
toddlers? The answer to that question is embedded in every page in this
book. The beginning of the answer lies in the ten principles on which the
book is based:

1. Involve infants and toddlers in things that concern them. Don't
work around them or distract them to get the job done faster.

2. Invest in quality time, when you are totally available to individual infants and toddlers. Don't settle for supervising groups
without focusing (more than just briefly) on individual children.

3. Learn each child's unique ways of communicating (cries, words,
movements, gestures, facial expressions, body positions) and
teach them yours. Don't underestimate their ability to communicate even though their verbal language skills may be non-
existent or minimal.

4. Invest in time and energy to build a total person (concentrate on
the "whole child"). Don't focus on cognitive development alone
or look at it as separate from total development.

5. Respect infants and toddlers as worthy people. Don't treat them as objects or cute little empty-headed creatures to be manipulated.

6. Be honest about your feelings around infants and toddlers. Don't pretend to feel something that you don't or not to feel something that you do.

7. Model the behavior you want to teach. Don't preach.

8. Recognize problems as learning opportunities, and let infants and toddlers try to solve their own difficulties. Don't rescue them, constantly make life easy for them, or try to protect them from all problems.

9. Build security by teaching trust. Don't teach distrust by being undependable or often inconsistent.

10. Be concerned about the *quality* of development in each stage. Don't rush infants and toddlers to reach developmental milestones.

These principles are shown in action throughout the book, especially in Part 1. They are supported by the information on infant and toddler development in Part 2. They underlie the information on programs in Part 3.

Care has been taken throughout the book to point out the pitfalls of promoting gender-role stereotypes. Narrowing children's expectations about what they are capable of starts right from the cradle as adults give messages in many subtle ways about what boys can and should do and what girls can and should do. If gender identification is to be a freeing factor, rather than a limiting one, in the next generations, attention must be given to adult expectations, behavior, and messages around infants and toddlers.

Although this book does not have a multicultural perspective, because it is based on a cohesive philosophy, we appeal to the reader throughout to take cultural differences into account. Many parents have little choice about child care, and people with a very different philosophy may find themselves in your program. Be sensitive to their needs and what they ask for their children. You don't have to give up your own way of looking at things, but if you try to see a point of conflict from a parent's perspective, you may feel ready to bend or negotiate on some points. Put yourself in the parents' shoes, and you'll be a better caregiver for their children.

This book is practical, not just theoretical. Therefore, specifics on what to do based on implications of theory abound throughout. Although this is not an "activity" book, and it does not use an "activity approach" to learning, there are a number of ideas for "things to do" with infants and toddlers spread throughout. We resisted the idea of writing an "activity book" because, without an underlying philosophy and a focus on relationships that come from caregiving, activities by themselves are useless. What infants and toddlers need are attention to their physical and psychological needs; a relationship with someone they can trust; respect; a safe, healthy, and developmentally appropriate environment; chances to interact with other infants and toddlers; and freedom to explore using all their senses. The purpose of this book is to show, in as visual a way as possible, just how all those elements fit together in a day-care program.

Part 1
Focus on the Caregiver

Chapter 1
Principles of Caregiving

This book emphasizes relationships—those between caregivers and very young children. Relationships don't just spring into being—they grow. They grow from a number of interactions. So this book is also about interactions—not just any kind of interactions, but what I call "three-r" interactions (those that are *r*espectful, *r*esponsive, and *r*eciprocal). Here is an example of a "three-r" interaction.

> A five month old is lying on the floor with several toys scattered within reach. She is contentedly surveying the six other infants and toddlers who are in the room with her. Reaching now and then, she caresses a toy first with her eyes, then with her hands. As we look more closely, we can see that some suspicious moisture has crept onto the infant's outer clothes in the area of her bottom. We are seeing a very contented, but a very wet, young person. A step is heard, and the infant's eyes travel in the direction of the sound. Then we see a pair of legs and feet traveling along in the direction of the infant. A voice says: "Jennifer, I'm wondering how you're getting along."
>
> The legs move over close to the blanket, and the rest of the person appears. She sees a kindly face come close. Jennifer smiles and makes a cooing noise. The caregiver responds, then notices the dampness of the clothing. "Oh, Jennifer, you need a change," she says. Jennifer responds by smiling and cooing.

Reaching out her hands, the caregiver says, "I'm going to pick you up now." Jennifer responds to the gesture and words with an ever-so-slight body movement. She continues to smile and coo. The caregiver picks her up. As they walk across the room, Jennifer reaches for a toy lying just out of reach on a shelf.

"I know you want that toy, but you have to wait a few minutes," says the caregiver with understanding. "First I am going to change your diapers," she adds with gentle firmness. She lays Jennifer on the changing table.

Jennifer's attention wanders around the room. The caregiver talks to her, bringing Jennifer's gaze back to her own face.

"Look Jennifer, I'm taking off the wet diaper." She shows her the diaper. Jennifer watches, but then starts to squirm, fussing a little.

"See where the diaper goes?" The caregiver once again retrieves Jennifer's attention by making a production of disposing of the wet diaper.

"Now the dry diaper, Jennifer. . . . " The caregiver shows her the fresh diaper. Jennifer reaches for it. "Yes, you can touch it," responds the caregiver.

"Lift up," says the caregiver, patting her bottom. Jennifer is distracted by a noise in another part of the room. The caregiver waits. Then when she has her attention again, she repeats, "Lift up, please." She raises Jennifer's bottom as she says this and slips the dry diaper under.

"Susan, look—I fixed it!" says a young voice.

The caregiver keeps her attention focused on Jennifer. "I can't come right now, Greg. I'm changing Jennifer. I'll be with you when I'm finished."

Jennifer has begun to squirm. She tries to roll over. "We're almost finished now." The caregiver pats her, bringing her back to the task. "Look, I'm fastening it now."

Jennifer squirms to look. "That's a girl, pay attention." The caregiver smiles.

"Okay, that's it; we're finished. Want to come up now?" She reaches out for her.

Jennifer stretches out her arms, making bubbling noises at the same time. The caregiver imitates her sounds. Both laugh. Then the caregiver picks Jennifer up in her arms and gives her a hug.

Notice the chain reaction as the caregiver responded to Jennifer, who responded to her, who in turn responded to her response. This scene illustrates a responsive interaction chain that is the basis of effective caregiving. A number of interactions such as this kind of diaper changing builds a partnership. This feeling of being part of a team instead of an object to be manipulated is vital to wholesome development. This scene illustrates principle 1.

Principle 1: Involve Infants and Toddlers in Things That Concern Them

Jennifer doesn't have things done to her. She and her caregiver do them together. If the caregiver had given Jennifer a toy to play with to keep her occupied while she changed her diaper, the whole tone of the scene would have been different. The partnership would have vanished, and in its place would have been a distracted child and a caregiver dealing with a damp bottom and a wet diaper instead of a whole child. Or if she had distracted her with other sorts of entertainment, the caregiver still would have had Jennifer's attention, but focus would have been on fun and games rather than on the task at hand.

The caregiver's primary goal in this scene was to keep Jennifer involved in the interaction as well as focused on her own body and on what was happening to it. Diapering then became an "educational experience" through which Jennifer increased attention span, body awareness, cooperation. A number of experiences like these give Jennifer an education in human relations from which she can build her whole outlook on life and people.

Why should diapering be the first example in this book? Diapering involves one-to-one interactions, and it occurs regularly. Imagine the amount of time spent in diapering each child each day. That time adds up. If the time spent together is quality time—that is, time when both partners are fully present, focused on the same task at hand—diapering can provide a lot of educational time.

There is a rumor that infants and toddlers have short attention spans. They can't pay attention to anything for very long, some people say. You can test that rumor for yourself. Watch an infant or toddler who is actually involved in something that concerns and interests him. Clock the amount of time he spends on the task or event. You may be surprised at what a long attention span infants and toddlers have when they are interested because they are involved. Consider how long Jennifer paid attention to her diapering because she was involved in the task.

Think about a time when you were involved in a respectful, reciprocal interaction. You don't have to be an infant to experience the focused attention of someone else. This can happen when someone is teaching you something. Or it can happen when you are in the doctor's office. Can you use your own experience to help you understand the benefits that babies derive by being involved in the things that concern them?

Principle 2: Invest in Quality Time

The scene between Jennifer and her caregiver is a good example of one kind of quality time. The caregiver was fully present. That is, she was attending to what was going on; her thoughts were not somewhere else. How often caregiving tasks are done routinely, with neither caregiver nor infant present any way but physically! This caregiver was quite conscious of quality time, as is evident by the way she handled Greg's interruption. How much more efficient it would have been to deal with him at the same time she was changing the baby. Obviously it is easy to diaper and talk to someone else at the same time. Yet she valued the time together with Jennifer and apparently had taught Greg about its value. He was probably so willing to leave her alone and wait his turn only because he had experienced quality time himself. Otherwise he might well have continued to try for her attention. He perhaps knew that when she finished with Jennifer, then he might have some minutes of quality time himself.

Magda Gerber calls the kind of quality time illustrated by the diapering scene "wants something" quality time. The adult and child are involved in a task the caregiver has set up. Diapering, feeding, bathing, and dressing fit into this category of quality time. If the caregiver pays attention to the child and asks in return that the child pay attention, the amount of "wants something" quality time adds up. In child care programs this can provide the one-to-one interactions that may be difficult to attain in a group setting. "Wants something" quality time is educational.

Another kind of equally important quality time is what Magda Gerber calls "wants nothing" quality time. This happens when caregivers make themselves available without directing the action, for instance, just sitting near babies, fully available and responsive but not in charge. Just being with toddlers while they play, responding rather than initiating, describes this type of quality time.

Many psychotherapists attest to the benefits of being fully present to another person without being directive; yet most of us seldom get this kind of attention from the people in our lives. Think for a moment of the delight of having someone's whole attention at your command for more than a moment or so. Can you remember a time when someone was fully available to you without being directive? What was that like for you? Can you understand from your own experience how that might benefit an infant?

This kind of quality time is easy to give, but often not understood or valued. Caregivers just sitting on the floor where babies and toddlers are playing sometimes feel as though they are not doing their job. They want to play the role of teacher, which they interpret as "teaching something." It is very hard for most adults to be around small children and not be directive. Being receptive and responsive is a skill most adults need to learn; it doesn't seem to just come naturally. Try it yourself. Choose a time when you will not initiate, only respond. See how long you can keep in the receptive, responsive mode.

Another kind of quality time, perhaps the most commonly understood, is shared activity. The initiating mode moves back and forth between adult and child during play times as the two enjoy each other's company. These times are often rewarding for the caregiver in ways that the other two kinds of quality time are not.

An interesting aspect of quality time is that a little goes a long way. No one wants (or can stand) intense interaction all the time—even when it is fun and games. Children (and adults) need to be private as well. In infant-toddler programs and in family day care time alone is hard to attain. Some children manage to be alone only by sleeping. Others can focus inwardly and ignore what's going on around them. The adult can help young children gain private time by providing small spaces (see Chapter 12, Physical Environment).

When people never have time alone, they get it by drifting off, by not paying attention, but being elsewhere mentally if not physically. This attitude becomes a habit, so that time spent constantly together tends to become time when the person is "only half there." "Half-there" time, even lots of it, never equals "all-there time."

Being able to "turn off" is an issue for caregivers as well as infants and toddlers. No adult can be expected to be completely present and responsive to others all day every day. Provision must be made for both adults' and babies' needs in programs if the adults are to be effective caregivers.

Of course every person's life is filled with time that is neither quality time nor private time. Children have to learn to live in a busy world of people. They are bound to get ignored, moved from place to place, or worked around sometimes. The point is that there is a difference between quality time and other kinds of time and that all children deserve and need some quality time in their lives.

Quality time is built into the daily routine when diapering, dressing, and feeding become occasions for close one-to-one interactions. In group care where a caregiver is responsible for several babies or a small group of toddlers, paying attention to just one child may be difficult unless caregivers free each other up by taking turns supervising the rest of the children. It is up to the director to ensure that each caregiver be freed at times from responsibility for children other than the one she is changing or feeding. That means that it must be permissible, even encouraged, for a caregiver to focus on just one child.

In family day care where there is no other adult, the caregiver has no one else to turn to when she feeds or diapers a baby. But caregivers can still focus on just one child by setting up a safe environment and encouraging the rest of the children to play on their own. Of course the caregiver must still keep a watchful eye on the group—a skill that can be developed with practice. It's amazing to watch an experienced caregiver give full attention to one child, but still manage to catch a dangerous or forbidden action going on in another part of the room.

Principle 3: Learn Each Child's Unique Ways of Communicating and Teach Them Yours

Notice how the communication between Jennifer and her caregiver worked. The caregiver talked directly to Jennifer about what she was going to do, using body movements that matched her words. Jennifer used her body, facial expressions, and voice to communicate her responses. The caregiver responded to her responses by interpreting, answering, and discussing. The caregiver did not carry on endless chatter. She said little, but what she said carried a lot of meaning, backed up by action. She is teaching Jennifer to listen, not tune out. She is teaching that talking is communication, not distraction. She is teaching words and language in context by talking naturally, not repeating words over and over or using baby talk. She also communicated with her body and with sounds other than words—and she responded to Jennifer's communication (sounds, facial expressions, and body movements). The communication between Jennifer and her caregiver went way beyond words.

Think about someone you know very well. Can you remember some ways that person communicates with you without using words? Facial expressions are obvious ways, but everyone has certain little gestures or actions that give hints about what he or she is feeling. If you make a list of the nonverbal means of communication of someone you know well, you'll see how he or she has a unique system, as we all do. No one knows a baby's or toddler's system as well as those people to whom he or she is attached. For that reason (and others) programs for infants and toddlers should encourage attachment between the children and the caregivers.

Eventually babies come to depend more on words to express themselves and have to rely less on other means of communication. They learn to express needs, wants, ideas, and feelings more and more clearly. They also learn to enjoy language for itself—to play with words, phrases, and sounds. Adult reactions and encouragement to use language facilitate their development. By late toddlerhood most children can express themselves in words, though, of course, they continue to use nonverbal communication throughout their lives.

It is important that young children see adults using words that match their nonverbal communication. If the face and body movements say one thing and the words say something else, children are receiving double messages, which get in the way of true communication. They not only have problems deciding which to believe, but they model after the adults and themselves learn to give double messages. Clear communication is important.

Principle 4: Invest in Time and Energy to Build a Total Person

Because parents realize that the early years are important ones in intellectual growth, they may expect to see some evidence that caregivers are providing "cognitive activities." Their concept of cognitive activities may be based on what they know about preschool. They may expect caregivers to teach such concepts as colors, shapes, even numbers and letters through an activity approach.

On the other side, caregivers, also concerned with intellectual development, may think that the way to promote it is through specialized equipment, exercises, or activities. Books and programs are readily available for a price to, as they say, "stimulate cognitive development." Catalogs and stores are full of toys, equipment, and gadgets advertised as making babies smarter. Of course providing a rich environment with interesting things to do is desirable. And yes, you can promote cognitive development. But be careful about falling into the trap of thinking that you can stimulate cognitive development without working on physical, social, and emotional development at the same time. It isn't the clever little toys that you provide or activities that you do with the children that make a difference. It's the day to day living, the relationships, the experiences, the diaperings, the feedings, the toilet training, and the playing that contribute to intellectual development. And those same experiences help the child grow physically, socially, and emotionally as well.

Think of how rich the experience of diapering was for Jennifer. She was immersed in sensory input—visual, auditory, tactile, olfactory. How often caregivers and parents are told to hang a mobile over the changing table so the diapering can be an "educational experience." Yet how limited an experience a mobile provides compared to what Jennifer was enjoying.

Principle 5: Respect Infants and Toddlers as Worthy People

Respect is not a word usually used with very young children. In fact until I met Magda Gerber, I had never heard anyone use that word in relation to infants and toddlers. Worries about respect usually go the other way, as adults demand (or wish for) children to respect them. There is no better way to gain respect for yourself than to model it for children.

What does it mean to respect a child? The diapering scene provides an example. Before the caregiver did anything to Jennifer, she explained what would happen. Just as a respectful nurse warns you before putting a cold instrument on your skin, so Jennifer's caregiver prepared her for what was to come. Until you realize the difference, the natural tendency is to pick up a child without saying anything. Babies are often carried around like objects—even when they are old enough to walk and talk. I have often seen adults pick a child up and put him or her in a chair or a stroller without a word. (I'm sure I've done it myself.) That kind of action is not respectful.

To clarify the concept of respecting an infant, try imagining how a nurse would move a fairly helpless patient from a bed to a wheelchair. Then just change the players, and imagine one is a caregiver and one is an infant. Except for the size and weight involved, if the adult is treating the infant with respect, the scene should look much the same.

To understand better the concept of respecting a toddler, try this. Imagine you have just seen a man fall off a ladder. Think how you would respond. Even if you are strong enough, you would probably not rush over and set him back on his feet. You'd start talking first, asking if he was hurt or needed help. You'd probably extend a hand if he indicated he was all right and started getting up. You'd comfort him if that were called for. Most people have no trouble responding respectfully to an adult.

Why then do adults rush over and pick up a fallen toddler without a moment's pause? Why not see first what it is the toddler needs? Maybe all that is required is some reassurance—not physical help. Perhaps the child is angry or embarrassed and needs an adult who can accept those feelings and allow expression of them. Perhaps the toddler needs nothing, and without adult interference will get up and go about his business on his own. More aspects of respect come out in the next scene.

Twelve month old Brian is sitting at a low table with several other children eating a piece of banana. He is obviously enjoying the experience in more ways than one. He has squashed the banana in his hand, crammed it in his mouth, and it is now oozing out between his teeth. He is relishing it. He reaches for his mouth with the very last piece and, plop, it falls on the ground. He stretches out a hand for it, but the caregiver is quicker. "I'm sorry, Brian, but the banana is dirty now. I can't let you eat it." Brian's eyes open wide, his mouth drops open, and a sorrowful wail comes forth. "That's all the banana we have," the caregiver adds as Brian reaches out to her for more. She sits back down at the table after having disposed of the dropped piece. She offers him a cracker, saying, "We're out of bananas, but you can have a cracker instead." Brian rejects the offered cracker. Aware now that he will get no more, he begins to scream.

"I see how unhappy you are," says the caregiver calmly but with genuine compassion. "I wish I had more banana to give you."

Brian's screams become more piercing, and he begins to kick his feet. The caregiver remains silent, looking at him as if she really cares about his feelings.

The other children at the table are having various reactions to this scene. The caregiver turns to them and explains, "Brian lost his banana, and he didn't like it." She turns back to Brian. He continues to cry. The caregiver waits. Sobbing, he gets off his chair, toddles over to her, and buries his head in her lap. She touches him on the back, stroking him soothingly. When he has quieted down, she says, "You need to wash your hands now." He doesn't move. She waits. Then gently she repeats, "You need to wash your hands, Brian. I'll come with you," she adds. Turning the table over to another caregiver, she gets up and walks slowly across the floor with Brian. Brian is licking globs of banana from his fingers. A last sob escapes from his lips as he reaches the sink.

The caregiver respected Brian's right to have feelings and to express them. She offered support without gushing sympathy. Because she did not distract him with great amounts of warmth or entertainment, he was able to pay attention to what was going on inside himself. He was learning that it was all right to respond honestly to the situation.

Sometimes adult attention is so rewarding that children associate anger, frustration, or sorrow with attention. They use their feelings to manipulate. We would all be better off to ask directly for what we need than to use emotional displays to get hugs and touching. That's why the caregiver remained available but let Brian indicate what he needed. She did not pick him up, but let him come to her. When he was ready for comfort, she was there to give it to him, but it didn't come so early on that he was not able to express himself.

Some examples of less respectful ways to respond to Brian would be:

"Stop that screaming—that's nothing to get so upset about— you were almost finished anyway."

"Poor little Brian, let's go play with the doggie that you like so much—look, Brian—see him bark—bow-wow!"

Principle 6: Be Honest About Your Feelings

In the last scene the child was encouraged to recognize his feelings. He was angry, and he was not asked to pretend to be something else. What about adults? Is it all right for caregivers to express their anger to young children? Yes. Children in day care need to be around real people—not warm empty role-players. Part of being a real person is getting angry, scared, upset, and nervous now and then. Here is a scene showing a caregiver expressing anger:

A caregiver has just separated two children who were coming to blows over a toy. "I can't let you hurt Amber," she says to Shawn, who is eighteen months old. She has him firmly but gently by the arm when he turns to her and spits in her face. Her expression changes from calm to anger, and she takes his other arm as well. Looking him right in the eyes, she says clearly, but with emotion in her voice, "I don't like that, Shawn. I don't want you to spit at me." She lets go, stands up, and turns her back and walks away. When she is a few steps away, she gives a quick glance back to see what he is doing. He hasn't moved, so she walks to the sink and washes her face. She keeps an eye out to make sure he doesn't return to hitting Amber. By the time she returns, she is calm. Shawn is climbing up the slide, and things return to normal.

This caregiver was saying honestly what effect Shawn's action had on her. Notice how she expressed her feelings. She didn't put on such a show as to hook him on doing it again for his own entertainment, a problem that can occur when displays of adult anger are dramatic and lengthy. She didn't blame, accuse, judge, or belittle Shawn. She merely verbalized her feelings and connected them clearly to the situation. She let Shawn know what made her angry and stopped him from continuing the action. Having expressed herself, she left the scene. In short, she neither masked her feelings nor blew up.

Compare this reaction to the times you've seen people angry with a child, yet smiling and talking in a honeyed voice. Imagine the difficulty a child has in reconciling the two sets of messages that he gets at the same time.

Principle 7: Model the Behavior You Want to Teach

All the caregivers in the previous scenes have been modeling behavior that is acceptable for children as well as adults. You've seen examples of cooperation, respect, honest feelings, and communication. Take a look at how this principle works in a more difficult situation—when aggression is involved.

Shawn and Amber are struggling over a rag doll again. A caregiver starts to move over near them. Before he reaches the pair, Shawn reaches out and gives Amber a slap on the arm. She lets out a wail. The caregiver kneels on the floor before the two children. His face is calm; his movements are slow and careful. He reaches out and touches Shawn, rubbing his arm on the same spot where he hit Amber. "Gently, Shawn, gently." At the same time he strokes Amber. Shawn remains silent. Amber continues to wail. The caregiver touches her again. "You got hit, didn't you, Amber? It hurt!" Amber stops crying and looks at him. All three are silent for a moment. The caregiver waits. Shawn clutches the doll and starts to walk away with it. Amber grabs it. The caregiver remains silent until Shawn raises his arm to hit again. "I can't let you hurt Amber," he says, catching the arm midair. He touches him softly. "Gently, gently." Amber suddenly jerks the doll and Shawn lets go unexpectedly. Taking the doll in triumph, she starts across the room. Shawn looks sad, but remains in the same spot. The caregiver stays near. "She has the doll," he observes. Amber sees a ball at her feet, drops the doll, and picks up the ball. She throws it and runs after it giggling. Shawn moves quickly over to the doll, picks it up, holds it tenderly, and coos to it. The scene ends with both children playing contentedly, and the caregiver is no longer needed.

Notice how this caregiver modeled gentleness—the behavior he wished to teach. A more common approach when an adult arrives on the scene of a dispute is to treat the children with even more aggression than they have been displaying themselves. "I'll teach you to play rough," growls the adult, jerking the child by the arm and shaking him. This approach models the very behavior the adult is trying to eliminate. (And shaking a young child is dangerous because the weight of the head whipping around on a young neck can cause damage.)

The caregiver in the Shawn versus Amber scene knew that both children needed assurance that control would be provided when needed. It is frightening to both aggressor and victim when there is no protecting adult around to stop the violent action. The aggressor needs to be dealt with gently and nonjudgmentally. The victim needs to be dealt with empathetically but not sympathetically (that is, acknowledging her distress without feeling sorry for her). Sympathy and a good deal of attention may reward victims. In that way they learn that being victimized pays off in adult love and attention. How sad that some children actually learn to become victims.

Principle 8: Recognize Problems as Learning Opportunities and Let Infants and Toddlers Try to Solve Their Own

The previous scene also illustrates this principle: let children, even babies, handle their own problems to the extent that they can. The caregiver could have stepped in and taken care of this tugging situation by creating a solution for the conflict. He didn't, however. He let the toddlers make a decision themselves. (Though he did, of course, keep them from hurting each other further.) Very young children can solve more problems than many people give them credit for. The caregiver's role is to provide time and freedom to work on the problem. That means not responding to every frustration immediately. Sometimes a bit of facilitating will move a child forward when he or she gets stuck on a problem, but the facilitating should be the least help necessary, leaving the child free to work toward his own solution.

In a movie called "On Their Own with Our Help,"[1] Magda Gerber illustrates this principle beautifully. A baby crawls under a low table, then tries to sit up. When he discovers he can't, he starts crying. He doesn't know how to crawl out again, and he looks very fearful. Instead of rescuing him (it would have been easy to just lift the table up), Magda guides him out— reassuring and directing him with both her words and her hands. Problems can be valuable learning opportunities. Programs in which babies learn to solve their own problems have a rich curriculum.

Can you remember a time when you were working on some problem that was quite challenging to you? How would you have felt if someone had come along and said, "Here, let me do that for you," and taken the problem out of your hands? Can you see a parallel between your situation and that of infants who get rescued from most of their problems by well-meaning adults who want to save them frustration?

Principle 9: Build Security by Teaching Trust

For infants to learn to trust they need dependable adults. They need to know that they will get their needs met in a reasonable amount of time. The scenes have shown examples of dependable adults who met needs as well as offered strength and support. They didn't trick the children.

One of the times adults are most tempted to deceive children is during good-bye times. When everyone knows that a child is going to suffer loudly with protests and wails when the mother leaves, some are willing to trick the child to avoid a scene. However, it is much better when the mother leaves a child by saying good-bye outright, and the caregiver accepts protests and wails. While providing security, support, and empathy, he or she can express acceptance of the baby's right to be unhappy. The baby learns that he can predict when his mother will go rather than worrying constantly that she has sneaked away when he was occupied. He knows that as long as she hasn't said good-bye, she is still around. He comes to depend on his knowledge that the adults around him don't lie to him or trick him. Learning to predict what will happen is an important part of building trust. Always being happy isn't.

Principle 10: Be Concerned About the Quality of Development in Each Stage

We live in the period of the hurried child (a phrase coined by David Elkind in his book by the same title). The pressure starts at birth as many parents anxiously await the time their child reaches each milestone, comparing his or her progress with other children or with developmental charts. The message is everywhere—"fast is better." Books advertise "Teach your baby to read." Institutes promise miracles. Children are pushed, pushed, pushed. When adults have this hurry-up attitude, babies are propped up before they can sit on their own, walked around by the hand before they can even stand by themselves, taught to ride a tricycle when they can barely walk.

Caregivers feel the pressure from every side—from parents, sometimes even from directors as they are urged to speed up development. Yet development cannot be hurried. Each child has a built-in timetable that dictates just when he will crawl, sit up, and start to walk. The way caregivers can help development is to encourage each baby to do thoroughly whatever he or she is doing. Learning is what counts—not teaching. The important learning comes when the baby is ready, not when the adults decide it's time.

Some programs write objectives for each child. A hurry-up program will write objectives that focus solely on the next step. However, it is possible to write objectives that help broaden the child's experience in the stage where he or she is. Doing something very thoroughly is the best preparation for moving forward.

Take crawling as an example. Instead of standing the child up and continually encouraging him or her to walk, it is better to celebrate the crawling. The only time in his life that he'll be so conveniently close to things on the floor is when he is so very curious about everything within reach and just beyond it. Caregivers can provide experiences and opportunities for him to develop not only his crawling but his curiosity.

If you are to help counteract the pushy approach, you need to sell parents on the idea that perfecting skills is more important than pushing children to develop new ones. The new ones will come when the child has thoroughly practiced the old ones. The age at which a child first walks in no way correlates with whether or not he or she will become an Olympic runner.

The ten principles for respectful adult-infant interactions carry with them regard for the individual: the very young child, even the infant, is treated as the full human being that he or she is. A good adult-infant relationship is built on a series of respectful, responsive, reciprocal interactions over a period of time. Such a relationship is the basis of good caregiving. It is also the basis of infant-toddler education, which is the subject of the next chapter.

Notes

1. Bradley Wright Films, 1 Oak Hill Drive, San Anselmo, California, 94960

For Further Reading

Ronda Garcia, *Home Centered Care: Designing a Family Day Care Program. A Guide for Caregivers and Parents* (San Francisco: Children's Council of San Francisco, 1985).

Magda Gerber, *Resources for Infant Educarers* (Los Angeles, Calif.: Resources for Infant Educarers, 1979).

Magda Gerber, "Respecting Infants: The Loczy Model of Infant Care," in Elizabeth Jones, ed. *Supporting the Growth of Infants, Toddlers and Parents* (Pasadena, Calif.: Pacific Oaks, 1979).

Chapter 2
Infant-Toddler Education

Day-care programs for infants and toddlers are necessarily educational, whether or not that is their primary purpose. There is no way to keep children for a number of hours every day without educating them. You can leave your car in a parking garage in the morning and expect to find it the same that night when you pick it up. But children aren't cars. Children are changed as a result of their day-care experiences. How they are changed and what they learn can come without thought or planning, or the changes can be planned for in a systematic way. This chapter looks at a philosophy of education appropriate for infants and toddlers in day care. Chapters 3 and 4 look at how you plan for that education.

What Infant-Toddler Education Is *Not*

Infant Stimulation

The word "stimulation" has become synonymous with the word "education" in the minds of many when talking about infants. Although infant stimulation is more of a special education concept, used for the disabled or at-risk infant, many group care programs feel pressure to incorporate it in their approach. No one has ever proved that a program of carefully designed stimulation has a particularly beneficial effect on the development of a normal child. They have proved that if you shock rats, they run mazes better, which is some of the research on which the infant stimulation approach is based.

In this book the word "education" does not mean stimulation. Of course stimulation is important—the right amount—for all of us, but even more so for babies. However, if you look at stimulation as something you do *to* babies, rather than something that happens because of a relationship and because of the way you meet a variety of needs, you might as well be raising rats to run mazes.

If you are primarily concerned with stimulating, with doing something *to* the baby, you ignore a vital requirement for learning and development: that babies need to discover that they can influence the people and things around them. Yes, they need stimulation, which they get from objects and, more important, from people. But they need to perceive their own involvement in these stimulating experiences. Their involvement comes when they are able to have some effect on—that is, interact with—the people and things that are part of the experiences. When stimulation is provided without regard to the baby's response, the baby is being treated as an object.

The attention on infant stimulation came partly in response to some crib-bound, institutionalized babies who failed to thrive. Being left alone, without much sensory input but more important without attachment, they naturally failed to thrive. But adding mobiles, music boxes, or fish tanks to the crib isn't the answer. Getting somebody to meet the baby's needs is what is called for—not merely providing stimulation.

In group care for infants, the problem is usually overstimulation rather than the opposite, as sights and sounds bombard the infants. So in order to meet individual needs, infant education for some may be cutting down the stimulation—the sensory input—rather than adding to what's already present in the environment.

Preschool

Education for toddlers in day care is often built on the model of part-time nursery schools, where the children come in for a few hours in the morning and engage in a variety of activities set up especially for their learning. These activities are often more appropriate to older children, so when they are offered to toddlers, the adults are disappointed. When presented with a nursery school curriculum, toddlers often look fairly incompetent because they don't conform to adults' expectations. They draw on themselves instead of on the paper, they put beans in their mouths instead of glueing them down into the puddles they've produced with glue bottles on paper, they cut their clothes instead of paper, and they explore toys and materials in ways that no one ever thought of before. Rather than find a more appropriate approach, or at least activities, some programs dedicated to this model seem to wait for the toddlers to grow up a bit and just tolerate them in the meantime. But while they're waiting, they spend a lot of time restricting children and teaching them to do these standard preschool activities. (By the time you finish this book, you'll have lots of ideas of what kinds of activities *are* appropriate for the toddler age group.)

Programs that regard toddlers as immature preschoolers have problems with more than just their education-as-activities approach. If they see prime time for education as the activity period—usually around 9 to 11 A.M. and perhaps after nap time—they get frustrated with all the noneducational time. Caregiving routines and transition times seem to extend endlessly and take incredible amounts of energy.

There's much more to toddler education than setting up activities, even very appropriate ones. As it does with infants, education for toddlers happens during caregiving routines as well as during free play time. Activities are just a small part of toddler education.

Education as Facilitating Problem Solving

This book proposes a different way of looking at infant-toddler education from either the stimulation or the activity-centered point of view. The educational approach in this book is based on a *problem-solving approach* in which babies and toddlers learn how to make things happen in their world. Sensory input, of course, is an important part of this approach, but education comes about mostly as a result of the children's actions. The children are in charge. The adults are *facilitators* rather than stimulators. Age appropriate activities are also part of this approach, but only one small part, not the whole curriculum.

What kinds of problems do infants and toddlers face? Watch an infant or toddler for just one hour, and you will go a long way toward answering that question. Note that infants and toddlers deal with a variety of kinds of problems, including physical ones, such as hunger or discomfort; manipulative ones, such as how to get a toy from one hand to the other or how to get one block to balance on top of another; and social and emotional problems, such as coping with separation from parent or caregiver or trying to interact with a peer who is not interested in interacting. Some problems are specific to particular levels of development and will eventually be solved. Others are specific to the situation and may or may not be solved. Still others are ones the child will be dealing with, in one form or another, throughout his or her lifetime. Education for children under three lies in learning to deal with this enormous variety of problems, learning various ways to approach them, and learning when they can be solved and when to give up. As babies continually experience the problems that come from everyday living, the problems they encounter in play as well as in being fed, changed, dressed, bathed, and put to sleep, they eventually become toddlers who come to see themselves as problem solvers. If they come to see themselves as good problem solvers, and indeed they are, they will have been, by the definition in this book, well educated.

The Role of the Adult

The primary function of the adult in infant-toddler education is to facilitate learning rather than to teach or train. Start by appreciating the problems babies encounter. Allow them to work on solving them themselves. Also, you, as caregiver, will present problems to the babies while you provide for their needs and set up the environment for their play. You facilitate infant education by the way you direct and respond to the problem-solving baby during "wants something" and "wants nothing" quality time.

The two kinds of quality time relate to two ways of being with an infant or toddler in an educational way, which I'll call "caregiver presence." To get an idea of these two ways of being, try this exercise. Find someone who is willing to be your mirror. Stand facing that person, and ask him or her to copy each of your movements. Then using your body, facial expressions, and hands, do something for the "mirror" to copy. You may want to move around. After you have been the doer, try being the mirror. When you finish, discuss the experience with your partner. What role did you prefer—doing or mirroring (leading or following)? What was hard about each one? What are the advantages and disadvantages of each?

This mirroring exercise shows the kind of reciprocal interactions that constitute the responsive relationship first discussed in Chapter 1. It also illustrates the two kinds of caregiver presence—active and receptive. Perhaps you prefer the active mode—being a leader, directing what is going on. Or perhaps you prefer the receptive mode—following the child's lead, being responsive. To be a good infant-toddler educator, you need to develop both modes, no matter what your preference. Knowing which you prefer can help you concentrate on improving the other.

Notice in the following scene how the adult's being receptive or active works when the child has a problem to solve.

> Jason toddles in crying loudly and holding his fingers out in front of him.
>
> "Oh, Jason, something happened to you," says the caregiver.
>
> Jason continues to cry and holds his fingers up for inspection. The caregiver touches his fingers gently. "It looks like you hurt your fingers," he says in a calm but understanding voice.
>
> Jason pulls his fingers away and tugs at the caregiver's pants, indicating he wants to show him something.
>
> "You want me to come," he verbalizes Jason's desire and follows him to an area behind a partition where another adult and several children are on the floor. Jason, sobbing, leads him directly to a cupboard with the door standing ajar. His cries change slightly as he nears the scene of the accident.
>
> "You pinched your fingers in the door?" guesses the caregiver.
>
> Jason, angry now, picks up a wooden block and gets ready to throw it at the cupboard door.

"I see you're mad, but I won't let you throw the block. You might hurt something," says the caregiver firmly, holding Jason's arm.

Jason seems to reconsider. He puts down the block and goes to the cupboard. Still crying, he closes the door and opens it again. He is very careful in his actions.

"Yes, you can do it now without pinching." The caregiver puts his actions into words.

Jason ignores the words and continues to open and close the door. The angry cries subside and pained whimpering takes their place. He sits down by the cupboard and remains there crying.

"Let's go put some cold water on your fingers," says the caregiver, bending over to Jason with his arms out.

This scene shows both active and receptive presence, with an emphasis on receptive. Only twice did the caregiver take the lead. Notice that the caregiver was calm and not overemotional, though he was able to empathize with Jason (to feel his hurt). Because he did not get drawn into the situation and could provide support to Jason in his pain, he facilitated Jason's problem-solving abilities. The scene might have been very different if the caregiver had given Jason advice or "taught him a lesson." The scene might also have been very different if the caregiver had offered sympathy. Imagine if he had picked up Jason and murmured phrases like, "Oh, poor Jason, you got hurt, poor, poor little boy." But the caregiver gave neither advice nor sympathy. Instead he gave his full, calm attention, both receptive and active, thereby providing Jason the support, strength, and acceptance he needed to pursue the problem he had encountered. This scene shows infant-toddler education at work.

The adult role of directing and responding to infant-toddler problem solving is made up of four skills. The adult must be able to ascertain the optimum level of stress for the child faced with a problem, provide appropriately for the child's need for attention, give feedback, and model desired behavior.

Determining Optimum Stress

Stress and frustration are an important part of infant-toddler education. They come naturally with problem solving. In order to develop physically, emotionally, and intellectually, children occasionally need something to fight against, to pit their will and strength against. In this way they can discover that they are competent problem solvers. With no stress, no frustrations, and no problems, children have no way to try themselves against the world. Consequently, their education is severely limited. A young parent, thinking about stress as a part of infant education, wrote the following:

I was watering my garden the other day, and I found out more about stress and development. I'd been watering every day for some time and found that some of my seedlings weren't growing deep roots. As I thought about it—if a plant doesn't have some stress factors so that it has to look for food and water, its roots won't grow as deep; therefore it won't be as stable in the world. Its foundation will be too shallow.[1]

The right amount of stress—not too much, not too little—promotes development. The optimum level of stress depends entirely on the individual. The caregiver must decide what optimum means for any particular child and then try to allow for it. Opportunities will arise naturally in daily life.

How can you decide what is enough stress? You can decide the optimum level of stress by watching the child's actions. Children under too much stress are not able to solve problems effectively; they may become greatly emotional, or they may withdraw.

You can also decide what is enough stress by being empathetic (imagining what a child is actually feeling) and by remaining calm and not being swayed by either the child's emotions or your own. Being calm gives a perspective that facilitates good decision making.

What should you do if children are either overstressed or understressed? Take a look at the problems each child faces. Perhaps there are too many of them, in which case some changes need to be made to cut down on the number. They may be too hard to solve, in which case the child may need more help.

If children are understressed, they may not be encountering enough problems in their lives—perhaps not enough is happening, the environment is lacking in variety or interest, or someone else is solving the children's problems.

Perhaps you can think of a time in your own life when stress was good for you. Can you relate your experience to that of an infant or toddler in group care? How good are you at telling the difference between optimum stress and too much stress in your own life? Does this ability relate to how you can tell when a child is having too much or too little stress?

Providing Attention

The way an adult responds to a child's actions is an important part of infant-toddler education. The adult response has a lot of power because infants and toddlers essentially live on attention from others, especially the others who are important to them. For each individual there is an optimum amount of attention—optimum again, not maximum. If the person gets enough, satisfaction results. If the individual doesn't get enough, he or she will seek it in a variety of ways.

Think about how you satisfy your own needs for attention. How aware are you of the ways in which you get people to pay attention to you? You might list some ways you get attention from other people.

Some typical ways that people get attention are by being attractive to look at, by being kind and sweet, by being smart, by misbehaving, by being loud, by talking a lot or very little, by being outgoing or by being shy, by being sick or helpless. Are some of these your ways? Are you satisfied with the ways you get attention? Would you want infants and toddlers to get attention in the same ways? Are you aware that girls are more likely to be noticed for what they wear or how they look, but boys are more likely to be noticed for what they can do—their capabilities? How long do you think it takes for children to fall into patterns of getting attention by taking on confining sex roles?

If babies find that smiling, cooing, and being peaceful are not enough, or toddlers find that playing and keeping a low profile do not bring them attention, they will try other behaviors. Children seriously in need of attention will eventually find out how to "push the buttons" of the important people around them. Adults must recognize when children are trying to get attention by upsetting them and when they are directly communicating their real needs. It is not always easy to tell the difference. Take a look at the following scene:

A caregiver is sitting in a comfortable chair feeding a six month old a bottle. A seventeen month old, Mike, at her feet keeps tugging at her arm and trying to reach the bottle. Another adult removes Mike and tries to engage him in play while explaining that his caregiver is busy right now. When she turns her back to settle a dispute in another part of the room, Mike walks over to another child and grabs the toy he is playing with. Both caregivers admonish Mike, who glows with the attention. As soon as they turn back to their various occupations, Mike goes to the doorway separating the play room from the kitchen. He hangs on the gate across the opening and fusses.

"You just ate!" responds his caregiver from her chair. "It's hard to believe that you're still hungry, but I'll get you a snack when I finish feeding Becky," she tells him, then settles her gaze back on the baby she is feeding. Mike walks over immediately and pulls all the toys off the shelf and stamps on them. Both caregivers admonish him. Again he glows with the attention. But when both withdraw it, he starts throwing toys over the gate across the open kitchen door. Again he has two adults' full attention. The free adult helps him retrieve the toys and put them back on the shelf while his caregiver in the chair watches and comments from time to time. When order is restored, she puts her attention back to the baby she is feeding while the other caregiver starts to change a diaper. The scene ends as Mike walks over and slaps a child who has been playing quietly in the corner all this time.

In this scene Mike continually got attention for undesirable behavior. It's easy to see that he knows how to get attention when he needs it, even when both caregivers are busy. There is no easy answer to this problem. However, if both caregivers are aware that he needs attention, they can concentrate on giving it to him when he is not misbehaving. Perhaps he'll have less need for adult attention when it's difficult to give it to him. The adults can also put into words what it is that he needs by saying things like, "I know you need my attention right now, Mike."

If you are generous with your attention during caregiving times, most children can go on about their business during play times when you can't respond to them in playful ways. They won't hunger for adult attention. But if a child has learned that misbehavior is satisfying in terms of the reward it brings, you must change your approach.

Start by ignoring undesirable behavior that is designed to attract your attention (without disregarding needs or safety, of course). At the same time pay lots of attention to behavior that is desirable. Be specific when you talk about the behavior—don't just throw out nonspecific global judgments like "good boy." Instead say things like, "I really like the way you're playing with that toy, Mike. You put the toy back when you finished, good for you, Mike. You're letting me feed Becky without interrupting. You're doing a good job of waiting. You're being gentle with Jason."

When behavior needs changing, positive reinforcement can be quite effective, especially when you are changing a learned behavior, that is, one that has been rewarded in the past, such as Mike's bid for attention.

But don't go overboard in using positive reinforcement. Attention and praise work and are powerful motivators. However, they can be addictive. Many activities are rewarding for their own sake. They lose that reward when adults add external rewards to the intrinsic ones. So when a toddler is playing and an adult constantly interrupts to praise him or her, the message is that the activity itself is not that great, so the child needs motivation. Eventually that comes to be the case as the child gets the message. It's easy to spot a child who is used to a lot of praise while playing. He is the one who constantly looks to the adult after each little accomplishment. He seems to constantly need someone to say, "Wonderful! You stacked that block on the other one." The accomplishment itself is empty without the adult praise.

When children are overpraised, they may lose touch with their own feelings and motives. They look around after every act to see if they did it right. They seek approval for everything they do. Activities and accomplishments are pleasing only for the rewards they bring from the outside. In short, these children cease to get pleasure and satisfaction from the activities themselves.

Abraham Maslow, in *Toward a Psychology of Being*, states that when a child is faced with a conflict between inner delight at his own accomplishment and the rewards offered by others, he "must generally choose approval from others, and then handle his delight by repression or letting it die, or not noticing it or controlling it by will power. In general, along with this will develop a disapproval of the delight experience, or shame and embarrassment and secretiveness about it, with finally, the inability even to experience it."[2]

Maslow is giving a powerful message about the use of praise in infant-toddler education. His message is quite different from the common practice of many caregivers, who lavish praise on children so they will feel good about themselves. My experience is that children feel better about themselves when adults limit their praise and respond to successes with words like, "You must feel good about finally getting that shoe off," which are an attempt to acknowledge the child's own inner delight.

Providing Feedback

Closely related to the subject of praise and attention is feedback. Part of infant-toddler education depends on the child getting clear feedback, that is, responses. Feedback comes both from the environment and from people. Children need to learn what effect their actions have on the world and on others. If they drop a glass of milk, it spills. That's feedback about the qualities of liquids. The child needs no further feedback about milk. Now what's needed is a response about how to remedy the situation. "The milk spilled. You need a sponge to sop it up" is a good response.

Some things children do result in caregivers expressing pain or anger. That expression is also feedback. For example, the child who scratches the caregiver can be told, "It hurts when you scratch me. I don't like it." The message should be clear if the feedback is to be useful to the child. If the caregiver responds to a scratch in a honeyed voice, smiling all the while but holding the child tightly as if angry, the child gets a mixed message rather than clear feedback.

Adults can also help provide feedback about the environment, as well as verbalizing the reaction they see in the child. In this way children learn to give themselves clear feedback. Here is an example of that principle:

Josh is playing with several other toddlers when his caregiver comes in the door. As Josh rushes over, he slams his elbow into a table. He approaches his caregiver crying. His caregiver says, "Oh, Josh, I saw that. You bumped your elbow on the table." Josh confirms his caregiver's statement by holding his elbow up.

"Me!" he exclaims.

"Yes," replies his caregiver. "Right here is where you bumped it." He touches the spot gently.

Josh goes back to the table where he bumped. "Table!" he explains.

"Yes," confirms his caregiver. "Right there—you bumped your elbow right there on the table." He knocks on the table. "It's hard."

Josh touches the table. "It hurt when you hit your elbow on it," continues his caregiver.

"Hard," repeats Josh. He cries less now. He concentrates on his elbow, then the table, then his elbow again.

Josh's caregiver helped him focus on what just happened, and Josh learned something about cause and effect. Josh was shown what hurt him and gained some understanding of the relationship of the pain to the source. His caregiver helped Josh understand the full experience, rather than letting him get lost in the pain; yet he didn't deny his pain or distract him from it.

Think of a time in your own life when feedback was useful to you in a problem-solving situation. Can you apply your own experience to that of an infant or toddler?

Modeling

Practice, don't preach! Model the behavior you want from the child. What you do speaks louder than what you say. For instance, if you want to teach the child to share, you need to *be* a sharing person yourself. You need to share your own possessions with others if that's what you expect a child to do. You can teach children to perform the actions of sharing by using rewards and punishments, or you can *make* them share by using your size and power. But neither of these approaches will make children sharing people. They will become sharing people (with lots of modeling) only after they gain the concept of possession. Gaining this concept is one of the tasks of toddlers (hence all the "Me!" "Mine!" statements you hear when you work with this age group).

Children model after other qualities of their caregivers as well—such as gentleness. Children who are treated gently are more likely to treat other children gently. Respect is another example. Children who are treated with respect are more likely to be respectful to others than children who are not.

Another example of modeling behavior is expression of anger. If you work all day, every day in an infant-toddler center, your own anger is bound to be an emotion you'll deal with at least occasionally. The children pick up how you cope. If you smile and sing and deny that you're feeling furious, they learn to hide their feelings too. (And they learn to give the same mixed messages you are giving.) But if you use the energy to confront the source and work on solving the problem, they learn that way of dealing with conflicts. Or if confrontation is not appropriate, they can learn your coping mechanisms, such as working out the feelings through talking about them, through redirection into physical exercise or expression, or through soothing activities. (For some adults washing dishes is as soothing as water play is to children.)

In short, modeling behavior is more effective than "teaching" it. Just think of the habits, mannerisms, attitudes, gestures, and expressions you use that came straight from your parent(s). We "pick up" behaviors and mannerisms without even being aware of it, and without being taught. As a caregiver, you must be conscious of the behavior you model, so that what you do and what you say are in accordance with one another.

Obviously, no one can be a model all the time. Everyone acts in ways they would rather not have children imitate. If you expect to be a perfect model, you set yourself up for disappointment. However, as you respond to your own weaknesses, your own imperfections, and your humanness, you are modeling. For example, when you make a mistake, you can show the children that mistakes can be forgiven by forgiving yourself. When you're feeling needy, you can tune in on your needs, modeling for the children that responding to needs is important. When you bring modeling to the conscious level of awareness, you can make decisions about it. Modeling is a powerful tool and can work either for you or against you. Because caregiving is already a difficult task, you might as well have all your tools working for you.

In summary, the adult role in infant-toddler education involves allowing for an appropriate degree of stress when a child is trying to solve a problem, responding appropriately to demands for attention, providing feedback, and modeling desirable behavior. The role of the infant-toddler educator can be carried out at any time—during caregiving tasks or when children are playing without direction.

The hardest part of infant-toddler education is trying to explain it to people who think learning comes only from schoollike activities. A good task to prepare yourself to be an infant-toddler caregiver is to prepare an answer to the question, "Do children learn anything in your program or do they just play?" You're bound to be asked that question at some point in your career or perhaps, "Is your program educational or just babysitting?" A short convincing answer should be right at your fingertips.

An Example of Infant Education

The focus of this chapter has been on the adult role in facilitating infant-toddler education. Kahlil Gibran sums up the kind of relationship between the "educator" and the child that has been presented here: "If he is indeed wise he does not bid you to enter the house of his wisdom, but rather leads you to the threshold of your own mind."[3] The following scene both illustrates and sums up this approach to infant education. Notice how the principles introduced in Chapter 1 are handled here in practice.

You're moving through a door in your mother's arms. You find yourself in a familiar room when a quiet voice says your name. You look into the eyes of your caregiver. At the same time you see and hear her, you notice her special smell, which is pleasantly familiar to you. You hold out your arms. She takes you briefly, then puts you on the floor.

Now you're aware of a smooth, cool floor. You're staring at your mother's shins. Up you get on all fours, and without giving much thought to where you are going, you take off. You leave the voices of your mother and caregiver behind. You notice a change under your knees. The smooth hard feeling has become soft and spongy. You stop for a moment to stick your fingers into the nap of the rug, then keep right on going past a ball and brightly colored scarf. You're headed for a shelf of toys you can see ahead of you. Whoops, what is that? A face comes into view. You stop to investigate. You regard this face quietly and at the same time feel a big presence come up close beside you. You ignore this adult and reach for the face. You touch the smooth skin, and the eyes come to rest on you. You feel good. You pat the soft hair, then have an urge to know what the hair will feel like on your lips. You reach down and touch your lips to the hair.

You sense the pleasure of the adult sitting by you. You look up for a moment, but this big face isn't as appealing or as reachable as the small face on the floor by you. You move back to your examination of the face. Then you begin to get more energetic about your explorations, you feel a big hand stroking your small one, and you hear a voice saying, "Gently, gently." You go back to your original soft stroking. Suddenly a small hand comes up and attaches itself to your hair. You move back, startled.

This movement puts you in a new position, and from this place you can see a big, bright ball. You move over to it. You reach out and touch it—it rolls away from you. You feel excited about this and crawl after it. You try to hold it, but it keeps getting away from you.

You stop for a moment and take your bearings. You're far from the rug now, and the toy shelf you were originally after has disappeared completely. You find that the ball has rolled to a small bed with a doll on it. You reach for the doll, pick it up by one foot, and drop it. You take the blankets off the bed one by one, comparing their textures. When you get down to the hard bare wood, you figure you've seen enough and move on. As you pass by the doll, you give a little attention to its face. You glance back to the small person on the rug, and a fleeting glimpse of that face crosses your mind. It's different from this one. You compare the two.

Suddenly you remember your mother. You have a tight feeling inside. Where is she? You sit straight up and look around. Not far away is a familiar pair of shoes, feet, and legs. You look up and up until you get to her face. Her familiar voice says, "Yes, I'm still here." You crawl over and touch her leg. Then you take off again.

You are aware now and then that there are other voices in the room. You don't pay much attention to them. You are busy trying on the hats that are in a box on the floor in front of you. You're very busy when you see your mother's legs again, then look up into her face. You hear her voice say, "I have to leave now. Good-bye." She leans over and kisses you on the forehead.

You sit up straight and still, wondering. You watch as your mother's feet move slowly away from you. A feeling of distress comes over you, but you remain stunned. You want to do something to stop her, but you can't. Her feet disappear out the door, and you can't see them anymore.

You feel a tenseness in your face and a pounding in your ears. You hear a loud noise and feel something come out of your throat. You're all alone in the world. You have just time to fully react to this feeling when a hand touches you and says, "Your mother had to go to work." You stop for a moment to consider what that means. But your mother doesn't come back, so you get the same feeling again, and your cries come pouring forth. The warm, familiar voice says, "You miss her." You don't really understand these words, but the tone of the voice captures your attention, and you feel understood. You crawl into the arms of your caregiver, who is sitting on the floor near you. You sob briefly; then you feel better.

Just beyond her you see a big, soft, floppy ball. It's a beach ball only half blown up. You reach out for it and grab it in your hand. Just as you are about to enjoy it, you find it in the hands of someone else. You are surprised and disappointed at the same time. You reach for it—but the person moves away. You follow and reach again. You just get your fingertips on it when it suddenly is yanked away again. You sit back in tears. A hand touches you, and a voice says, "You don't like it when Kevin takes the ball." That voice conveys such understanding that your feeling changes. You cry a few more sobs, look at the face, and crawl away.

You find yourself at a small table with a puzzle on it. Kevin is just removing two pieces. You push the puzzle with your hand, and it falls on the floor with a great big delightful noise. Kevin looks at the puzzle, then at you. You take the piece he has in his hand. He looks surprised. You pick up a piece on the floor and begin to bang the two together. Then you shove the puzzle under the table and crawl under after it. You turn on your back and contemplate the textures of the unpainted side of the table. A feeling of peace comes over you as you lie there.

You crawl out and over to a low platform. You want very much to get up on it, but you don't know how. You make several attempts to crawl up, but it is just a little bit too high. You are about to give up when a voice says, "Maybe a cushion will make it easier for you." A flat, firm cushion appears between you and the platform. You sit back to think this over—but only for a minute. You climb up on the cushion, and from there you can easily get onto the platform.

What a great feeling to be up there! You take only a moment to let it sink in, and then crawl back down. You want to try to get up there again. You manage the climb the second time and get the same feeling. You repeat this sequence a number of times until the pleasure of it begins to wear off.

You notice a caregiver is bringing out something new in another part of the room. Curious, you head over to see what it is. You forget you were on the little platform. You miss the cushion and find yourself sprawled on the floor. You're surprised and upset. You let out a loud series of cries. You have your eyes closed, so you don't see your caregiver come to your side. You hear a voice say, "You fell down." You lie there a moment, gathering your scattered feelings before you attempt to pick yourself up. The adult waits. You wait. The adult says, "Do you need some help?" You respond by getting up by yourself.

An image of your mother flashes across your mind, and you think you might need her very much in the next instant. But the toys the other caregiver is getting out are appealing, and you continue to crawl to the other side of the room. You are vaguely aware of a little sensation in your leg that wasn't there before, as well as a slight throbbing in one cheek. By the time you reach the toys, these sensations are no longer important—all you can think of is exploring these new objects in front of you.

Notice that this infant encountered some problems that could be solved alone and some that required help. The adults were both active and receptive. The infant felt some stress, but never so much that it prevented problem solving. Needs for attention (which were never very great in this scene) were satisfied in ways that did nothing to encourage undesirable behavior. The infant received feedback—both from actions on the objects in the environment and from the adults present. And the adults consistently modeled the behavior they wanted to teach.

Look now at a scene where a toddler is experiencing an educational situation.

You are two years old, and you have just said good-bye to your father. You watch out the window as he gets into his car and drives off. Tears roll down your cheeks, even though you know he will be back. You've been through this often enough now not to be terrified, but you still feel sad about the departure. You feel a warm hand in yours, and you and a caregiver stand side by side by the window even after the car has disappeared. Then you are offered a tissue from a box, which you take and use to wipe your nose. You are about to throw the tissue on the floor when you are directed gently to a wastebasket, where you deposit the used tissue. "Want to hear a story?" asks the adult, motioning to a cozy corner of the room where another adult sits with several children snuggled into soft cushions. You join the group, plopping down on the caregiver's lap. She moves the book so all can see, including you, and continues on with the story she was in the middle of. Before she has finished, you get off her lap and wander over to the bookshelf and select another book. "Here," you say as you thrust it into her face.

She moves your book, looks into your eyes, and explains, "I'll read that one when I finish this one." You sit beside her, turning the pages of the book until she has finished reading. Then she reaches for your book.

"Me!" you tell her, holding it away from her.

"Oh, you want to read it to us?" she asks. She sits back and waits. You open the book and begin pointing to objects, naming them. She is interested in what you are saying. She adds a few words for objects you don't know the names of. One child, who can't see the pictures, leaves the group. Two others move in closer. One climbs on the adult's lap.

"No!" you shout, shoving the child. You're stopped firmly. The caregiver looks into your eyes and says, "I can see that you don't want Roberto on my lap." You feel understood, but Roberto is still there, and that frustrates you. But while you are worried about that, another child takes the book you had been reading and trots off with it. You run after her saying "my book" emphatically. She drops it, and you pick it up and return and sit down and resume "reading," glad to have the book back. You're still concerned that Roberto has taken your place, but you continue turning pages and naming objects. When you get to the beginning (you've been reading it backward), the caregiver says to you, "It's time to wash your hands for breakfast."

You jump up right away. Hand washing is your favorite activity. You find a crowd at the sinks, but by pushing slightly you manage to get close to one. You're vaguely aware that you're supposed to wait, not push, but no one really noticed. You remember another time when you pushed hard and were taken away and told not to push. You've learned to avoid that situation.

The water feels oh so good on your hands. You reach for the soap and lather all the way up your arms. You stand for a long time rubbing the soap in your hands and arms. Then you rinse and soap up again. By now the sinks are nearly empty. You rinse and soap up once more.

"Time to rinse off and dry," says the caregiver who was reading to you. She stands near you with a towel. You rinse off your hands reluctantly, leaving soap on your arms.

"How about your arms?" she suggests.

You put your arms under the running water. She hands you the towel and then turns to help another child. While her back is turned, you run water over the towel and start wiping out the sink. Then you push the end of the towel into the indentation of the drain and turn the water on harder. You're watching delightedly as the sink begins to fill with water. Right before it runs over onto the floor and your shoes, the caregiver gets back to you. She quietly corrects the problem, hands you a dry towel, and directs you to the breakfast table.

You settle down at the table with a feeling of satisfaction, and very clean arms and hands. You grab a cup from the child next to you and begin pounding it on the table, looking toward the caregiver who is offering cups to seated children. The child next to you grabs his cup back, and you are about to scream when the caregiver says, "If you want my attention, just say my name." You say her name and are offered the choice of a red or blue cup. You take the blue one and show it to the child next to you, who has the same color. The caregiver smiles at you and says, "Yes, they're the same, aren't they?" You return the smile and sit back in your chair, ready to enjoy the breakfast you can smell in the kitchen.

This child encountered some problems and created some. The adults were both active and receptive in facilitating the child's problem solving. Needs for attention were met in ways that didn't encourage undesirable behavior. The child received feedback from both the environment and the people in it. Although nothing in this scene looked like a school-type activity, the child was nevertheless receiving an education as he or she dealt with a variety of problems, problems that belong to the physical, social, emotional, and intellectual realms.

This chapter has focused on problem solving as an approach to infant-toddler education. It has examined the adult role in facilitating problem solving in very young children, including determining optimum individual stress level, adult attention, feedback, and modeling. The two chapters that follow examine how the educational approach explained in this chapter can become a curriculum, that is, a plan for learning, in a program.

Notes

1. Personal letter from Patti Wade, October 1978.

2. Abraham H. Maslow, *Toward a Psychology of Being*, 2nd ed. (New York: Van Nostrand, 1968), p. 51. Reprinted by permission of the publisher.
3. Kahlil Gibran, *The Prophet* (New York: Alfred A. Knopf, 1965), p. 56.

For Further Reading

Magda Gerber, "Conflict Resolution with Infants," *Educaring* 4(4), Fall 1983, p. 3.

Stacie G. Goffin, with Claudia Q. Tull, "Problem Solving: Encouraging Active Learning," *Young Children*, March 1985, pp. 28–32.

Seymore Levine, "Stimulation in Infancy," *Scientific American*, May 1960, pp. 436, 624.

Chapter 3
Caregiving as Curriculum

Curriculum is a major issue because we now know that infants and toddlers are competent learners and that the early years are an important foundation for learning in the later ones. Gone are the days when child care was merely custodial, without concern for each child's development. *Education* must be a primary concern, and if you are to educate, you must have a *curriculum*, that is, a plan for learning.

The problem is that curriculum doesn't look the same in infant-toddler programs as it does in educational programs for older children. One difference is that you can't just educate the mind because there is no way to separate intellectual needs from other needs at this beginning level. Therefore, curriculum modeled after school programs where intellectual needs are the main concern is inappropriate for the very young.

Another problem is that the curriculum is so broad in infant-toddler programs that it is very difficult to define. I had that difficulty with this chapter and the next. The curriculum is really everything that happens in the program; therefore, this whole book is about curriculum. To try to talk about curriculum in just two chapters is difficult. Yet we need to learn how to talk specifics in order to educate parents and policymakers about infant-toddler programs. They must be made to understand that infant-toddler programs are educational when they are designed to meet the children's needs—all their needs. They need to understand that there is a plan for learning, though the adults are not primarily teachers. This chapter and the next, as well as the curriculum chart in Appendix B, provide those specifics.

If you approach infant-toddler education as facilitating problem solving, then the curriculum occurs naturally during the two main activities of the day: caregiving and free play. These are when children encounter and solve problems. The basis of the curriculum is interaction—with people (adults and peers) and with objects. This chapter concentrates on interactions with adults as they occur during caregiving times.

Adult-child Relationships

I have emphasized the importance of the adult's attitude toward caregiving in previous chapters. Because caregiving activities provide regular times when each child has full adult attention on an individual basis, the adult needs to be fully present, providing "wants something" quality time.

One important component of the curriculum as it occurs both during caregiving times and free play times is attachment. Learning and attachment are related. Through caregiving interactions, attachment grows. When caregiving times are quality times, much learning takes place. Diapering, for example, becomes not just a chore, but a vital part of the curriculum. Life-long learnings and attitudes can be initiated on the diapering table. Likewise, feeding is another vital part of the curriculum. Not only does it promote attachment between infant and caregiver, but it provides a variety of sensory experiences, much pleasure and satisfaction, and an opportunity to learn social and self-help skills. Dressing, grooming, and washing are other opportunities for providing sensory experiences, developing self-help skills, as well as promoting attachment.

Young children need attachment, a tie to a special person, who in turn gives them a feeling that they are important—that they matter. Although most infants and toddlers in day care are attached to their parent(s), if they are to spend long hours a day away from them, attachment to caregivers is additionally beneficial. Both caregivers and children gain from attachment because communication is enhanced and needs are understood. The caregiver is rewarded by the child's feeling for him or her, and the child gains a feeling of importance. Through attachment, the child knows that he or she is being cared *about* as well as *for*.

Attachment is promoted by assigning one caregiver to several infants and young toddlers in what is called a "primary caregiver system." The idea behind this is that, if caregivers see three or four children each as their own special charges, they can promote a stronger attachment than might happen if attachment were left to chance. Naturally, shifts change, and caregivers come and go. Nevertheless, if attachment needs are recognized, much can be done to provide for them.

Older toddlers are more likely to become attached if they are grouped with a consistent caregiver who pays special attention to them. Naturally, with children over two, the groups can be larger than just the three or four appropriate to younger children.

In the following scene with eight infants and young toddlers and two caregivers, consistent feeding by one caregiver, who is released from other duties to give his full attention to the baby he is feeding, promotes attachment. Notice in this scene not only how the caregiver builds attachment, but also how the children use their attachment to the *other* caregiver. When a threatening situation arises (when a stranger walks into the room), the children head for the person to whom they are attached.

A slender middle-aged woman is sitting low in a beanbag chair. On her lap is a baby who has climbed there to pat her cheek. Clinging to her shoulder is a toddler who is also trying to climb on her lap. The baby pushes gently at the toddler to try to keep him off. "No," says the toddler, who continues to hang on tight. A short distance away two toddlers are banging wooden spoons on empty margarine cartons. A third child sits looking on, quietly opening and closing a small cardboard box that has a big plastic bead inside. Just beyond the seated woman is a large pen that fences off one corner of the room. In it two very young infants are lying on their backs, waving their arms and looking at each other and at the scattering of toys close to them. In another area of the room, a man is seated in a comfortable chair, quietly giving a baby his bottle. His full attention is on the baby he is feeding, while the woman is obviously taking charge of all the rest of the children in the room. She focuses on the two children interacting with her, but she also manages to spread her awareness to the other children.

A large bearded man in a uniform walks into the room. The child who was opening and closing the cardboard box starts to cry. All action immediately stops except the arm waving in the one corner and the feeding in the other. The climbers and the bangers sit with their eyes on the stranger. The crying child starts creeping backward toward the woman in the beanbag chair, never taking her eyes off the man's face. When she reaches the comfort and safety of the familiar lap, she climbs on, clutching at her caregiver's blouse. The woman puts her arm reassuringly around the child and speaks first to her and then to the man. "That's Josh's father, Melanie," she says matter-of-factly. Then to the man, "Hello, David. You're early today. Josh is still in the nap room, but he is probably just about starting to wake up. Oh, by the way, be sure to check his log—he didn't eat much lunch today—see what's written down. He may be ready for something to eat when he gets home. Also, as I recall, he was tired this morning, but couldn't sleep. He's been grumpy all day, but had a long nap this afternoon."

The man thanks her and leaves the room to get his son. The action starts up again. Melanie crawls down and goes back to her cardboard box. In the corner pen both infants have started whimpering, and one occasionally breaks into a loud cry. The woman gets up, telling the children around her that she is going to do so beforehand. She goes into the pen to talk to the two needy babies. "Yes, I know, Nathan," she says to the one crying loudest. "You need to eat. I'm going to feed you just as soon as Darryll finishes and can take over for me." And then turning to the other child, who has settled down a bit with her presence, "And then it's your turn to eat. I don't think you're too hungry yet, are you?" Turning back to the first infant, "It's hard to wait, I know."

Notice that this scene shows examples of how attachment can work in an infant-toddler center. Notice, too, that in this center caregivers kept daily logs on "their" children so that parents can receive a comprehensive and detailed report when they arrive to pick them up. This record keeping also serves to make the caregivers pay special attention to "their" children.

Determining children's needs is the first step in performing caregiving tasks. This is easy when the child is old enough to tell you. But those who are too young to express themselves beyond squirming and crying can cause you some real anguish. It is easier when you are attached to the children or know them well enough to understand their unique ways of communicating.

Whenever a child communicates a need to you, either directly or indirectly, ask yourself, "What is it this child really needs?" This is a much easier question to ask than it is to answer, especially in the urgency of the moment, when a young baby is already screaming.

The best approach, if the need is not immediately obvious, is to ask the child. If the child is a toddler and has learned to express his or her needs directly, it is easy. But with a young infant, you may have to work hard to figure out what the need is. Nevertheless, asking directly is a good approach. Ask aloud. Talk to the infant, expressing your desire to understand what he or she needs. Listen, look, and feel for the answer. If you're beginning to learn the child's system of communication (the third principle in Chapter 1), you may get your answer directly from the child. By taking this approach, you're beginning to set up a two-way communication pattern that will serve the child well for the rest of his or her life. Children (even the youngest) who are encouraged to express their needs can become quite skilled at doing just that.

Adults sometimes develop a singular approach to responding to a child's crying. "Oh, he's tired" may be one caregiver's standard response. "He needs a nap." Another caregiver may wish to feed all cranky children. A problem arises when a baby with one need has an already satisfied one met. For example, when a child is uncomfortable, restless, sleepy, or irritable and food is given, the child's ability to identify the real need may be impaired.

This is more apt to happen with infants than with toddlers because comforting with a bottle is so easy for many babies. Food becomes a substitute for cuddling, attention, or rest. How many adults reach automatically for food when they have some kind of need? This behavior is learned in the early years.

Some needs cannot be met by caregivers. For example, some infants cannot go to sleep without crying, which seems to release tension and relax them. In those cases the best approach, when you're sure these infants need sleep, is to put them in a crib and let them know that you understand if they are unhappy about being put there. By accepting the crying, you don't have to make yourself responsible for stopping it.

In day care it sometimes happens that an adult's or the group's needs conflict with individual needs. A child must be awakened from a nap because it is time to go home or fed early for some reason. Or an infant must wait to be fed because several others are simultaneously making demands. Once again the best approach is to let children know that their needs have been recognized and then accept the fact that they may cry until it is their turn for attention. If you can think of the crying as good—as a sign that children are communicating their needs—it is sometimes easier to accept. When it is the crying child's turn, you will, of course, give him or her your full attention.

Children are resilient, and they can cope with their individual needs being put second sometimes. However, it can be harmful to children when needs other than their own are *usually* put first. To avoid the effects of institutionalization, caregivers must be very careful to make sure that individual needs are taken into consideration. Infants and toddlers must not be put on a rigid schedule that meets program needs rather than their own.

This institutionalization effect can be a danger when toddlers are mixed with older children who have learned to subordinate their individual needs to the dictates of a daily schedule. For most of us, our first away-from-home experience was school, where we subordinated our wide range of needs to more narrow educational goals, to the group, and to the schedule. School must not be the model for programs for very young children.

Think for a minute about how you determine your own needs and get them met. Can you remember a time when you required something that you could not get by yourself? How did you communicate this need? Were you direct about it? Was your message received? Did you get the results you wanted? Perhaps you can relate your own experience to that of infants and toddlers in day care.

The key to effective caregiving is the good relationship described in Chapter 14. Anne Morrow Lindbergh in *Gift from the Sea* says:

> A good relationship has a pattern like a dance and is built on some of the same rules. The partners do not need to hold on tightly, because they move confidently in the same pattern, intricate but gay and swift and free, like a country dance of Mozart's. To touch heavily would be to arrest the pattern

and freeze the moment, to check the endlessly changing beauty of its un-
folding . . . now arm in arm, now face to face, now back to back— it does not
matter which. Because they know they are partners moving to the same
rhythm, creating a pattern together and being visibly nourished by it.

The joy of such a pattern is not only the joy of creating or the joy of
participating, it is also the joy of living in the moment. Lightness of touch
and living in the moment are intertwined. One can't dance well unless one
is completely in time with the music, not leaning back to the last step or
pressing forward to the next one, but poised directly on the present step as
it comes. [1]

Take a look now at an example of a good relationship in one of the primary
caregiving tasks—feeding an infant. Imagine yourself in a small body with
a bib around your neck.

Hear a familiar voice say to you, "Here's some applesauce for
you." Look around and see a spoon, a hand, and beyond it a
small dish of applesauce. Take time to really perceive all this. Feel
the coziness as well as the anticipation. Hear the same voice say,
"Are you ready?" See the spoon come up to your face. There is
plenty of time for you to open your mouth for the bite. You feel
the applesauce in your mouth. You taste it. You notice the texture
and the temperature. You thoroughly explore this bite before you
swallow. Some goes down your throat; some runs down your chin.
You look up to find the familiar face. Seeing the face adds to
your pleasure. You open your mouth again. You feel a scraping
on your chin. The next bite comes into your mouth. You explore
it. You compare it to the first bite. You take your time and get the
most out of this bite before you swallow it. When you swallow, you
get an excited feeling—an anticipation of the next bite. You look
at the face again. You reach out, and your fingers touch
something soft and smooth. All of these feelings are present as
you open your mouth for the next bite.

Come back now from your imagining. Reflect on this experience for
a moment. Now compare that imaginary experience with this one:

You feel yourself plopped into a high chair without a word. A
strap is put around your middle, and you are left alone with an
empty tray. You look around and see a number of other babies.
You pound on the tray. It's cold and hard, as is the back of the
chair. You feel impatient. It seems like forever that you are sitting
there. You squirm and twist. Suddenly there is a spoon in between
your lips, forcing them open. You look toward the source of the
spoon, at the same time tasting applesauce. You wiggle your
tongue around, swallowing down the bite. The spoon again comes
between your lips, and your teeth are forced open. You take

another mouthful while looking into an expressionless face of a person who seems to have her mind somewhere else. You enjoy the taste and feeling of the applesauce—pushing it around in your mouth and out between your teeth—down your chin. You feel metal scraping your chin. More applesauce comes into your mouth. You are about to swallow this mouthful when the spoon arrives again. You take a second mouthful into the first, which you haven't swallowed yet. You work on swallowing while you feel scrape, scrape on your chin as the spoon gathers up what is running down. More applesauce arrives in your mouth. You swallow a little of the big load, and you get ready to swallow more. But before you can, the spoon finds its way in between your teeth again. Now your mouth is fuller than before. You sense a bit of urgency to get this down before the next load. You try to hurry, which only slows you down. More applesauce squishes out and runs down your chin. You feel the spoon—scrape, scrape, scrape—and more applesauce comes into your mouth. Hold onto that feeling now and stop imagining.

Just think what the long-term effects of a number of feedings like the second one might be! How much better it is to be fed sensitively, by a caring person.

Notice how the first experience encompassed the ten principles of caregiving. The infant was involved in how the task progressed. The infant and caregiver were sharing quality time—that is, both were paying full attention to each other and the task at hand. They were interacting responsively. They were communicating. The infant was being respected. It's not easy to always feed every infant in day care in the manner of the first feeding, but it is certainly a goal worth striving for.

Feeding

Day-care programs for infants and toddlers, both centers and family day care, should make every possible provision for nursing mothers. Both mothers and infants benefit, even though it may be less convenient for caregivers. Help the mother feel welcome, and provide a place for her and her infant to be quiet and comfortable.

Bottle-fed infants deserve the same kind of one-to-one attention and physical closeness that breast-fed infants receive. A well-organized center will find ways to release a caregiver to sit and feed an infant while holding him or her, without requiring that the caregiver jump up and down to take care of other children's needs. In family day care this "release time" is harder to come by, but caregivers who make it a priority to hold each baby while feeding can find ways to work it out.

Feeding time should be quality time. One reason is that, during feeding, attachments are formed between caregivers and children. For this reason, caregivers should feed the same babies daily insofar as possible.

When infants begin to feed themselves, the mess level rises dramatically. Most caregivers are willing to put up with the mess because they value independence. They want children in their care to learn self-help skills. Accepted practice in this country is to let or even encourage children to take over their own feeding as soon as they are able. Usually when a baby grabs the spoon, he or she is given one and allowed to try getting it to the mouth. Here are some hints to help children learn to become self-feeders.

1. Use child-size unbreakable utensils.
2. Provide finger food. Chunks of soft food that can be picked up in the hands, such as banana, can be a welcome treat to the child who is just learning to use utensils.
3. Give only small amounts of food. Better to let children ask for more than to discourage them with too large a portion. It's also easier to clean up a smaller amount.
4. Allow time for play and experimentation, but be aware of your own limits. End the meal for the child before the play begins to bother you. A tension-free setting promotes self-feeding skills.

Eating is an emotional process. Adults bring to a feeding situation feelings, ideas, and traditions that have nothing to do with the immediate experience but come from their own history and culture. People have strong feelings about what should or should not go on at the table. For some, the taboos about what cannot be done are deeply ingrained and very important. The way they eat seems to define who they are. For others, the resentment of the taboos is equally strong. The point is that eating is connected with strong feelings and that these feelings affect the way an adult approaches or reacts to children eating.

It is also important to recognize that not all cultures view early independence, self-feeding, and big messes in the same way. Although you may not wish to do it yourself, you should respect the fact that a parent may continue spoon-feeding a child long past the age you approve of.

Understanding each child's signals, giving some choices, defining limits clearly, reacting honestly, and interacting responsively are all keys to pleasant feeding experiences. Ending a meal for children when their hunger has been satisfied is important. Children cannot be expected to restrain from playing with their food if they are full and it is still in front of them.

The following scene shows some of the principles mentioned here in action:

Four toddlers are seated at a low table intently watching a caregiver who has several plastic cups in his hand. He turns to the child on his right and holds out two cups. "Do you want this one, Susan, or this one?"

The cups are different colors and shapes. One has a handle. Susan reaches for one of the cups. The caregiver puts the other one on a table behind him and brings a pitcher around in front of him.

"Now everyone has a cup," he says, looking around at the expectant children. "Here is the juice." He smells it. "It smells like apple juice to me."

He pours a small amount of juice in a pitcher and hands it to Manuel, who is sitting to his left. Manuel grabs the pitcher and pours with great excitement, missing his cup. The caregiver hands him a small sponge. "Here's a sponge for the spill," he says calmly. Manuel pays little attention to the sponge, but it is close enough to the spill that the liquid runs into it and becomes absorbed. Manuel looks carefully at the juice left in the pitcher and then with precise movements pours the small amount into his cup. He abandons the pitcher and concentrates on the cup, with a satisfied look on his face.

"Your turn, Kim," says the caregiver, refilling the pitcher and passing it to her. She takes the pitcher, pours some, then shoves the pitcher toward the next child, who receives it gratefully.

The child next to him bangs his cup yelling, "Me!"

"You want your juice, Kiwon," says the caregiver.

"No!" says Kiwon, emphatically.

"Maybe you're ready for some cereal," speculates the caregiver, reaching for a bowl with dry cereal in it.

"No!" repeats Kiwon.

"Well!" says the caregiver, stumped. In the meantime he refills the small pitcher, which is still going around the table.

Kiwon points at the counter behind them. On it a box of raisins is in full view.

"Oh," says the caregiver. "You want raisins, right?"

"Raisins!" repeats Kiwon carefully. When he receives a handful, he crams a number into his mouth and sits contentedly chewing and sucking on the raisins without removing his fingers.

This caregiver was able to give the children some choices without setting out a whole smorgasbord. He communicated with each child and read signals. He was sensitive and responsive. He set limits.

Perhaps you have not seen toddlers eating at a table instead of in high chairs. Seating them together provides a more social experience than seating them in rows in high chairs. And they have more choice about leaving when finished. They don't have to wait for an adult to take them down. If independence is a value, this simple technique goes a long way toward promoting it.

Diapering

Did you think the diapering episode in Chapter 1 was too idealistic? The following scene doesn't go so smoothly, but it is based on the same principles as the first one.

The scene is a small center. The room is set up for the toddlers who are now occupying it. One is a small boy playing contentedly with an empty can and a wooden spoon. He sees a pair of feet and legs approach. The child looks up as a voice reaches him. "LeRoy, I smell something! I think you need changing," says a caregiver.

"No!" responds LeRoy.

"LeRoy, you need a clean diaper," says the caregiver, holding out her hands. LeRoy ignores her. "I can see you don't want to be changed, but I'm going to do it anyway. Do you want to walk or shall I carry you?"

LeRoy gets up and walks in the other direction. "Okay, I'll carry you," says the caregiver firmly, picking him up. He struggles in her arms. "Would you rather walk to the changing table?" she says, putting him down. He reluctantly moves toward a corner of the room. When he reaches the changing table, LeRoy turns and tries to run off in the other direction.

"I'm sorry, but you just have to put up with this," says the caregiver, holding him firmly and lifting him to the table. "First we have to get your jeans off," she says, struggling with suspenders. LeRoy squirms under her grasp. "I know—you really don't like this." She continues undressing him, then unfastens the diaper. He tries to stand up. She holds him down firmly. "I know you want to stand up, but you have to wait just a minute. See, I'm putting the diaper here—she shows him where she disposes of the diaper. He twists to look, finally showing some interest in what is going on.

"Look, I'm going to wipe your bottom with this." She takes advantage of his momentary interest. He squirms as he feels wetness on his bottom. He struggles to sit up. "Almost finished." The caregiver is obviously hurrying. She puts the clean diaper in place. He lifts his bottom as she slides it under him.

"I like the way you help me, LeRoy." She smiles at him. "There, all done—let me just pull your pants up again." He willingly puts his arms into the suspenders.

"Get down!" he demands.

"Yes, I'll put you down now," says the caregiver, holding out her arms as he sits up. She puts him on the floor. He runs immediately to the can and wooden spoon he was playing with before. He looks relaxed and happy—giving no hint that he just went through some kind of ordeal.

Notice that the caregiver did not give up. She tried to involve LeRoy in the task, even though it wasn't easy. She acknowledged his feelings and verbalized them for him. She respected his feeling annoyed and wanting to be active. She worked quickly with as little fuss as she could manage. In short, she treated LeRoy as a human being—never as an object. She treated him with respect.

All children go through periods of being uncooperative, as LeRoy did in the preceding scene. It is important that they do so, even though it is hard on the caregivers. Resisting is a sign of growth; by resisting, children assert their individuality. They learn something about the push toward independence that will one day make them individuals who no longer need the kind of care they now receive.

Toilet Training

Part of the job of toddler caregivers who work with children over two years of age is toilet training. Toilet training happens as a part of normal development because children want to be like the other children they see using the bathroom. The key to ease in toilet training is readiness. Children must be physically ready, which means they can hold on and let go at will. In addition, children must be mentally ready, which means they know what is expected. And finally, children must be emotionally ready, which means they are willing. When these three conditions are present, toilet training occurs naturally as caregivers ask for cooperation, just as they do in all caregiving routines.

Most programs are concerned with cooperating with the parent when it comes to toilet training. At Napa Valley College Child Care Center, in California, the policy is not to initiate toilet training until the parent suggests it; then the staff is assured that the child will find consistency at home and at the center. Consistency may be more difficult if the parent is from a culture that views toilet training as a first-year task. Although staff may not be willing to try to "catch" children and put them on the potty before they consider them really ready, it is important to respect a different view. Here are some hints for making toilet training easier.

1. Help children feel physically secure by providing potties (if licensing allows) or very low toilets, if possible. The easier it is for children to get on and off by themselves, the more independence is promoted.

2. If appropriate, ask parents to dress children in loose, simple clothing they can remove themselves (elastic waistbands rather than overalls, for example).
3. Be gentle and understanding about accidents.
4. Avoid power struggles. You can't win them, and children can be left with long-lasting effects if toilet training has been a highly emotional affair.

Washing and Bathing

Most programs leave bathing up to parents except under very special circumstances. Some parents become insulted if their children are sent home cleaner than they arrived. Cleanliness can be a great point of conflict between parents and caregivers if they have different standards. Parents may be angry if a child with hard-to-wash hair comes home with hair full of sand. Cultural issues can give people different perspectives on the subject of cleanliness, so respect ideas that differ from your own.

Hand washing before meals is not such a touchy issue as bathing. Hand washing is popular with most children and can even be the highlight of the day for some toddlers. Short attention spans lengthen appreciably when toddlers are sent off to wash. Hand washing can be the most pleasant self-help skill to learn if low sinks are available and toddlers are allowed to use them at leisure. In fact, hand washing can become a major activity because toddlers greatly enjoy the sensory properties of soap and water.

Dressing

Caregivers can promote autonomy by setting up tasks in such a way that the child makes maximum contribution. You can easily see examples of this principle in dressing activities. For instance, when taking off the socks or booties of even a very young baby, you can pull them half off and ask the child to finish the job. It takes little coordination when the task is set up like this. Even young babies get real pleasure and satisfaction from helping out. The idea is to simplify the task just the right amount so that the child gets practice in the dressing and undressing process. At first it takes longer to work cooperatively, but as child and caregiver come to see themselves as a team, the earlier patience pays off. By toddlerhood, children who were encouraged to help dress and undress themselves have become proficient, needing little help except with such things as buttons and starting zippers. Here is a scene that shows how it would be if the caregiver did not aim for teamwork.

Imagine yourself a young toddler. You are about to be taken outside for a walk. Without anything being said to you, you feel your arm being grabbed. You're thrown off balance. Then you find yourself being hauled over to a coat rack. Your arm is held tight and then thrust into a sleeve. Your thumb gets stuck and stretches back as the sleeve comes up your arm. Then you feel yourself being swung around. You feel annoyed. When the other sleeve comes up your other arm, you stick your thumb out on purpose. Then you become all floppy. You feel a tighter grip on you, and some tension transfers from the hands holding you. You become even floppier. Finally a face comes down near yours, but the eyes look only at the zipper that is resisting getting on the track. You feel the struggle with the piece of metal; then suddenly the zipper moves upward. It stops only when it touches your neck and feels cold, uncomfortable, and tight. The face disappears, and you're left standing alone while the child next to you is readied in the same impersonal way.

Not a very enjoyable experience, was it? This child was being treated more like an object than a person. Can you remember a time in your own life when you were treated as an object? If you can, then you know why it is important not to treat a child (of any age) that way.

Napping

It is important that infants be allowed to rest according to their individual needs rather than according to someone else's schedule. Infants' sleep patterns change—sometimes from day to day as well as over a period of time. No one napping schedule will fit all babies in a program, and each baby's personal schedule changes from time to time.

Not all babies express their need for rest in the same way. Experienced, sensitive caregivers learn to read each child's signals, which may range from slowing down and yawning to increased activity and low frustration threshold.

Parents are the best source of information about their baby's sleep patterns and needs. Experienced caregivers are aware how useful it is to know that the baby woke up extra early that morning or got less sleep than usual over the weekend. They understand fussy behavior in a different light if they know the reason for it.

Each baby should have a personal crib located in the same spot every day. That kind of consistency and security may help the baby feel at home faster. Decisions about when to put a baby in the crib and how long to leave him or her there depend on the adult's perception of the particular child's needs. Some children need to be confined for some time before they can fall asleep, even when they are very tired. They may play or cry before sleeping. Other children fall asleep immediately. The waking up period also takes some adult judgment. Does the child wake up energetic, active, and ready to play, or is there a long transition period between sleeping and waking during which the child may need to remain in the crib?

Reading a young child's signals about rest needs is not always easy. Again, the parent is a good source of information. Find out what kind of self-calming behaviors a child has and encourage them. Some children stroke a blanket; others twist their hair. The most common self-calming behavior is thumb sucking. Ask how the child naps at home. Can you use some of the same devices or rituals the parent uses? Perhaps a favorite toy or blanket provides comfort.

Once again, cultural factors may enter into attitudes about sleeping. Some cultures see being alone in a dark room as the way to promote independence. Others feel that babies should not sleep alone. You may not agree with an attitude that is different from your own, but be sure to respect it. If you can't do what the parent wants, talk about it with him or her. Negotiate, discuss, exchange viewpoints. Don't just ignore a parent's wishes and do what you think is best.

As children move through toddlerhood and nap only once a day, they can learn to rest according to a group schedule. However, individual needs are still important, and provision should be made for the toddler who needs a quiet time earlier in the day, if not an actual nap.

Toddlers who feel nervous, scared, or lacking in trust may have sleep problems that consistency would help alleviate. A favorite toy or blanket may also provide needed security. Sometimes a caregiver can do nothing at the moment to promote security, but must acknowledge the child's insecure feelings and wait until he or she eventually learns that it's a safe place. In some programs, the children who need it have a back rub to help them go to sleep. Here are some further hints about how to help toddlers get to sleep:

1. Provide visual privacy for those children who need it. Some toddlers are too stimulated by being near another child to go to sleep.
2. Provide a quiet, peaceful atmosphere. Some programs use soft music to help. Start winding down before naptime.
3. Make sure all children get plenty of fresh air and exercise. Being tired is the best motivator for napping.
4. Don't let children get overtired. Some children have a hard time settling down to sleep when they are exhausted.

If adults regard caregiving tasks as vital learning experiences, they are more likely to approach them with patience and attention. In group care, even when the adult-child ratio is good, an infant's main opportunity to enjoy a long period of one-to-one interaction is during caregiving times like feeding, diapering, and dressing. If those times are used well, babies require far less adult attention during other periods of their day. Babies can go about their play (interacting with the environment and with the other babies) with no more than general supervision from an adult who may be watching a number of babies.

As toddlers develop self-help skills, this built-in one-to-one time disappears. Therefore, caregivers must provide it some other way even to the oldest toddlers. The fact that required ratios of adults to children may change when children are about two adds to the difficulty of giving the kind of individual attention each child needs. Some get it by being charming and appealing to adults. Others get it by exhibiting unacceptable behaviors. Some don't get it at all. One way to ensure that all children are getting individual attention, once the caregiving tasks are no longer such a focus during the day-care day, is to keep brief anecdotal records. If during naptime you write a single sentence about each child in your care that day, you'll soon see the patterns. You'll see that some children stand out because of their behaviors. Some children are practically invisible, and it's hard to think of anything to write about these youngsters. Once you see these patterns, you can make better conscious decisions about how to make sure that all children get individual attention each day.

When infants and toddlers are treated with respect and caregiving is done with a teamwork approach, relationships grow— relationships that help children learn about themselves and the world. They come to anticipate what will happen to them and realize the world has some predictability. They learn they have some power to influence the world and the people in it. They begin to make sense out of life. When used to their fullest, these times can become focuses in children's days—something they look forward to, their chance to "dance" with their partner.

This chapter has examined the role of attachment in determining needs as well as the importance of a relationship in order to make caregiving activities a viable part of the curriculum. But caregiving is only half the story. The next chapter explores the role of free play in comprising the other half of the curriculum.

Notes

1. Anne Morrow Lindbergh, *Gift from the Sea* (New York: Pantheon, 1955), p. 104. Reprinted by permission of Pantheon Books, a division of Random House.

For Further Reading

Educaring. Published quarterly by Resources for Infant Educarers.

Magda Gerber, "Respecting Infants: The Loczy Model of Infant Care," in Elizabeth Jones, ed., *Supporting the Growth of Infants, Toddlers and Parents* (Pasadena, Calif.: Pacific Oaks, 1979).

Magda Gerber, *Resources for Infant Educarers* (Los Angeles, Calif.: Resources for Infant Educarers, 1979).

Chapter 4
Play as Curriculum

A main ingredient of any infant or toddler program should be play. Early childhood educators have long recognized play as vital to growth and learning. It is natural to young children and should be regarded as an *important* use of their time, not as something secondary or optional.

The benefits of play are enormous and go far beyond the kinds of things we talk about so easily, like developing skills and learning concepts. Play offers children opportunities that come from nowhere else. Through play, children get involved in open-ended exploration. They are not confined by rules, procedures, or outcomes. Children at play have self-direction. They have power. Through total absorption during play, they make discoveries they might otherwise never make, they work on problems, they make choices, and they find out what interests them.

Seymour Papert in the foreword to *Mindstorms* talks about a play theme that started when he was a toddler, continued throughout his childhood, and has been an important influence throughout his whole life. Here is what he says about "The Gears of My Childhood":

> Before I was two years old I had developed an intense involvement with automobiles. The names of the car parts made up a very substantial portion of my vocabulary: I was particularly proud of knowing about the parts of the transmission system, the gearbox, and most especially the differential. It was, of course, many years later before I understood how gears work; but once I did, playing with gears was my favorite pastime. I loved rotating

circular objects against one another in gearlike motions, and, naturally, my first "erector set" project was a crude gear system.

I became adept at turning wheels in my head and at making chains of cause and effect: This one turns this way so that must turn that way so. . . .

He went on to use his model for learning mathematics. He feels that "working with differentials (gears) did more for my mathematical development than anything I was taught in elementary school." From his own experience he formulated what he still considers the fundamental fact about learning: "Anything is easy if you can assimilate it to your collection of models. If you can't, anything can be painfully difficult . . . what an individual can learn, and how he learns it, depends on what models he has available."

Children collect models through play. Papert talks about how children learn through models: "You can *be* the gear, you can understand how it turns by projecting yourself into its place and turning with it. It is this double relationship—both abstract and sensory—that gives the gear the power to carry powerful mathematics into the mind." He goes on to explain that no one told him to learn about gears. It was his own idea—indeed, a passion: "I remember that there was a FEELING, LOVE, as well as understanding in my relationship with gears."

What are the implications of Papert's story for caregivers? Should all children be encouraged to play with gear sets? He says, "To hope that every child might have the experience I had would be to miss the essence of the story. I FELL IN LOVE WITH THE GEARS . . . something very personal happened and one cannot assume that it would be repeated for other children in exactly the same form."[1]

Papert's story has great implications for promoting free play with the adult in the facilitator role. Papert obviously had someone who capitalized on his early interest and helped him in his pursuit. He or she probably provided further materials. But the important point is that *he* made the choices. Papert's interest, his initiative, provided the push. And what he gained was a set of models that served him throughout his academic career in learning the abstractions of mathematics. Early play in Papert's life (as in all children's lives) provided an important foundation for later learning and understanding.

The way we respond to infants and toddlers at play by giving them freedom, by helping them pursue their special interests, and by providing resources may result in children gaining lifelong models such as Papert's gears.

Letting free play remain free is difficult for some adults once they recognize how important play is for infants and toddlers. They want to set up objectives and plan for, indeed, control outcomes. This is especially true for programs for low-income children.

I remember visiting an infant-toddler program and watching the children playing freely with the toys available. They were involved and interested, and I was impressed with what I saw. But then the director arrived breathless, apologized that things were late in starting that morning, and proceeded to organize groups, get out "activities," and herd toddlers into chairs around tables. Here, they were drilled on names of objects in pictures, told to match shapes, and shown how to make circles and squares out of play dough. The adults, who had earlier been playing a background role, except when there was a call to be responsive, suddenly took charge of everything. The focus became very objective oriented. I looked later at individual education plans and discovered that cognitive objectives were defined very narrowly (for example, "shown pictures of a dog, a horse, and a cat, child will identify two out of three"). No wonder playtime was so objective oriented.

One reason that adults sometimes want to control toddler play is that they don't understand it. They understand preschool play because it looks involved and productive and fits into categories such as "dramatic play" or "art" or "block play." But toddler play may not look like much. Toddlers may not look involved. They dabble at things, wander around, often carrying objects with them. But if you watch carefully, you see they are not uninvolved, nor are they in transition. They are walking and carrying. They are making choices. In addition, perhaps they are enjoying the sensory changes as they move around. Sometimes they are keeping in contact with the person they are most attached to (touching home base).

Toddlers are easy to satisfy as long as they have room to move and things to examine and manipulate. They may seem to have short attention spans because of their gross motor focus and this need to change location. However, they can also get very involved, especially in problem solving or a self-chosen sensory activity. I have watched toddlers at a sink with soap, water, and paper towels for up to half an hour. (That's not a short attention span.)

The Adult Role in Play

Children learn from other children. By interacting with their peers, infants and toddlers learn much about the world, their power in it, and their effect on others. Through the kinds of problem-solving situations that present themselves in child-child interactions, youngsters come to learn such valuable skills as how to resolve conflicts. The adult's role in these child-child interactions is to encourage them, then step back until needed. Sensitive caregivers know when to intervene. Timing is crucial. If you step in too soon, valuable learning is lost. But if you step in too late, children can hurt each other. Timing and selective intervention are important skills for caregivers to acquire in order to facilitate infant-toddler social play.

Adults promote free play by providing time, space, and materials. The adult should remain available while infants and toddlers are playing, giving "wants nothing" quality time. They should restrain from interrupting the child who is really absorbed in play. Absorption is a quality we should value.

Adults can be part of the play, but they must remain in a playful mode, open to what happens, without setting up goals or playing for particular results, or the play ceases to be play and becomes an adult-directed "activity." You'll see examples throughout this book of adults in a "wants nothing" mode, playing with children.

Adults can also engage in mutual play with children for their own enjoyment. But be careful about becoming a child's major entertainment device. Some children get hooked on adults playing with them and are unable to play with other children or on their own when the adult steps back.

Adults also provide safety. Without safety, there is no free play. Children can feel comfortable only when they know no one will let them get hurt.

Adults can provide help with problem solving, but only when a child gets stuck and can't continue the problem-solving process.

A problem arises when a program stresses free play and asks adults to spend a good deal of time in a "wants nothing" mode, being available but not directive during free play time. It looks as though the adults are not doing anything. Here is a scene that shows adults facilitating free play.

> The play area is set up for older toddlers, who are busily exploring what has been put out for them. Two adults are sitting on the floor on opposite ends of the play area, and a third adult is sitting on a low chair by a table set up with play dough. At one end of the room, a group of children is carrying around large plastic blocks. One seems to have a plan in mind; two seem to be just interested in the transporting activity, without regard to where they are going. A fourth child has built a four-block enclosure and is sitting in the middle of it. A fifth child is walking across the blocks that are lying flat on the rug. A tussle starts as the child in the enclosure defends his structure from one of the transporters, who is determined to take one of his blocks. The adult moves calmly close to the action. When the conflict continues, she says quietly, "Josh doesn't want you to take his block."
>
> The other child ignores her and keeps pulling on the block that Josh is now sitting on. "How about this one?" says the adult, offering the child a similar block. The child hesitates a moment, then moves toward the block the adult is holding. The conflict resolved, the caregiver moves back to her original spot.
>
> At the other end of the room, a group of children is playing in a housekeeping area. One has gathered an armload of dolls and is trying to climb the stairs to the low loft, where there are several doll beds. He can't manage the stairs with his arms so full and is beginning to look frustrated. The caregiver walks over to him and suggests it would help if he could see the stairs. He

drops the doll in front of his face and starts to climb, but staggers slightly. The caregiver holds his arm with one hand and with the other hand touches the stair rail, saying, "You need a hand here to help you." He immediately gets the idea and drops the dolls in one arm. He then grabs the rail and carries the other armload of dolls upstairs, returning quickly for the ones he dropped. In the meantime, the caregiver has gone to sit on the floor and is drinking pretend coffee that another child is offering to her in a plastic cup.

The children at the play dough table are contentedly poking, prodding, and patting the play dough. They are ignoring the caregiver who is sitting there, and he sits quietly, not interrupting them.

Contrast that scene to this one:

This playroom has two main areas of activity at the moment. On a rug sit a group of toddlers with a caregiver directing a "circle time." She has been singing songs and doing finger plays, trying her best to get the toddlers to join in. None of them is singing. A couple of them are listening as they squirm around. Half the group is busy trying to escape to the toys in the other part of the room. Another caregiver is directing the escapees back to the circle, saying, "Circle time isn't over yet." Then the caregiver in charge gets out a flannel board and begins to tell a story. She briefly captures most of the group's attention, but then one boy comes up and tries to take the figures off the flannel board. The others can't see, so they get squirmy, and two start wrestling.

In the meantime in another area of the room, a third caregiver has a group of toddlers around a table. Each has a piece of paper with his or her name printed in bold letters. Each has a squeeze bottle of glue and a container of cutout shapes. The adult is explaining that they are going to "make a picture for their mothers." Before she has finished her explanation and given directions, one of the toddlers has begun sucking on the glue bottle while another has squeezed a huge puddle on his paper. A third drops the container on the floor and laughs as the papers fly out. While the caregiver is dealing with these mishaps, two other children leave to join the circle, and the remaining children squeeze glue to their hearts content. One finger paints in it, then rubs his head with his gluey hands.

The toddlers in both scenes are making choices, but in the second scene choices aren't part of the plan. The adult energy is heavily taxed by being in charge and by maintaining the limits set by the adult-directed activities they have chosen. Although the first scene shows far more adult-approved child behavior (due to the nature of the choices offered, all of which are appropriate for the age group), the second scene may appeal more to some people. In the second scene the caregivers are *doing something.* They are being teachers. They are playing the role most people expect them to play.

The outsider can understand a program where children are engaged in adult-directed "learning activities" but may be critical of one where caregivers just sit on the floor and respond. Parents may prefer that caregivers *teach* and look like they are in control of what is happening. They may not understand the role of facilitating learning through self-directed free play. Further, the caregivers themselves may feel like babysitters when in the "wants nothing" mode during free play time. They may resist this role. All these factors work against a curriculum in which free play is a main ingredient. Caregivers need to find ways to articulate what they are doing so they can counteract the pressure that comes from all sides to *teach* infants and toddlers rather than let them play. What caregivers do that is more important than teaching is to structure the environment so that it is conducive to play.

An important environmental factor is group size. Larger groups tend to be overstimulating, and quieter children get ignored. It's much harder for children to get truly absorbed in play in a large group than in a small one, even when the adult to child ratio is good.

Mixture of ages is another environmental factor. Adult preferences in age mixtures in groups vary. Some programs work well with a variety of ages; others work equally well with most of the children about the same age.

If you do mix ages, be aware of protecting the youngest children. In the case of infants mixed with toddlers, you must protect those who can't move around from those who can. One way to do this, if they are in the same room, is to fence off a portion of the room for the immobile children. Don't just keep them in playpens and cribs. They need floor space and room to stretch and move, as well as interactions that come from several infants and adults sharing floor space.

Sometimes the mixture is toddlers with preschoolers. In that case, the toddlers need to be protected from equipment they aren't mature enough to use, as well as from conflicts that they can't win. You can't just stand back and let the children solve their own problems if one is two and the other almost five. The two year old will probably need some help to hold his or her own.

Most programs and family day-care homes set up the environment so that it's clear what activities take place in it. Play space is usually separate from the rest of the areas. (See Chapter 12 for more explanations of the other areas of the environment.)

Caregivers aren't providing structure by directing the play itself, but they structure the play environment. You can do away with most rules by setting up the environment so that a good deal of undesirable behavior is eliminated. For example, if the children aren't allowed to play in the kitchen, put a gate across the access.

Make sure that everything in the environment is touchable and even mouthable. You can expect older children not to put things in their mouths, but infants and toddlers learn through mouthing. Sanitize toys periodically rather than restricting children from their natural inclinations.

Provide for gross motor activity inside as well as outside. Toddlers run, climb, roll, and jump all the time—not just when invited to. You should think of your toddler play area as a gym more than a classroom and set it up for active play.

Provide plenty of softness, both for the active play and for the quiet times. Cushions, pads, mattresses, and foam rubber blocks on the floor invite children to bounce, roll, flop down, as well as cuddle and snuggle with books or stuffed animals.

Provide hard surfaces as well. A vinyl floor provides a contrast to carpeting and is interesting to crawlers as well as beginning walkers. Hard surfaces also clean up easier when you set up such activities as cooking or perhaps water play. (A thick bath mat under a plastic dishpan gives toddlers a chance to play in water without making too big a mess.)

Make available toys that can be used in many ways—rather than toys meant to be used in only one way. Large foam blocks are an example. They can be hauled around, stacked, put together to make a structure, or sat upon. There is much more to do with large foam blocks than, say, a battery-operated or wind-up toy that puts the child in the role of a spectator.

Let children combine toys and materials as much as possible. If they want to haul stuffed animals into a block structure they have built, let them. If they take pots and pans out of the play stove to put the play dough in, let them.

Of course, you can't let everything be combined. Play dough in the water play table makes a mess nobody wants to have to clean up and wrecks the play dough besides. If you don't want something combined, make a clear environmental limit. (For example, water play can take place only in the pan on the table. You can't carry water in cups to the rug area.)

Determine what is the right amount of toys to make available. Don't put out more than you can stand to pick up. Watch out for overstimulation. Excited toddlers who have too many choices are more apt to make themselves and everyone else unhappy than those who have just enough to do. Bored toddlers in a nearly empty room create as many behavior problems as those in a room overstuffed with toys and people. Be aware of what is the optimum amount of things to do. You can judge the right amount by the children's behavior. The optimum amount changes with the day, the group, and even the time of year.

Take advantage of happenings. For the infant or toddler, these happenings can be simple and still be satisfying. Perhaps it is leaf raking in the play yard. Let the children watch or help, then play in the pile of leaves afterward.

Set up some happenings. A favorite at Napa Valley College Lab School Infant Center was an ongoing collage. A large piece of contact paper was put up on the wall (sticky side out), and the children stuck various items on. The continual rearrangement of the elements of this collage showed clearly how much more important the process is than the product at this age.

Some happenings that toddlers enjoy are modified versions of preschool activities. For example, easel painting can be done with plain water on chalk boards or thick soap suds (colored with food coloring) on plexiglass easels. Sponge painting can become squeezing sponges in trays with a little water covering the bottom.

One clever caregiver who knew how much infants and toddlers enjoy pulling tissues out of their box made a toy consisting of a tissue box filled with scarves tied together. Another simple activity the very young enjoy is crumpling tissue paper. (Use white so that if it gets wet, you don't have dye all over everything.)

Simple food preparation tasks (mashing bananas or peeling hardboiled eggs) can delight toddlers. Even snapping spaghetti can be involving and satisfying for toddlers.

The environment should be set up to provide choices. Free choice is an important ingredient of play. Here is a scene that shows a playroom set up to encourage free play with numerous choices.

One end of the room is fenced off. In it three infants are lying on their backs, waving their arms, and looking around. A caregiver sits near them, rearranging brightly colored scarves to be within the reach of each child. A floppy beach ball is also available. One of the infants grabs it, waves it in the air, and lets it go. It lands near another of the infants, who regards it briefly, then turns back to gaze at the red scarf standing puffed up near his face.

Beyond the small fenced-in area is a larger space where nine young toddlers are playing. Two are busily engaged in crawling in and out of the rungs of the ladder that is lying flat on the floor. One leaves to sit in an empty laundry basket nearby. He climbs out, turns it over, then crawls under it. He lifts it up to look out at two children who are trying on hats from a collection they have found in a box near a shelf of toys. One of these children puts three hats on his head, then picks up two in his hands and runs over to the fence and throws the hats, one by one, into the area where the infants are lying. He giggles delightedly at the reaction he gets from the surprised infants. The other hat player in the meantime has loaded several into the back of a small toddler trike and is riding around the room. He stops at a low table where several children are squeezing zip-lock bags full of different substances. He looks at the caregiver sitting there when she says to one of the squeezers, "You really like the soft one, don't you?" He briefly pokes one of the bags. Finding it interesting, he abandons the hats and the trike and sits down at the table to explore the other bags.

In another area of the room, a girl is hauling large plastic-covered foam blocks from one corner and piling them on the couch, which is pulled out a few feet from the wall. Then she climbs up on the couch and proceeds to throw the cushions over the back until she has nearly filled the space. She gets down, walks around, and jumps on the pile she has made.

In another part of the room, a child is sitting with a caregiver on a large mattress (which actually is two sheets sewed together and filled with foam rubber scraps). The two are "reading" a book together. They are joined by one of the bag squeezers, who plops down on the adult's lap and takes the book away. It is quickly replaced by the other child, who has a stack of books next to her on the mattress.

In this scene, the children have a number of choices. It is also an important prerequisite to learning. J. McVicker Hunt talks about the relationship of learning to choice in terms of what he calls the "problem of the match." He says that learning occurs when the environment provides experiences just familiar enough so that children can understand them with the mental ability they have already attained, but just new enough to offer interesting challenges.[2]

Learning occurs when there is optimum incongruity between what is already known and a new situation. If the situation is too new and different, children withdraw, become frightened, ignore it, or react in some way other than learning. If it is not novel enough, children ignore it. They won't pay attention to that which has already become so much a part of them that it no longer "registers."

The question is, how can you set up an environment so that it has elements of "optimum incongruity"? How does anyone know exactly what a match is for each child in his or her care? The answer is to have some knowledge of ages and states (see the chart of developmental curriculum in Appendix B). The developmental information in Part II should help too.

The other answer is by *observation*. When you watch the children, you have a good idea what kinds of things to put into the environment for your particular group. By providing a number of choices of appropriate toys, objects, and occurrences and letting the children play, you give them the opportunity to move to novel situations and novel uses of materials. No one is more creative than infants and toddlers when it comes to inventive uses of materials and objects. They have a need to learn, a desire to understand. Caregivers can capitalize on this need to let them guide their use of the environment (within reason, of course). By directing children with either praise or pressure, we distract them from the inner delights mentioned by Abraham Maslow in Chapter 2. Children get these inner delights from struggling with a problem that matches their learning level.

Sooner or later children in an interesting, challenging environment are bound to find a problem that they want to solve, but can't. They "get stuck." If they can't figure out the next move, the adult can intervene by providing a tiny bit of help. Sometimes it's hard for adults to wait when they solve a problem so easily. But if they wait, they provide children the best learning opportunities. Don't rescue children from problems; help them problem solve.

And don't push children. Here's another view of "getting stuck." Sometimes children get stuck by becoming satiated with something. They have had enough of some activity. *Adults* decide children are bored and want to do something about it— quickly! Many adults have a great fear of boredom for infants as well as for themselves. This fear has perhaps been heightened by the trend for infant stimulation and pressures for academics before kindergarten. Yet boredom is educational and can be considered part of the learning plan of any program. As Maslow says:

> The single holistic principle that binds together the multiplicity of human motives is the tendency for a new and higher need to emerge as the lower need fulfills itself by being sufficiently gratified. The child who is fortunate enough to grow normally and well gets satiated and *bored* with the delights that he has savored sufficiently, and *eagerly* (without pushing) goes on to higher, more complex, delights as they become available to him without danger or threat. . . . He doesn't have to be "kicked upstairs," or forced on to maturity as it is so often implied. He *chooses* to grow on to higher delights, to become bored with older ones.[3]

Children cannot push themselves on until they have done very thoroughly what it is they need to do. Until they have reached the state of boredom, they are still motivated by unfinished business and can't move on. Boredom, when they finally attain it, provides the push to move on—but the push comes from within, not from without. They can then leave behind the old level, the old needs, and deal with the new ones, giving them their full attention. When the push to move on comes from without—from the adult or the environment—children never quite satisfy themselves. They may move on to the next stage, task, or activity with leftover feelings from the previous one, perhaps unable to give full attention to the new.

This idea of children deciding for themselves when to move on is the basis of the play yard design of Jerry Ferguson, who is an architect as well as an early childhood educator.[4] Ferguson designs environments uniquely suited to allowing infants and young toddlers to decide when and whether they are old enough to leave each developmental area. For example, she designed a play yard for the Pacific Oaks Infant-Toddler Program in Pasadena, California, in which the very youngest infants were in a low-stimulation area in the middle yard cut off from the rest by a variety of barriers. In this area was a grassy place, completely safe for tiny babies. Beyond the grass was a sandy place with a tunnel at the end connecting the sand to a more challenging play yard. Between the grass and the sand there was also a low wooden walkway designed to present a sufficient barrier to infants who were not yet ready to cross it. Children who were just beginning to move around had to conquer the raised walkway before they could get to the sand. They could test the sand from the safety of the walk before deciding to go into it, and they did this, sometimes for a week at a time, before they were ready. By the time they chose to go into the sand, they were able to handle the risks it presented, and the sand then became a safe environment for them. The tunnel at the other end, though obviously open, presented a formidable barricade, and few children chose to go through it until they were nearly ready to walk.

Thus, by the time the infants were able to leave the safe inner yard (by their own choice), they were developmentally ready for the bigger challenges of the yard beyond. This yard was designed for the beginning walker and good crawler and was interesting and safe, yet challenging (that is, optimally risky). Beyond was the most challenging yard, with climbing equipment and wheel toys for the toddlers. Although all the children who left the inner yard could return to it, few did so except for occasional visits. They chose to play where the environment had more to offer them.

Jerry Ferguson stresses that her approach works only because the infants have learned to take some responsibility for their own well-being. They come to depend on their ability to make choices, which means they have had the opportunity to gain experience in making decisions.

Infants and toddlers learn a great deal by being in an environment that offers the freedom to explore and discover. The adult role is to set up that environment and to remain available but nondirective while the children play, intervening selectively to prevent children from hurting each other and to help them work at solving problems.

This chapter ends the first section, which focuses on the adult's role. The next section examines the progression of development in each of seven areas, starting with attachment.

Notes

1. Seymour Papert, *Mindstorms: Children, Computers, and Powerful Ideas* (New York: Basic Books, 1980), pp. vi–viii. Reprinted by permission of Basic Books, Inc., Publishers.
2. J. McVicker Hunt, *Intelligence and Experience* (New York: Ronald Press, 1961), p. 267.
3. Abraham H. Maslow, *Toward a Psychology of Being*, 2nd ed. (New York: Van Nostrand, 1968), pp. 55–56. Copyright 1968 by Litton Educational Publishing, Inc.
4. Jerry Ferguson, "Creating Growth-Producing Environments for Infants and Toddlers," in Elizabeth Jones, ed., *Supporting the Growth of Infants, Toddlers, and Parents* (Pasadena, Calif.: Pacific Oaks, 1979).

For Further Reading

Stephanie Feeney and Marion Magarick, "Choosing Good Toys for Young Children," *Young Children*, November 1984, pp. 21– 25.

Magda Gerber, "Good Play Objects for Babies," *Educaring* 7(3), Spring 1986, pp. 4–6.

Anna Tardos, "Facilitating the Play of Children at Loczy," *Educaring* 6(3), Summer 1985, pp. 1–7.

Mary Jane Tonge, "Hanging Out with Babies at Play: Vignettes from a Participant-Observer," in Elizabeth Jones, ed., *Supporting the Growth of Infants, Toddlers, and Parents* (Pasadena, Calif.: Pacific Oaks, 1979).

Connie K. Williams and Constance Kamii, "How Do Children Learn by Handling Objects?" *Young Children*, November 1986, pp. 23–26.

Part 2
Focus on the Child

Chapter 5
Attachment

Once the umbilical cord has been cut, the newborn is a separate individual. That child's life depends on the attention, the care, and the love of those around him or her. Babies depend on the closeness of adults in order to get their needs met. That closeness comes through a process of attachment, called by some "falling in love."

Attachment is a two-way process that is deeper and lasts longer than just a relationship. Through attachment, two individuals come together and stay together. The mother is almost always the first and primary attachment the baby makes, but more and more babies are also becoming strongly attached to their fathers early on. Babies can make secondary attachments to people other than their parents. When they go off to day care at a young age, these secondary attachments become important.

Attachment to caregivers differs from that to parents in many ways. One obvious way is in duration. The long-term, even lifetime attachment one expects as a parent gives way to a much shorter period for caregivers. From day one, caregivers know that the children will leave their charge long before they grow up. The departure may come without warning because parents' lives and need for child care sometimes change suddenly. This expectation of the permanence of the adult-child relationship is a big difference between being a parent and being a caregiver.

Parental attachment, this feeling of closeness, starts right at birth for some. In the ideal situation, where parents and alert newborn are allowed time together to get acquainted, what's called "bonding" may occur as they fall in love in a very short period of time. You might even call it "love at first sight."

"Love at first sight" sometimes occurs between caregivers and children, too, as an adult and child are drawn to each other at first meeting. More commonly, however, attachment grows more slowly over time as the parties in question get to know each other and learn each other's special ways of communicating.

Babies are designed to promote their own attachment. Think for a moment about the variety of behaviors that attract adults to them. If you have ever heard the cry of a newborn, you know that it elicits feelings in the people who hear it. It is hard to ignore and at once becomes one of the infant's strongest signals to the people responsible for its care.

Another strong attachment behavior most babies have at birth is the ability to establish eye contact. When newborns look right into their eyes, most people melt. And if you touch the little fingers, they are likely to curl around your big one. If you talk to alert newborns, they are likely to turn toward the sound of your voice. And if you move away from them slightly, their eyes will follow your face. All these behaviors promote attachment.

And, of course, babies look so cute, especially as they grow older. They make you (if you're the object of attachment) feel *so* special. This preferential response starts early—even at birth as babies distinguish their mother's voice from other voices. Studies show that babies react differently to the people they're attached to right from the beginning. Later this preferential response becomes obvious as babies cry when the object of attachment leaves the room. They follow the person with whom they have the attachment, first with gaze alone, then, when they are mobile, by crawling after. Here is a scene showing some of the attachment behaviors mentioned during a feeding.

A small baby is screaming, lying on the floor on a blanket in the family room of the home where he is cared for. A reassuring voice comes from the other room. "I know you're hungry! I'm coming!" The cries cease at the sound of the voice. Then when no one appears, they start again even louder.

The family day-care provider hustles into the room carrying a warm bottle. "I'm sorry you had to wait!" The screaming continues. "I know, I know. I'm going to pick you up now so you can eat." She bends over with her arms outstretched. The screaming slows up. She lifts him gently and walks across the room to sit down in a soft chair.

As he is picked up, the baby's whole body shows his anticipation of what is to come. He stiffens and his arms wave in excitement. He looks intensely into his caregiver's face.

Once settled into the chair, he begins to squirm frantically, his mouth searching for the nipple. As it comes into his mouth, he closes his eyes, clenches his fists, and sucks furiously. "There you are. That's better, isn't it?" coos the caregiver.

He begins to relax after a few minutes, and both adult and child settle back, moving around until comfortable. "You were really hungry, weren't you?" The baby continues to suck without stopping. Both begin to look more and more relaxed and contented.

The baby eases up a little. His fists unclench, and one hand reaches out, groping. The caregiver touches his hand with her finger. He wraps his fingers around her finger and holds on tight. The caregiver snuggles him a little closer and kisses the top of his head. He opens his eyes and looks up at her. She looks back, a warm smile on her lips. He stops sucking and lets go of the nipple. With his gaze fixed on his caregiver's eyes, his mouth breaks into a big grin. Then he snuggles in even closer and continues to suck contentedly, his little fist wrapped around her finger, his eyes looking into hers.

These two are a unit. Both feel that this is an intimate moment of a close partnership. This infant has the capacity to elicit delight from another; this in turn gives him pleasure. The example of the feeding experience illustrates some of the repertoire of behaviors involved in attachment. Through these mutually responsive behaviors, which include touching, fondling, and eye contact, as well as feeding, infants and adults form an extremely close relationship. Infants need this relationship because they cannot physically attach themselves to people in order to get nourished and cared for. They are dependent. Attachment is nature's way of ensuring that someone will care (in the emotional sense) and provide care (in the physical sense).

Have you ever tried to get close to someone who was indifferent? As an adult, you can usually choose to establish a relationship with someone or not. Infants, however, do not have that choice. If they are to thrive, it is *vital* that the process of attachment be provided for, even if it takes a great deal of time and effort.

Not all babies enjoy an ideal relationship that fosters the attachment process; the infant and caregiver do not respond to each other in ways that bring mutual delight, as well as the care necessary for the infant. What about a relationship that is less than ideal?

Sometimes infants are born without a strong set of attachment behaviors. They may not be responsive or attractive. Adults may find it neither rewarding nor satisfying to interact with such babies or to meet their needs. Not only may these infants lack a set of pleasing behaviors; they may even reject any advances. They may constantly stiffen when cuddled or cry when touched. Some babies are just not responsive. They may be too active to attend, or too passive. In these cases, it is up to adults to promote attachment.

Caregivers can promote attachment by setting as a goal to develop a relationship. That means being persistent and not being put off by the baby. Sensitive caregivers find ways that cause less discomfort to hold the babies who reject them. They continue to touch and talk to these babies despite rejection. They use caregiving times to interact and pay attention to the child at other times as well. Sometimes just observing such babies regularly and in depth will help caregivers develop a feeling for babies that they feel indifferent or even negative about. That feeling is part of the attachment process.

Caregivers also find ways to help too active or too passive babies attend. They discover ways to reduce stimulation or increase sensory input, depending on what is needed.

Center-based programs can provide for attachment needs through a primary caregiver system in which babies are assigned to a particular caregiver. Group size is important if babies are to be responded to consistently and sensitively in order to promote attachment. More than about twelve babies works against attachment.

Sometimes the attachment problems lie with the parents. The infant may be born fully equipped with attachment behaviors, but the mother may fail to respond. Indifference, for whatever reason, can be devastating to an infant. The infant doesn't give up for a long time and may develop a set of behaviors that elicits a negative response from the adult, which is better than no response at all.

If the baby has no attachment or negative attachment, that is cause for alarm. Outside help is required. Day-care workers may perceive the problem and refer the family, but it is beyond their realm of responsibility to solve it.

You may suspect this problem when a baby in your care does not thrive in the same way the other babies do. He or she may not be gaining weight or reaching milestones within a reasonable time. This failure to thrive may be related to a variety of other causes instead of an attachment problem. A clue that attachment is the problem is a lack of attachment or your having trouble getting attached. You may see that the baby is unresponsive to everybody. Or perhaps you see him or her responding exactly the same to everyone—parent, stranger, and caregiver.

What happens if there is no attachment? A significant answer came from Harry Harlow, who learned something about attachment without even setting out to study it. He was interested in isolating rhesus monkeys so that they could live in a disease-free environment and not infect one another. He raised fifty-six newborn monkeys in separate cages, away from one another and their mothers. He was surprised to find that they grew to be very different adults from the rest of their species. They were unsocial, indifferent, and aggressive compared to other rhesus monkeys, who are normally social and cooperative. None of the monkeys raised in isolation mated.[1]

Let's examine the implications for child rearing. Although virtually no one attempts to raise a child in total isolation, children are too frequently raised without enough human physical contact, without opportunities for interaction, and without consistent treatment. This kind of deprivation occurs in some institutions. In such a situation, the problems are multiple. Though the infants have contact with adults who feed and change them, the adults may vary from day to day, and the infants may be unable to distinguish one from the other or may find that their attachment behavior when they are being cared for brings no consistent response. They find no one to call their own—no one whom they can influence. Eventually, such children give up and no longer try to influence anyone. Lacking not only attachment, but adequate physical contact, these infants are deprived of the variety of sensory input that comes with a healthy relationship. They become passive and noncomplaining, their development slows, and they may fail to thrive. Researchers believe that it is important for babies to have established a consistent attachment to at least one person before four to six months of age.[2]

Studies of children in institutions have kept many people from considering group day care for infants. But infants in day care are different from infants in orphanages. They have parents (at least one). Most of them arrive in day care attached, and they remain attached. But we have learned from those sad orphanages of yesterday. We know now how vital attachment needs are. We know too that infants need ongoing, reciprocal, responsive interactions when they are outside their own homes for significant periods during the day. We know that infants in day care retain their attachments to their parents.

Evidence on the effects of day care on the development of attachment in infancy is still sparse, though some answers are beginning to come. The research shows that infant day care is not detrimental to development if the quality of care is exemplary. That means, among many things, that the caregivers are nurturing, responsive adults who meet each infant's individual needs. Quality care is vital. Infants not only deserve, but *must have*, fine care—not just good enough care.[3]

Milestones of Attachment

Important milestones of attachment, which relate to both mental and social development, are reached when infants begin to discriminate between just any human face and familiar faces. Within the first few months of life, the baby can clearly indicate recognition of his mother (or other primary caregiver). At first he follows her with his gaze, sometimes crying when she leaves. Later, when he is mobile, he crawls after her in preference to others. He knows that this is the person(s) who meets his needs.

Once babies can distinguish their mother or caregiver from other people, two new worries begin. First, at about eight to ten months of age, they begin to fear strangers. Second, now that they know who mother is, they worry about losing her. This latter fear usually appears by about ten to twelve months. Both of these fears indicate infants' ability to discriminate and recognize difference and are therefore obvious signs of mental growth. Corresponding to this second developmental fear is babies' inability to understand that objects that are gone from sight still exist. Jean Piaget called this "object permanence"; it will be discussed further in Chapter 8. Infants' worry about losing their mother is understandable. They cannot foresee that a separation is only temporary. Knowing this, it is easier for caregivers to understand the desperation of the protest when a baby is left behind as mother walks out the door.

It may be helpful here to emphasize the interplay between dependency, mental development, and trust in this process of attachment. When an eighteen month old child is clinging to his mother and crying for her not to go (obvious dependent behavior), he is also saying I *know* I need you (a mental function). As his mental capacity grows, and his experiences teach him that he can trust his mother to return, from attachment comes trust as he learns that the world is basically a friendly place where he can get his needs met. From attachment also comes autonomy or independence as babies grow and begin to take over the caregiving by learning self-help skills. They also find it easier and easier to let go because they know that their mother (or father) will be back. This ability to trust a relationship is the foundation for independence—a focus of the toddler period.

Separation anxiety is what this worry about leaving the parent or other primary caregiver is called. Separation anxiety is usually at its peak as the baby nears the end of the first year of life. If the child enters day care just at this time, the beginning can be very difficult. Children do better if they enter before or after the peak of separation anxiety.

Not only infants suffer from separation anxiety; toddlers can experience it as well. Here is a scene in which a toddler in day care for the first time works on his separation anxiety.

> Adam's mother is sitting in a corner of the play yard. Two year old Adam is on her lap. He watches the other children play from his very safe vantage point. Periodically, his mother tries to get him interested in joining the others. He resists all her efforts. She finally sits back. Obviously, she is prepared to stay until he is comfortable.
>
> From time to time, Adam's attention focuses on the rabbit cage quite near where he and his mother are sitting. Finally, he slides off her lap, runs to the cage, sticks his finger in, poking at the rabbit, then pulls his finger out and runs back to his mother. He does not climb back on her lap, but stands close, resting a hand on her leg. Again he approaches the rabbit cage, staying longer this time. He once again returns to his mother. He follows this same pattern for at least ten minutes.

Then his attention moves to several other toddlers who are playing on a low climbing structure. He stands by his mother, watching them. They move to where a caregiver is putting out a water table. His gaze follows them. Then he looks back to the now empty climbing structure. He lets go of his mother's leg and moves slowly in the direction of the climbing structure. He climbs cautiously up a wide ramp, then runs back down, straight to his mother. Again he stands by her, watching the children now splashing in the water with their hands. It takes him another ten minutes to consider joining them, but consider he does, and he begins to move in their direction. He stands on the periphery, watching everything that is going on.

When he finally joins them and tentatively puts his hands into the water, his mother gets up to leave. Immediately he runs back to her.

"I'm sorry, Adam, but I really have to go now. I know that you'll be just fine here." She bends down to kiss him. A caregiver has joined the two and begins talking to Adam about saying good-bye to his mother. She's down on her knees looking into his eyes and touching him lightly on the shoulder.

Adam begins to cry. His mother walks toward the building, and he follows her, crying more loudly. The caregiver goes too. Once inside, the parade heads for the door. The caregiver tells Adam that they will watch from the window and directs him away from the door his mother goes out. His cries are much louder now. He waves until his mother's car is out of sight; then he sits down and sobs brokenheartedly.

"I know it's hard to see her go," says the caregiver, obviously understanding what he is feeling. She sits on the floor by him and strokes his back gently.

He stops crying briefly, then starts again, quieter this time. He leaves the window and goes over to stand by a frog in an aquarium on the wall opposite the window. He continues to stare out the window. The caregiver sits at a low table where several other children are playing with simple puzzles.

Adam has stopped crying now and just stands by the frog, gazing into the aquarium periodically, then out the window, then at the caregiver. He makes a short trip over to the window, looks out, goes to stand by the caregiver briefly, then goes back to the frog. The children at the table leave the puzzles and go to play with a wooden train that is on the floor in another part of the room. Adam moves closer to the caregiver, who is still at the table organizing the puzzles. He stands next to where she is sitting in a low chair. He watches the children, glances at the frog, and then focuses on the caregiver, who is talking to him in a calm, matter-of-fact voice about the puzzles on the table. Finally, he begins fiddling with one of the puzzle pieces. Later he goes off to join the children who are still pushing wooden train cars around on the rug.

This scene shows several aspects of attachment behavior in toddlers. Adam gained courage to explore and participate by using his mother as home base from which to move out. He checked in periodically to renew the energy he needed to move out. His mother was able to provide this period of support during this first hour in the program. Then when she left, he was able to use the caregiver in the same way, though the attachment was significantly less.

Notice too that Adam had warning that his mother was leaving. She did not sneak away while Adam was busy, though she was probably tempted to. She surely knew that her leaving would upset him. She could have avoided being witness to that upset by sneaking out, but she would have not been building trust if she had. By saying good-bye, she teaches Adam that she will not leave without warning, but rather that her departure is predictable, at least to the extent that it follows a good-bye ritual. Eventually, he'll learn to confine his worries to the times of actual separation rather than wondering constantly and uneasily whether or not his mother has slipped out on him.

In this scene, the caregiver expressed what she perceived he was feeling in words, accepting the fact that he was unhappy. She offered support but did not try to distract him from what he was feeling. She helped him cope with the separation by suggesting he watch the car drive away. For some children, waving good-bye helps the separation. Perhaps they need to be able to *do* something, or perhaps they just need to see for themselves that mother is really gone—not just in another room. Here are some hints for helping toddlers with separation:

1. Help the parent understand that once the good-byes are said, the departure should be immediate. Some parents have as much or more trouble than their toddlers separating. Help the parent know that you understand it is hard to leave, but it is easier on the child if departure is quick once the good-byes are said.
2. Allow the child his or her feelings, but don't get involved in them yourself. Separation feelings are hard for some adults because they trigger issues they may want to forget. One way caregivers respond to this situation is by trying to get rid of the child's feelings, through distraction or by minimizing them. ("Come on now—it's not that bad—she'll be back before you know it.")
3. Have an interesting, even enticing environment that calls out to children so that when they are ready, they can readily get involved in something. One center did an informal study of what attracted children during separation (what they separated to—adults, other

children, or objects). Objects won, hands down, although adult proximity helped.

Attachment is vital to infants' and toddlers' development and should be promoted in day-care programs. At the same time, caregivers should realize that parents may fear their children may gain secondary attachments outside the home at the expense of their primary ones with parents. Caregivers can help ease parents' fears by letting them know they are unfounded. The secondary attachments are in addition to the primary ones—not replacements for them (more on this subject in Chapter 14). Separation anxiety and all the feelings that go with being left in day care are also of concern to both parents and the caregivers who have to help the children cope until they feel comfortable. But it may comfort parents to know that these feelings are a sign that attachment is strong and that it will hold. Children learn to cope with separation, and this skill can serve them for a lifetime.

The next chapter is about perception. Perception relates to attachment because attachment depends on an infant's ability to perceive. Only when infants can discriminate their sense impressions of one person from another can they become attached. Chapter 6 examines how the progression of sensory discrimination occurs.

Notes

1. Harry Harlow, "The Nature of Love," *American Psychology 13,* 1958, pp. 59–60.
2. John Bowlby, *Attachment and Loss, vol. I: Attachment* (London: Hogarth, 1969), p. 386.
3. J. Kagan, R. B. Kearsley, and P. R. Zelazo, "The Effects of Infant Day Care on Psychological Development," *Evaluation Quarterly* 1(1), pp. 143–158.

For Further Reading

M. D. Ainsworth and B. A. Wittig, "Attachment and Exploratory Behavior of One-Year-Olds in a Strange Situation," in B. M. Foss, ed., *Determinants of Infant Behavior*, vol. 4 (New York: Barnes and Noble, 1969).

J. Bretherton and E. Waters, eds., "Growing Points of Attachment Theory and Research," *Monographs of the Society for Research in Child Development* 50 (1–2, Serial No. 209).

B. M. Caldwell, C. M. Wright, A. S. Honig, and J. Tannenbaum, "Infant Care and Attachment," *American Journal of Orthopsychiatry* 40 (1970), pp. 397–412.

F. C. Portnoy and C. H. Simmons, "Day Care and Attachment," *Child Development* 49 (1978), pp. 239–242.

Daniel Stern, *The Interpersonal World of the Infant* (New York: Basic Books, 1985).

Chapter 6
The Development
of Perception

The link between motor experience and sensory or perceptual awareness is strong. As infants move, they take in different sensory experiences. As they become aware of various perceptual differences, they move to accommodate to them. This interaction between movement experience and perceptual awareness is vital as infants begin to make sense of their world. This chapter will take a look at perceptual or sensory abilities. The next chapter will discuss motor skills. Keep in mind that they are always interacting and influencing each other.

To become more aware of your own perceptions, so that you can better understand those of an infant, try the following exercise:

> Choose something you like the taste and smell of (a sprig of mint, a piece of apple), and take it to a place where you can be undisturbed.
>
> Block out all your senses except smell and taste. Then pay attention to what you have brought along to smell and taste. Concentrate first on your sense of smell only, then on your sense of taste. When you have fully explored these, put the substance away. Notice how the sensation fades. When the flavor is gone, move on.
>
> Become aware of your body. Sense the places on your body where your clothes touch, where you feel pressure. Pay attention to these sensations. Alter your position, and note the changes you feel.

Be aware of your body in relation to the space it occupies. Feel
the space around you. "Sense," without touching, where your
body ends and the space begins. Explore the relationship between
your body and this space. Try expanding and contracting your
body; alter the space it takes up.

Now move your attention from your whole body to your hands.
Explore around you with your hands, noticing the textures and
forms your fingers encounter. Pay attention only to what your
fingertips feel.

Move your focus from your hands to your ears. Pay attention to
everything that is coming in through your ears. Now pick out the
noise closest to you, and listen to it carefully. Next, shift your
attention to the noise that is farthest from you. Now see if you can
concentrate on sounds coming from inside you. Finally, turn on
all the noises at once and take them in without sorting them out.

Now move your attention to your eyes. Open your eyes. Look
around. Focus on an object near you. See if you can make the
object disappear by looking only at the spaces around it and
between its parts. Concentrate on these negative spaces for a
minute or so. Then take in more objects. Look at them carefully.
Then concentrate on the space around and between them. Shift
your focus from the space back to the objects and back to the
space again. Try concentrating only on background, then on
foreground, then on a single object. Let your eyes go out
of focus.

Come back to your normal perceptive state.

Now reflect on the order in which you experienced your senses. If
you did the exercise the way it was set up, you went from perceiving through
very localized physical contact (your taste buds) to generalized physical contact (your skin). Then you went on to perceive with two senses that extended
beyond physical contact—hearing and seeing. With these you took in events
or objects at a distance.

Infants learn to use their senses in much the same order. They first
depend most on perceptions that are direct and physical—especially those
that come in through their mouths. An infant's mouth is his or her main
learning tool in the first months of life. As infants grow, they learn to
"extend" themselves by tuning in to the senses that bring information from
a distance.

This ability to "tune in" to experience and concentrate on certain
aspects of it allows an organizational process to develop. This process is
neurological—it cannot be seen. But we *can see* infants adjust to their experiences. Even though all the senses are operating, infants initially do not
realize that the information they receive from these senses has continuity.
They cannot yet perceive the repetitiveness of events or interpret them. In a

short time, however, connections between separate events are clarified. For example, crying infants will calm down as they realize that hearing a particular voice or seeing a particular face means that food or care is about to be given.

This book talks about only five senses, but it is interesting to speculate about possible other senses and whether infants may have many more sensory abilities than we retain as adults. Examine the following passage from *The Metaphoric Mind,* a book that argues that we have not five or six, but twenty or more senses.

> Some human beings clearly detect minute changes in gravitational and magnetic fields. Others can detect the energy created by a flow of material in pipes, movement through soil, or electrostatic currents in the air. As adults these people are considered unique, mystical, or deviant in some other way. It may well be that these people have simply retained an awareness of senses they possessed as children.[1]

Hearing

Newborns can hear at birth (and even before). They can sense the direction from which sound comes as well as its frequency and duration. Researchers have found that sounds of five to fifteen seconds seem to have the most effect on the infant's level of activity and heart rate (the two measures most frequently used to reflect an infant's awareness of a change in an event). If the sound lasts over several minutes, the infant becomes less responsive. In other words, an infant is more attentive if you speak and then be quiet than if you make long speeches.

Newborns recognize the sound of their mother's voice. Experiments have shown that infants only twenty weeks old can discriminate between the syllables "bah" and "gah." Listening to people's voices and noting differences seems to be an early skill. The way infants react to sounds or any other sensory stimulation, however, depends a great deal on the situation in which they experience them. A loud or strange noise may be frightening, but the presence of a familiar, comforting caregiver transmits a sense of security and allows the infant to remain calm and open to learning.

Infants need the opportunity to experience a variety of sounds, and they need quiet times in order to appreciate the differences in sounds. If the noise level in the environment is too high, the infant spends a lot of energy tuning out and focusing. The optimum noise level varies with each child. Sensitive caregivers can determine what is more or less right for the individual after they get to know the child. Part of this awareness comes from knowing your own optimum noise level.

Some adults like background music, and others don't. However, a point to consider is this: if you want an infant to focus on a sound, that sound should be isolated and have a beginning and an end. For example, if a music box or record player is constantly playing, the infant eventually stops listening because the sound is no longer interesting. Caregivers should be sure that mechanical toys and other noisemakers do not become substitutes for the human voice. Infants can determine a great deal from the inflection of a person's voice, and attending to the human voice and its inflections is the beginning of language development.

Toddlers have a greater ability to tolerate higher noise levels, so they can be in slightly larger groups than infants. However, toddlers too vary individually, and some children are greatly overstimulated by multiple sounds. These children may be unable to focus when surrounded by noise. One way to help solve this problem is to have quiet spaces where one or two overstimulated children may retreat when they choose to. I've seen pillow-lined closets, tents, and even large wooden boxes available for this purpose.

Toddlers, as well as infants, benefit when the sounds they hear most are live, human voices directed to them personally. Other appropriate sounds in the environment include voices of all sorts (children and adults), music (both live and recorded), and the sounds that naturally go along with free play in a rich environment. Helping children tune in to the sounds of nature, a worthy activity, is often accomplished on short walks, depending, of course, on the environment in which the center or family day-care home is located.

Be aware of talking to one sex more than the other. Boys and girls need equal treatment if they are to grow up feeling like equals.

Smell and Taste

Less is known about smell than about the other senses. Researchers know that it is present at birth. Newborns can distinguish the smell of their own mothers from that of other women who have just given birth, so smell obviously plays a role in attachment. (Mothers also often report that the smells of their babies are pleasing to them.)

Newborns respond to unpleasant strong odors such as ammonia or acetic acid by turning away but seem insensitive to less-interesting odors that are fainter. An increase in breathing rate and activity level can be noted when odors are present in the air, and the greater the saturation of the odors, the greater the heart rate and activity level.

Much animal communication is carried by odors, and it's possible that the infant and toddler smell emotions in others, though that statement is more speculation than fact.

An environment rich in smells adds to a toddler program. They can be part of the daily program, such as food cooking, or they can be introduced by caregivers in such ways as "smell bottles." Be careful of making things that aren't edible smell delicious—such as chocolate shaving cream or peppermint flavoring in play dough—unless the toddlers are well conditioned to the idea that play dough and shaving cream are not for eating.

Taste does not seem to be present at birth, but by two weeks the infant can distinguish between sweet and bitter, and prefers sweet. Salt taste is recognized soon after and will be accepted if the infant is hungry. A ten day old infant can show surprise if water is substituted for the expected milk, but there seems to be a correlation with whether the baby has been well fed: infants whose diets have been inadequate do not seem to notice taste differences rapidly.

Be careful not to condition infants to the taste of salt and other additives. There is no reason to spice food for the very young—the natural flavors are appreciated and enjoyed if not covered. Most of us have learned that food in its plain state "needs something," and we are suffering for that acquired taste as blood pressures soar and great numbers are on salt-restricted diets.

Tasting can be an important part of the toddlers' day as they are exposed to a variety of foods at meals and snack times.

Touch

Sensitivity to discomfort and pain increases rapidly after birth. Some parts of the body are more sensitive than others. The head, for example, is more sensitive than the arms and legs. Individual babies vary in their sensitivity to touch, and for some touch is unwelcome. Caregivers need to learn ways to handle those "touch defensive" babies in ways that cause minimal discomfort. One such way is to lift such young infants on a pillow instead of picking them up as you would other babies. Some babies and toddlers respond better to strong touch than light touch, which seems to pain them.

Where and how we touch is bound up in culture. It is a good idea to find out what is forbidden or disrespectful in cultures different from your own if they are represented in your program. For example, some cultures never touch children on the head, and to do so upsets parents. Consider the message mainstream America gives when one person touches or pats another on the head. How would you feel if your boss patted you on the head? Pats on the head are reserved for the very young or dogs, never for an equal or a superior. Though it seems very natural to most adults, perhaps it would be more respectful to restrain from patting babies and young children on the head.

Be aware if you are differentiating between boys and girls in the way you touch the children in your care. Sometimes people unconsciously touch one sex more than the other. Try to be equal in your treatment of both sexes.

Tactile perception (touch) relates to motor abilities (movement skills). As babies increase in their ability to move around, touch gives them more and more information about the world. And they seek this information almost emphatically. Any environment for infants and toddlers should be all touchable and mouthable (the mouth also gives the very young a good deal of information). And while you are filling the environment with plastic toys (that are both touchable and mouthable), don't forget to provide as well some natural substances that the children can explore—wood, for example, or wool. (One educational approach, Waldorf Education, believes that young children should experience *only* objects [toys] made from natural substances because artificial ones—things that look like one thing but are really something else—fool the senses.

Give toddlers words for what they are feeling—soft, warm, fuzzy, rough, smooth. And be sure they have plenty of soft objects in their environment. Some programs occur in predominantly hard environments because hard surfaces and objects last longer and are more sanitary. However, reducing softness is not a way to increase cost-effectiveness because a hard environment changes the whole program. At Napa Valley College Child Care Lab School, toddler behavior improved appreciably when the environment was softened.

Provide a variety of tactile (touching) experiences for toddlers. Even though they are up and around, they haven't outgrown their need to explore the world with their skin. Here are some ideas for offering toddlers tactile experiences that involve their entire body:

1. a "dress-up" area filled with silky, slinky, furry, and other textured clothes
2. a sensory tub filled with such things as plastic balls or yarn balls (securely fastened so children don't get tangled in loose ends) to climb into
3. swimming in plastic pools in the summer
4. sit-in sandboxes
5. mud baths (Nothing more is needed than a warm day, a hose, some dirt, and the willingness to clean up afterwards. The toddlers themselves know what to do with the mud.)

One program, less inclined to deal with mud but nevertheless interested in trying new ideas, made Jell-O cubes from eight years worth of leftover Jell-O, put them in a plastic swimming pool, and let the children wallow around with bathing suits on. This would work only if children didn't eat the Jell-O. I don't know how you'd be sure of that. (Be aware that some individuals and cultures frown on using food as a play material.)

If you're willing to let children wallow about getting whole body tactile experiences, be careful you don't tread on cultural values. Some cultures have strong prohibitions against children getting dirty or messy.

Other kinds of tactile experiences are designed mainly for the hands (or hands and arms). Some simple, one-step cooking allows children to have a tactile experience. Other possibilities include water play, sand play, play dough, and finger painting (which has several variations, such as shaving cream [not for the youngest toddlers], cornstarch and water, and chocolate pudding [not if food is frowned on as a play medium]). Be sure you emphasize the process and not the product. The point of finger painting is to feel the paint and squish it around, not to make a pretty picture to take home.

Be careful not to exclude girls from these tactile activities because they might get messy. (Some people tolerate messy boys easier than they do messy girls.) And be aware that some toddlers do not want to get messy. Don't blame parents for this. It may be that the parent has discouraged messiness (for personal or cultural reasons). But sometimes the reluctance comes from the child's personality or stage of development. Many toddlers go through a period of refusing to get their hands messy.

Not all tactile experiences have to be messy. Many excellent programs for toddlers have very limited messy experiences—no one expects you to encourage children to muck around in mud or Jell-O unless you really want to set up that kind of experience. Some simpler but also valuable experiences include a pan of cornmeal with spoons and sifters; a pan of birdseed (just to feel) or birdseed with pitchers, spoons, and cups; and a tray of salt to feel (and perhaps some little cars to run around in it).

Just letting children go barefoot provides them with a variety of experiences as they encounter different textures underfoot. You can also provide contact paper, sticky side up, to walk on. A favorite foot activity at Napa Valley College Child Care Lab School is foot painting. Children step barefooted in a pan of paint and then walk on strips of butcher paper.

Seeing

We know more about sight than about the other senses, probably because most people depend so heavily on it. Infants can distinguish light and dark at birth. The pupillary reflex (the automatic narrowing of the pupil in bright light and widening in dim light) can be seen at birth, even in premature infants. Within a few hours infants are capable of visual pursuit. Their fixed focus seems to be about eight inches away. In other words, infants are equipped to see the mother's face while breast-feeding.

Within a few weeks, infants can discriminate among colors and prefer warm ones (red, orange, yellow) to cool ones (blue and green). Eye movements are somewhat erratic at first, but they rapidly become more refined. By the end of the second month, infants can focus both eyes to produce a single, though probably blurred, image. By the fourth month, they can focus their eyes and see clearly. Their ability to see is then comparable to that of an adult, though of course they have to learn to perceive and interpret what they are seeing.

Most newborns find all people and objects placed in front of them interesting—though some are more so than others. The human face is the most interesting of all (because newborns' visual abilities are clearly designed to promote attachment).

Infants of all ages need to be able to see interesting things. However, in the first weeks, eating and diaper changing provide sufficient visual input. As infants get older, a variety of visual material becomes more appropriate because it encourages them to move around in their world. Something interesting to see becomes something interesting to reach for and eventually to move toward. Too much visual stimulation, however, can lead to a "circus effect." Infants become entertained observers rather than active participants and grow into passive toddlers who demand entertainment instead of inventing their own. Children used to outside entertainment are drawn toward television—the ultimate entertaining visual experience.

An entertained observer is quite different from a scientific observer. Entertained observers get hooked on a constant flow of novel visual stimulation. They get bored quickly and demand constant visual change. They may become television addicts. Because they experience such a strong assault on one sense (the visual), they ignore the fact that they are not actually involved physically or socially with the world around them. This eventual habit of observation and lack of involvement is detrimental to the development of a wide range of abilities.

Take cues from the infants themselves when setting up an environment that develops visual skills. Otherwise it's hard to know how much sensory input is too much and when interesting new visual experiences will be welcome. If infants cry at certain things, too much may be going on, or they may not yet be ready to leave what they were paying attention to. If they are very quiet, they may be concentrating on something in particular or may be "turned off" by too many events. When infants find their world interesting and are allowed to explore it at their own pace, they learn to entertain themselves in the process of discovery.

Toddlers' visual worlds are larger as they move around more. They also have a better understanding of what they are seeing. To get an idea of what toddlers' visual environments are like, get down at their level and look around. Things look very different down there.

To cut down on visual stimulation for toddlers, put low barricades to block areas of the room. Adults can see over the barriers in order to supervise, but children experience a visually calming room. (Barriers can also muffle sound to some extent.) Some rooms invite children to really focus on what's available; in others, toddlers get overexcited and have a hard time focusing.

Pictures add visual interest to a toddlers' environment (though of course pictures also belong in an infant environment). Hang them low enough for the toddlers to see at their own eye level. Change them periodically, but not constantly, because toddlers appreciate seeing the familiar on a regular basis. Choose pictures that clearly depict familiar objects or other children in action. Be sure to represent different races in your picture display. Also be aware of the sex of the children in the pictures you hang. Don't show pictures that are predominantly little girls looking pretty and doing nothing and little boys involved in engaging activities. We've all been brought up on books that had that particular bias. Let's not pass it on to the children in our care.

One way to hang pictures is with clear contact paper that covers the picture and extends out beyond to stick to the wall. This way the picture is sealed in with no loose corners to pick at and tear and no tacks to swallow.

Aesthetics is a worthy, but often unconsidered, goal when designing a visual environment for infants and toddlers. Children are more likely to grow up with an eye for beauty if the adults around them demonstrate that they value aesthetics.

Caregivers need to be sensitive to each infant's sensory needs and provide for the development of all the senses. The infants' task is to learn to interpret the sensations that come in through their senses. They don't just take in information; they learn to perceive it. They learn to hear and eventually to listen. They learn to discriminate the feelings on their skin, the various tastes in their mouths, the smells around them, the sights they take in. They learn to "make sense" of sensory information. Responses or reactions to this information from the senses depend on muscles—on motor skills, the topic of Chapter 7.

Notes

1. Robert Samples, *The Metaphoric Mind* (Menlo Park, Calif.: Addison-Wesley, 1976), p. 95.

For Further Reading

T. G. R. Bower, *Development in Infancy,* 2nd ed. (San Francisco: W. H. Freeman, 1982).
T. G. R. Bower, *A Primer of Infant Development* (San Francisco: W. H. Freeman, 1977).

Chapter 7
The Development of Motor Skills

W ithout muscular coordination, our perceptions (and thoughts) would be locked inside, if, indeed, they would occur at all. Life depends on muscles. Without our eye muscles, we would see little, if anything. Without our hand muscles, we could do little about what we did see. Without the intricate muscles of our throat, tongue, and other organs of speech, our communication would be severely restricted. Without our heart muscles (or a substitute), we would have no life at all.

Infants' abilities to use their muscles are quite different from those of adults, but the potential is obviously there. Infants are born with an internal blueprint for developing the basic skills and abilities that we as adults possess, and they go right to work doing just that soon after birth. Within a year and a half or so, they have learned most of the basic motor skills—sitting, walking, arm/hand coordination—that they will need throughout their lifetime. They spend the next years perfecting, expanding, and refining the original postures and movements that they learned early.

The Progression of Gross Motor Development
Reflexive Movements

Newborns can make few voluntary movements beyond the gross random movements of arms and legs. Most of their first movements are reflexive; that is, the muscles react automatically in the presence of different kinds of stimuli. The refined and complex movements that they make are also reflexive in nature.

Reflexes serve several functions. Some, like blinking, swallowing, and clearing the face for breathing, are protective. Others, such as kicking the legs alternately (reciprocal kicking), are precursors of later skills, in this case, walking.

Pediatricians and other infant specialists pay attention to reflexes because they indicate brain growth. As the growth of the brain shifts from the brain stem to the cortex, reflexes change or disappear. Figure 7.1 illustrates some of the reflexes described below.

Reflexes Present at Birth

Normal babies have the same breathing reflex that adults have, as well as a cough and gag reflex that keeps the breathing passage clear. Their eyes blink and squint, and pupils narrow just like adults. They pull away from painful stimuli. They coordinate sucking and swallowing. These are all normal reflexes that are present at birth that remain throughout the person's lifetime.

Other reflexes are specific to newborns and change or disappear as they mature. Some of those are discussed below. The ones outlined here are the most visually obvious and the most often checked when infants are being examined by physicians because they indicate normal development as well as the rate at which the newborn is maturing.

> Stepping: If you stand newborns on their feet, they will respond to the pressure by stepping.
> Palmar grasp reflex: A newborn's hands curl tightly around any object placed in them.
> Babinski reflex: If you stroke the sole of the foot, the toes will fan out, and the big toe will extend.
> Moro reflex (also called the startle reflex): If newborns are startled by a sudden change of position or a noise, they fling their arms out with fingers spread wide and then draw their arms (and, to a lesser extent, legs) back toward the body in a clutching motion.
> Rooting and sucking: If you touch the cheeks of newborns, they begin to search for a nipple with their mouth. When the mouth is touched, they start to suck.
> Hand-to-mouth reflex: If newborns' mouth and palm are touched, they put their hand in their mouth. This is useful for clearing mucus in the early days, because, when they suck on their fist, they can swallow easily.

Righting reflex (also called the china doll reflex): When newborns are held upright, they try to keep their head up and eyes open.

Tonic neck reflex (sometimes called the fencer position): When the newborn's head is turned to one side, the arm on that side extends, and the opposite arm flexes, making the baby look like a fencer. This reflex may eventually help the baby use the sides of the body separately.

Swimming reflex: When newborns are placed in water, they make swimming motions.

Reflexes That Appear After Birth

Other reflexes make their appearance during the first few months. As the new reflexes appear, some of the original ones begin to disappear.

Reciprocal kicking (bicycling): If infants are held out by an adult, they begin kicking their legs alternately. Usually this appears in the first month.

Neck righting: If the infant's head is turned, the body follows. This reflex begins to appear about the time the tonic neck reflex disappears.

Parachute reflex: If infants begin to fall forward from an upright position, they try to catch themselves—arms go forward with hands outstretched. This reflex appears about the time the Moro reflex fades.

Landau reflex: If babies are held under the stomach only, they extend their arms and legs. This extension, which indicates the strength of the back, is a precursor of walking. It is complete at about one year.

Not only is it interesting to see how reflexes serve as the basis for later movement; it is useful for caregivers to know what reflexes indicate about infants' behavior and development. For instance, it is sometimes useful to know that babies have not chosen to move in a certain way (for example, rooting before starting to suck), but that they have to do so.

Furthermore, the appearance of certain reflexes and the absence of others can indicate differences in development, as can reflexes that remain instead of fading. This aspect of development is well understood. When parents or caregivers notice that a baby is showing what seems to be inappropriate reflexive behavior, they may want to discuss what they have noticed with a developmental expert or a doctor. For more information about informal screening by noting reflexes, contact your local cerebral palsy agency or association.

FIGURE 7.1
Reflexes at and after birth

At birth

Moro reflex
(startle reflex)

Palmar grasp

Tonic neck reflex

Rooting reflex

After birth

Landau reflex

Reciprocal kicking

Parachute reflex

Voluntary Movements

Eventually, infants make motions that are not automatic, but voluntary. These movements are generally divided into two broad types: gross motor, having to do with large muscles and big movements, and fine motor, having to do with small muscles and more delicate movements.

Various large muscles contribute to the infant's ability to move in two directions: *up* (to an upright position) and *around* (on a horizontal plane). The two are intertwined because the child needs to get up to move around and needs to move around to get up. Little by little babies gain control over these muscles. The first muscles to develop are those that control head movements. As babies perfect the skills involved in turning the head from side to side and lifting it up, they strengthen the shoulder muscles. As they begin to move around and squirm, lifting their arms and legs, they develop the trunk muscles. All this preparation is for turning over, just as turning over is preparation for (that is, strengthens the muscles necessary for) sitting up. A child will learn to come to a sitting position without ever having been propped up. The ability to sit comes from developing the muscles prerequisite to the upright position. Infants get ready to sit by learning to move the head and by turning over. The building of the muscle systems is vital; practice at sitting is not.

A general principle involved in motor development is that stability is the means to mobility. Infants cannot move until they gain a good solid base from which to move—whether the movement is vertical, as in sitting and standing, or horizontal, as in crawling and walking. This same principle operates on another level as well. Chapter 5 pointed out that exploration (mobility) is related to psychological stability (trust in attachment).

The plan for developing muscular stability is a part of the infant's makeup—as is the plan for mobility. Nobody has to "teach" either sitting or walking. When normal babies have gone through the necessary muscle development, they will be able to sit and walk without any lessons or practice.

Figure 7.2 shows the major milestones of gross motor development. Use it with caution. Such charts are based on averages, and no individual baby is average. The sequence of motor development is mostly standard, but within it lies a good deal of room for individual variation in timing and style.

Promoting Gross Motor Development

Caregivers can do several things to promote gross motor development in infants. Try to keep children in the position in which they are freest and least helpless during their waking hours. Dr. Emmi Pikler's research shows that even the youngest babies change position an average of once a minute.[1] So if they are strapped into an infant seat or a swing, they are not able to do what they would do naturally if free. Avoid contraptions that confine infants. (Car seats are, of course, a necessary exception.)

FIGURE 7.2
Gross motor development milestones:
birth to thirty months

Raises self by
arms in prone position
2.1 months
(range 0.7-5 months)

Prewalking progression
7.1 months
(range 5-11 months)

Pulls to sit
7.3 months
(range 6-8 months)

Pulls up on furniture
8.6 months
(range 6-12 months)

Stands alone
11 months
(range 9-16 months)

Walks alone
11.7 months
(range 9-17 months)

Walks backward
14.6 months
(range 11-20 months)

Jumps off floor
23.4 months
(range 17-30 months)

Source: Adapted by permission from the Bayley Scales of Infant Development. The Psychological Corp., 1969. New York.

Don't teach gross motor skills, but encourage infants to practice what they know how to do. Babies get ready for the next stage by doing thoroughly whatever it is they are doing in the present stage. Trying to teach babies to roll over or walk keeps them from fully exploring and perfecting the skills they already have. They reach each milestone just when they are ready, and their own inner timetable dictates when that will be.

Don't put babies into positions they cannot get into by themselves. The process of *getting into* a position is more important than *being in* the position—the process promotes development. Babies get ready for standing by sitting and crawling, not by being stood up.

Don't shield babies from all physical stress. The body needs a certain amount of stress to grow. Don't rescue babies when they get in an uncomfortable position, but wait and see if they can get out of it on their own. Of course, you don't want to leave babies in great distress alone and unsupported, but you don't want to always make everything easy for them either. Reasonable—optimum—stress stimulates growth, increases motivation, and strengthens the body as well as the psyche.

Above all, *facilitate* development in the gross motor area—don't *push* it. Because we live in a "hurry-up" culture, some people are most anxious for babies to reach milestones "on time" or even "early." "In time" is a better motto for milestones. Each baby has his or her own timetable. There is no reason to impose someone else's. The question to ask is not, "Is this baby progressing rapidly in development?" but "How well can this baby do whatever he or she is doing?" Note how well babies use the skills they have and if they are progressing in their use of those skills. With these two concepts in mind, you will not have to be so concerned about where they fit on the chart.

Promoting gross motor development in toddlers follows the same principles as that of infants. Toddlers need freedom to move and experience a variety of ways of using the skills they possess. Large muscle activity cannot be saved for outdoor time, but must be both allowed and encouraged inside. A soft environment, pillows, mattresses, foam blocks, and thick rugs (indoors) and grass, sand, pads, and mats (outdoors) help toddlers roll, tumble, and bounce around. Various kinds of scaled-down climbing and sliding equipment (both indoors and out) allow the toddler to experience a variety of skills. Wheel toys (these can be saved for outdoors for the older toddler) give a whole different kind of experience as toddlers learn first to walk them and later to pedal them. Large, light-weight blocks encourage building skills as toddlers carry them around and form them into walks, houses, and abstract structures and then practice gross motor skills on them.

Wandering, carrying, and dumping are gross motor skills that toddlers practice a great deal. Rather than seeing these as negative, caregivers can provide for them in the curriculum. Some programs have things available to dump (and put back). One center even suspends from the ceiling a bucket of objects whose sole purpose is dumping (and refilling). Wandering usually involves picking up objects, carrying them to another location, and putting them down. Sometimes they are actively discarded, and sometimes just dropped—abandoned as if forgotten. The map in Figure 7.3 shows the path of a two year old over a period of twenty minutes. The black dots represent each time the child picked up or put down an object. Notice the territory he covered and the number of times he picked up and put down objects. This is not atypical two year old behavior, although, if you observed a four or five year old wandering like this, you'd wonder why he or she was not able to settle into an activity. (Of course, toddlers can settle down and focus for long periods too. For example, I've watched lengthy hand washing episodes more than once. I timed one that lasted half an hour.)

The closer to three toddlers get, the less likely they are to spend good parts of the day moving from one place to another. But early in toddlerhood this constant movement is part of gross motor development, and the environment, both indoors and out, should be set up to accommodate that need.

Notice whether you are encouraging gross motor movement more in boys than in girls. Girls need strong, skillful bodies as much as boys do.

Molly Sullivan, a family day-care provider in Berkeley, California, has some further suggestions for interacting with older toddlers in ways that further encourage gross motor activity. She suggests that older toddlers are intrigued with the theme of being caught and taken care of as well as running away and experiencing freedom. You can play out this theme on a gross motor level by making a game out of it. Children will often initiate it themselves. What Sullivan calls "loving chases" or "loving wrestles" are part of this game. Don't restrict these activities to boys; they are just as appropriate for girls.

If your children aren't engaging in gross motor activities, Sullivan has some suggestions for getting them started that involve such simple devices as exercising yourself. Run from one point to another, jump up and down, jump onto piles of pillows, roll, crawl, somersault, or walk backward. Once you start this, children will take it up, and you can begin imitating them instead of continuing to initiate.

Play circle games and sing songs with movements. Dance. Here is a wonderful place for multicultural input. Ask parents for suggestions of very simple games, songs, and music to dance to. You can expand beyond "Ring Around the Rosy" and "Jack in the Box." Just be sure you keep it very simple and always a choice. (Don't require the whole group to participate.)

Outside, dig holes in the dirt to see what you find. Go for walks and hikes. Make your goal to examine every interesting thing along the way rather than to cover distance.

The Progression of Fine Motor Development

The small muscles that a baby gradually gains control of include those of the eyes, mouth, speech organs, bladder, rectum, hands, fingers,

FIGURE 7.3
Map tracing a two year old's movements

feet, and toes. The development of the manipulative skills (hands and fingers) will be considered here.

The sequence in which infants learn to manipulate objects shows how complex this ability is. Figure 7.4 illustrates the developmental sequence. At first, newborns generally hold their hands in tight fists (although the clenched fist is more relaxed in those babies who were treated to gentle birth procedures). They hold on to any object put into their hands, gripping so tightly that they can, if held up, support their own weight. But they have no control over their grasp and cannot let go at will. For this reason, it's not a good idea to put a rattle into infants' hands. They cannot let go, no matter how much they want to. At some time before six months (usually a little over two and a half months), the tight fists remain relaxed most of the time, and the hands are open.

During the first three months, more of the hand and arm movements become voluntary. Infants begin to reach for objects, first with their eyes, then with open hands. By around three and a half months, they can often close on an object within reach. They may also begin to play with their own hands about this time. The way they grasp at first is distinctive: they use all the fingers together as if they had a mitten on, drawing objects into the palm of the hand. This motion is called the "palmar grasp." Although at this stage the palmar grasp is a voluntary movement, it comes from the earlier palmar grasp reflex present at birth. After learning to pick up objects with one hand, infants soon begin to pass them back and forth between the two hands. By the sixth month, they have begun trying to use thumb and forefinger in what is called a "pincer grasp." They can then manipulate objects with more skill and a variety of motions.

By about the ninth month, infants have perfected the pincer grasp and can pick up small objects with great adeptness. Playing with the hands—picking up and dropping objects for a helpful adult to retrieve and playing patticake—provides pleasure. The dropping game shows infants' joy in and awareness of now being able to let go. By the ninth month, infants may also be using their forefingers alone—poking, hooking, and probing. Eventually, they can differentiate the uses of the hands and can then do two different activities at once (for example, holding something with one hand and maneuvering with the other).

By eleven months, infants can hold crayons and mark on available surfaces, and they can probably get a spoon to their mouths. By a year, the variety of movements has come a long way from the compulsive grasping that was present at birth. Infants can take covers off objects, undress themselves to some degree, take one thing out of another, and take things apart and move them around. They continue to expand their manipulative skills, refining and perfecting their movements. From here on, individuals vary greatly.

Much fine motor development in toddlers comes from encouraging them in self-help tasks. As they get more adept at eating with utensils, pouring their own milk, taking off their own shoes, and zipping up their

FIGURE 7.4
Fine motor development: manipulative skills, birth to twenty-one months

Grasps and holds ring
.8 months
(range .3-3 months)

Hands predominantly
open and relaxed
2.7 months
(range .7-6 months)

Reaches for dangling ring
3.1 months
(range 1-5 months)

Closes on dangling ring
3.8 months
(range 2-6 months)

Fingers hand in play
3.2 months
(range 1-6 months)

Palmar grasp
3.7 months
(range 2-7 months)

Neat pincer grasp
8.9 months
(range 7-12 months)

Patticake (Midline skills)
9.7 months
(range 7-15 months)

Scribbles spontaneously
14 months
(range 10-21 months)

Source: Adapted by permission from the Bayley Scales of Infant Development. The Psychological Corp., 1969. New York.

jackets (with a start from an adult), their ability to use their hands and fingers grows.

In addition, toys and materials add to their chances to practice as they play with what you provide them (such as dress-up clothes, dolls and doll clothes, play dough, button and zipper boards, latch boards, stringing beads, nesting toys, simple shape sorters, snap together blocks, telephones, paint and paint brushes or water and paint brushes, crayons, felt pens, scissors, paper, simple puzzles, blocks, small figures, cars, and trucks). The tactile experiences mentioned in "Touch" in Chapter 6 also promote fine motor development. Almost any toy or material you make available encourages fine motor development. See Appendix B for age-appropriate fine motor toys, materials, and activities. Be sure that you encourage boys and girls to engage equally in fine motor activities. Take a look at Scotty and the number of motor experiences (fine and gross) he is getting in just a few minutes.

Scotty stands in the sandbox, looking around him. He bends over and picks up a sieve and spoon that are lying at his feet. Then he plops down, legs out straight, and starts spooning sand into the sieve and watching it pour out on his knees. He continues to hold the sieve but drops the spoon as his attention is drawn to a child on a tot bike who has just pulled up to the edge of the sandbox. The child gets off the bike and stands by it, watching something going on beyond the fence. Scotty trips across the sand, sieve still in hand. When he reaches the edge of the sandbox, the sieve drops out of his hand. He seems unaware of that development. He concentrates his effort on getting his feet, first one, then the other, over the board that makes up the edge of the sandbox. He stands by the bike; the child who rode up on it is on the other side of it.

Disregarding the other child, Scotty swings one foot over the bike and straddles it. The other child, who has been watching him, frowns, makes a small noise, and looks around the yard as if to find someone to help him claim the bike. No one responds to his look, so he makes no further protest. Scotty walks the bike away, leaving the child standing there in the same spot.

Scotty alternates between standing and walking the bike and sitting on it and scooting it with his feet. (There are no pedals on the bike.) He keeps on the walk, which is a bumpy asphalt and slightly uphill. He joins a group of two other bikers, and the three move together toward a wide, gentle ramp. They ride up the ramp, stop at the top, and then coast down together. Scotty then leaves the group, walks the bike over to the gate, and stands looking out. He gets off the bike and starts to climb the gate. An adult walks over and gently redirects him to a climbing structure nearby. He starts to climb, but when the adult walks off, he follows her. He stops halfway across the yard when he comes across a group of children washing dolls in dishpans on a low table. He grabs a sponge lying on the table and squeezes it, watching the soapy water drip out. He puts the sponge into the pan, holds it up dripping, and squeezes it again onto the tabletop. He scrubs the tabletop briefly, then puts the sponge back into the water. He takes a doll out of another tub and puts it on top of the sponge in the tub in front of him. Another child reaches over and takes the doll back, and there is a slight tussle as Scotty tries to keep the doll. He lets go when he hears a call for snack time. He gives the sponge in the tub a pat, which splashes water onto his face. He smiles, pats it again, then races tripping across the yard to the snack table, where he is just in time to pour his own juice from a small, half-filled pitcher.

Scotty encounters many chances to build his skills in walking, running, climbing, and balancing just by being in an environment with equipment and choices. He is also building fine motor skills as he practices grasping, holding, scooping, pouring, and squeezing with the toys and materials available to him. These experiences not only help him develop his perceptual skills, but also contribute to cognitive development.

This chapter has looked at the progression of gross and fine motor development, including the reflexes present at birth and those present after birth. It has examined both voluntary movements and milestones of gross and fine motor development. The chapter also included suggestions for ways to promote motor development in infants and toddlers.

Notes

1. Emmi Pikler, "Data on Gross Motor Development of the Infant," *Early Child Development and Care* 1 (1972), pp. 297–310.

For Further Reading

T. G. R. Bower, *Development in Infancy*, 2nd ed. (San Francisco: W. H. Freeman, 1982).

T. G. R. Bower, *A Primer of Infant Development* (San Francisco: W. H. Freeman, 1977).

Emmi Pikler, "Data on Gross Motor Development," *Early Childhood Development and Care* 1 (1972), pp. 297–310.

Molly Sullivan, *Feeling Strong, Feeling Free: Movement Exploration for Young Children* (Washington, D.C.: National Association for the Education of Young Children, 1982).

Anna Tardos, "The Pikler/Loczy Philosophy," *Educaring* 7 (2), Spring 1986, pp. 1–7.

Chapter 8
The Development of Cognition

The abilities related to knowing and understanding are called cognition. One of the biggest challenges facing infant-toddler caregivers is conveying the message that their programs do promote cognitive development even though nothing "intellectual" is apparently going on.

Many people understand cognitive or intellectual development only in terms of their own school experience. Because of that fact, they look for school-like activities, even in infant-toddler programs, in order to be assured that cognitive development is being promoted. However, cognitive development in the very young does not occur because of school-type learning activities. How it does occur is the subject of this chapter, which will look first at the sequence of development and then at how to promote cognition in infants and toddlers.

How do infants develop knowing and understanding? Initially, experience is perceived directly with the senses. For infants to acquire the ability to comprehend this sensory information, they must be able to distinguish between the familiar and the unknown; later they will begin to consider, to formulate, and eventually to form mental images in this process of experiencing and clarifying the environment.

Because part of this process is internal, certain assumptions concerning cognition must be inferred by observing obvious physical movements. Infants begin by exploring the world with their bodies. They internalize what they take in through their senses and display it in their physical movements. Through such simple acts as mouthing, grasping, and reaching, infants gather vital information. You can see infants practicing these acts, repeating them over and over. They rather quickly refine them. For example, when newborns first bring the mouth toward a nipple, the mouth opens wide and ready. With only a few trials, they learn just what size opening the nipple requires and adjust the mouth accordingly in anticipation of what will go into it. They have refined a simple action. Soon they will judge how far to reach and what shape the fingers must take to pick up a cup or a toy. Much later, as adults, they may refine their actions further in order to reach without looking and strike a particular chord on the piano or input data on a computer keyboard. All these muscular refinements had their beginnings in that tiny mouth adjusting itself to the appropriate size for the nipple. In this example, cognition has been tied in with fine motor development. You can think of other examples where cognition is tied in with gross motor development, with social development, and with emotional development. Learning and thinking are behind all areas of development.

The knowing process, cognition, also incorporates language abilities. As young children experience the world through their senses and body, their needs for labels to categorize and remember these experiences develop. Once they attain labels for experience, they have increased the ability to communicate desires and accomplishments. This expanded ability to communicate and store information opens up young children to additional opportunities for understanding the world.

The Progression of Cognitive Development
The Sensorimotor Experience of Knowing

The theorist who has contributed the most to our understanding of cognitive development in infants and toddlers is Jean Piaget. He named the first stage, that of the child up to two years of age, the sensorimotor stage. This name, which means the coordination of sense perception and muscle movements, is appropriate because that coordination is the beginning of thinking.

The coordination of the information from the senses and from the body is the basic definition of the sensorimotor experience. Babies turn their bodies toward the lights and sounds they have perceived. They grasp, suck, and cry. At first many of these acts are reflexive, and their consequences are accidental. A little arm swipes at a blanket or a toy, and it moves. A head turns to free the face from a corner of a blanket that has fallen over it.

Soon, however, babies learn to make adjustments in their behavior. They begin to act more purposefully. They learn, for example, that sucking on a rattle may be interesting, but only sucking on the breast or bottle tastes good and satisfies hunger. Along with practicing movements, they begin to combine them. For instance, they begin to suck and look at the same time.

They learn to bring their hands to their mouths and suck on them. They begin to touch their hands together and look at their fingers. They gradually begin to watch their hands as they touch objects and bring them to their mouths. These abilities become combined and coordinated—seeing and reaching for the same object, then grasping and sucking the same object. This happens as babies come to recognize cause and effect. These physical movements that lead toward understanding and knowing can be diagramed as follows:

> Reflexes → accidental movement → repetition and practice → coordination and combination → cause and effect → organized, planned, thinking behaviors

Gradually, babies come to know that they can control the interaction between themselves and objects. They like this new piece of knowledge, and they keep testing it out. They want to repeat interesting activities. Through this testing, babies come to know that shaking a rattle produces a sound, but shaking a spoon does not. They soon learn, however, that banging a spoon will make a noise, and they like that and keep doing it.

When babies are practicing and combining these first actions, they are in love with their own body—fascinated by what they are feeling and doing. Eventually that fascination moves from their own body to the effects of their actions on the environment. They get interested in what happens when they shove their arm out and hit a toy. A new understanding develops with this shift of focus from self to environment, from action to consequences. Babies begin to realize that they and the objects in the world are separate.

You can see this same progression of development a bit later in toddlers having art experiences. At first, children are most interested in what it feels like when they scribble or scrub with a paintbrush on paper. Later they start looking at the product of their action—the drawing or painting. Some children don't focus on the product until after three years of age.

Knowing they are in a world full of objects and part of it, but not the whole of it, is a great step forward in understanding for infants. Nevertheless, their ideas of objects differ greatly from those of adults. Infants acknowledge the existence only of things they can see, touch, or otherwise know with their senses. When you hide his favorite toy, the infant does not look for it because he believes it no longer exists. ("Out of sight, out of mind" applies to the thinking of the very young infant.) If you bring the toy out of hiding, it has been re-created for him. This understanding of the world makes a game of peek-a-boo extremely exciting. What power—to create and uncreate a person in an instant. No wonder peek-a-boo has universal fascination. What the young infant lacks is what Piaget called "object permanence." Eventually, infants become aware that objects continue to exist even when they can't see them. But gaining this awareness is a gradual process.

At about one year of age, children begin to think in a more sophisticated way and to use tools. Give them a stick, and they will use it to gain an out-of-reach toy. Give them a string with something they want at the end, and they know just what to do. Novelty becomes an end in itself. Children will deliberately manipulate the environment to find out what happens.

With all this experimenting children develop some new abilities: the ability to anticipate where an object will be when they drop it, the ability to remember an action after a short interruption, and the ability to predict. For example, watch an eighteen month old child who has had experience with a ball. She may roll the ball off a table and turn her head to the place where it will land. Or if the ball rolls under a chair, she may look for a way to get it out again. Or if she rolls a ball toward a hole, she will run to the hole to watch the ball drop into it.

The next step in the development of understanding comes when infants can find solutions mentally. After enough experience using their sense perceptions and muscles, they can begin to think of ways of acting and try them out in their head before doing them. They can think of past and future events. You can see they are using mental images and connecting thoughts to experiences and objects that are not present. They can throw an imaginary ball or contemplate the solution to a problem before they begin to tackle it.

The sensorimotor stage can be summarized as follows:

1. reflexes, simple inborn behaviors (crying, sucking, grasping) (1 month)
2. repeats and combines simple behaviors (reaching, grasping, and sucking on an object) (1–4 months)
3. plans (intention) a movement to have something happen (pulls a string to bring a toy closer) (8–12 months)
4. experiments with known things in order to create new events (A ball rolled off the table will bounce. What will a book do?) (12–18 months)
5. imagines events and solves problems, uses words (pretends to throw a ball and calls to a parent, "here come ball") (18–24 months)

The Preoperational Stage

The beginning of language and the ability to pretend signal the end of the sensorimotor stage and the beginning of the next, which Piaget called the preoperational stage. Although the stage stretches from about two to seven years of age, I will deal here only with the beginnings, because this book covers birth through three years of age. Toddlers may be in either the sensorimotor stage or the preoperational stage, and many are in transition between them.

Much of what has been written in English about Piaget's preoperational stage talks about its limitations because it has been written for preschool teachers rather than infant-toddler caregivers. The comparison is of children in the stage of concrete operations, which is the stage from seven to eleven years. However, when you compare a sensorimotor child with a pre-operational one, you have a different perspective.

Preoperational children can use mental images for their thinking processes. Thinking, though still tied to the concrete, is not limited to sense perceptions and body movements. Although toddlers don't practice this very much, they *can* think while standing or even sitting still. (However, they still need to be gathering a great number of concrete experiences *to think about*, so don't let anyone pressure you into sitting toddlers down in order to educate them.)

Because of their increased ability to hold and store mental images, toddlers entering the preoperational stage have increased memory of past events. Although yesterday may not yet be in their vocabulary, they *can* remember yesterday—and the day before.

Their sense of the future also increases as their ability to predict grows with their experience in the world. They continue to use trial and error to gain in this skill, not only in the concrete world ("I wonder what will happen if I pour sand in the sink"), but in the social one as well ("I wonder what will happen if I pour sand in Jamie's hair"). Sometimes these experiments are both social and physical and are thought out on the conscious level ("If I pinch the baby, will he cry?"). Sometimes children don't make such clear decisions, but are still problem solving in a trial and error way ("I wonder if hitting Erin will get an adult over here to pay attention to me" or "If I break enough limits, can I get my caregiver and mother to quit talking to each other so we can go home?"). What appears to be "naughty behavior" may in reality be this scientific testing.

Look at the behavior of four children as it relates to Piaget's stages. See if you can determine which stage each child is in. Also practice looking at real infants and toddlers and noticing the behaviors that relate to Piaget's stages. Being able to talk about Piaget gives you good arguments to resist the pressures to provide inappropriate "school-like" academic experiences in the name of educating infants and toddlers.

> The first child is lying on his back on a rug surrounded by a few toys. He turns slightly toward a ball lying near his arm. He stretches, and the movement causes him to accidentally touch the ball. It moves, making a sound. He startles at the sound and looks toward the ball. He lies still again; his gaze wanders. Then he moves his arms again—a big, sweeping gesture—and the ball moves again, making the same jingling sound. He again startles, and a look of surprise comes on his face. You can almost hear his question, "Who did that?" He looks at the ball, looks around, and looks at the ball again. Then he lies still. A few moments later his

arms come up and out again, this time tentatively waving. He misses the ball. Nothing happens. He lies still again. He repeats the action—again tentatively. This time his hand passes in front of his eyes, and a spark of interest comes over his face. He looks intently at his hand, and you can almost hear him saying, "What's that thing? Where did it come from?" He moves his fingers, and delight comes into his eyes. "Hey, it works!" he seems to say. His arms continue to wave, taking the fascinating fingers out of his line of vision. He breezes by the ball again, causing it to make just a whisper of sound. His eyes search for the source of the sound.

The second child is sitting on a rug near the first, but they are separated by a low fence. She has a rubber toy in her hand and is banging it up and down on the floor, giggling at the squeaks issuing forth. The toy bounces across the rug as she lets go, and she crawls happily after it. She stops to explore a string with a large bead on the end of it, then moves on after the rubber toy. She bounces it several more times before throwing it down, this time ignoring it as it bounces away. She returns to the string. She ignores the interesting bead on the end, but glances to see where the other end is. The string disappears into a pile of toys on the lowest shelf at the edge of the rug. She expectantly pulls the string and laughs delightedly. Then she catches sight of a bright red ball that has rolled out from the pile of toys that fell off the shelf. She crawls over to it and begins to smack it with her hand, making noises while doing so. She seems to expect the ball to move. When it doesn't, she tries again with more force. The ball moves slightly, and she moves after it. She is getting more and more excited, and as she approaches the ball, one hand accidentally swipes it so that it rolls some distance and disappears under a couch in the corner of the room. She watches it roll, starts after it, but stops when it disappears. Looking puzzled, she crawls over to the edge of the couch, but does not lift up the ruffle at the bottom to check underneath. She looks a little disappointed, but then she crawls back to the rug and the squeaky rubber toy. As the scene closes, she is once again banging the toy against the floor and laughing at the noise it makes.

The third child stands holding an empty pitcher in his hand. He goes over to a box of toys, reaches into it, and brings out a small plastic bowl, an egg carton, and the lid to a peanut butter jar. He sets these in a row on a low table and pretends to pour something in them from his pitcher. He is careful in his actions and methodically fills each container, including each compartment of the egg carton. Then, seemingly satisfied that the task is done, he tosses the pitcher aside with a joyous shout. He starts across the room in another direction when he notices a plant standing on a table. He immediately runs back to where he left the pitcher and rummages through a pile of dolls and blankets hiding it from his view. He finds it, carries it over to the plant, and carefully pours pretend water into the pot. He abandons the pitcher again and picks up a doll. He scolds the doll, bangs it on the floor several times, then wraps it in a blanket, and lovingly puts it to bed in a box of toys. As he bends over the box, he spies a picture book with fire engines on the cover. He looks at the pictures for a moment, then puts the book on his head and races around the room screaming in what seems to be an imitation of a siren. As he passes by a toy shelf, he sees a wooden fire truck. He pulls it out and proceeds to push it around on the floor. He stops and looks at the holes on the truck where the little fire fighters are supposed to sit. No little fire fighters are in sight. He pauses for a moment, looks around, then goes to the pitcher once more. The scene ends as he carefully fills each hole in the fire truck with whatever pretend liquid the pitcher contains.

The fourth child is sitting at a table putting puzzle pieces in a three-piece puzzle. When she gets stuck, she looks to a nearby adult, who gives her verbal hints about how to turn the pieces. When she completes the puzzle, she turns it upside down and smiles at the clatter of wooden pieces hitting the tabletop. She works the puzzle again, faster this time, with no help from the adult. When she finishes the puzzle, she puts it back on a low shelf and moves to another table where several other children are poking and squeezing play dough. She asks for a piece, and when none is forthcoming, an adult intervenes, helping each child give her a bit off the hunks they are playing with. She sits contentedly poking and prodding her play dough, periodically conversing with the other children about what she is doing. Her monologue relates to what they are saying about their own play dough, but it is not in direct response to anything they are saying. There is little interaction at the table, though there is lots of talking. The child we are focusing on rolls her play dough into a ball, then sits looking at it for a minute. Then she begins to pat and shape it, obviously with purpose in her actions. When she has produced a lopsided lump, she sits back, satisfied, and announces to no one in particular that she is finished. She gets up and walks away. As she leaves the table, another child grabs her piece and incorporates it into his own. This act goes unnoticed. The girl, seeing a cart of food being wheeled into the room, runs to the corner to a row of sinks and begins to wash her hands. We leave her thoroughly soaping her hands and arms and obviously enjoying the experience.

When observing children, we can only infer from their physical behaviors what they are thinking. Yet, using Piaget's way of looking at early cognitive development, we can guess what is going on inside these children's heads and see the progression from unintentional, even accidental, behavior to purposeful behavior that involves problem solving, mental images, representational thought, and pretend.

Promoting Cognitive Development in Infants and Toddlers

The prerequisite for promoting cognitive development is security and attachment. Through the attachment process, infants develop skills such as differentiation as they distinguish the person(s) they are attached to from others in their world. Attachment also shows intentionality as infants and toddlers use all their behaviors to bring the attached person(s) close and keep them there. Clinging, crying infants or toddlers are exhibiting strong intentionality (a mark of early cognitive behavior) as they try to get the parent to remain. This may be annoying, and it is not usually recognized as cognitive behavior; yet in truth it is very purposeful and intelligent.

Meeting other needs is also part of the prerequisites for promoting cognitive development. Children with unmet needs put their energies into trying to get someone to meet them, which focuses their cognitive development in a narrow way. But children whose needs are met consistently will feel trusting and comfortable. And children who feel comfortable will *explore the environment.* From continual exploration comes cognitive development.

You promote cognitive development by inviting and encouraging exploration in an environment rich in sensory experiences. When given the opportunity to play with objects in any way they wish, children encounter problems. As mentioned earlier, problem solving is the basis of infant-toddler education as it is outlined in this book. Allowing infants and toddlers to solve the kinds of problems they run into during the course of a day promotes their cognitive development. Free choice ensures that children find problems that are meaningful to them. Solving someone else's problem is not nearly as interesting to most of us as solving the ones that are related to something that really matters to us.

It helps problem solving if adults do such things as adding words (labeling sensory input—"That rabbit feels soft and warm" or "That was a loud noise" or "That sponge is soaking wet"). In addition adults can help by asking questions, pointing out relationships, reflecting feelings, and generally supporting the child.

Encourage children to interact with one another during problem solving. The input infants and toddlers get from their peers can both be useful and offer more than one way to a solution. Piaget's view is that interaction—with objects and with other people, especially peers—promotes cognitive development.

Include dramatic play props for toddlers. Through pretend, they build the mental images that are so important for the thought process.

Resist pressure to teach or to introduce academic kinds of experiences. Children will learn the names of colors and shapes in the course of normal conversations if you use them naturally ("Please bring me the red pillow" or "Do you want a round cracker or a square one?"). A better use of your time than teaching colors and shapes is to help children learn a variety of approaches to meeting their needs (both physical and social) and making things happen in the world. The concepts will then be imbedded in real life experience and therefore have meaning, rather than ending up as an academic exercise.

Number concepts can also be learned in a natural context. More or less have real meaning when things are being handed out—such as apple slices. Mathematical concepts come as toddlers play with blocks and sand, compare size and weight of objects, make other comparisons, and figure out relationships.

You will teach reading in your job—but at a toddler level, that is, in a developmentally appropriate way. Your job as a reading teacher of infants and toddlers is not to teach the alphabet but to promote oral language development as well as provide plenty of experiences from which to build concepts so that later, when they see a written word such as "bean," they'll have many associations with it. It won't be empty of experience and therefore feeling. Children who can recall planting, watering, debugging, picking, snapping, washing, and eating beans really understand what the word means. The word "bean" has meaning as well as rich associations (called connotations). Later, when the children are ready to decode written words, they have real life experience with the words they're reading about.

You can help give children an appreciation of reading and an idea of what it is all about by reading book after book to them. The idea and the joy of reading are important prerequisites to reading itself.

One of the easiest and most effective ways to promote cognitive development is to pay attention to children when they exhibit thinking through problem solving. Of course, many times their choice of solutions gets them in trouble, but even then you can point out that they were problem solving.

Infants and toddlers are naturally creative. If you don't hinder them with too tight limits and an impoverished environment, they will give you lessons in how to use toys and materials in ways you never thought of. Curiosity is part of this push for creativity and needs to be valued and nurtured. Infants and toddlers are newcomers to the world, and they want to know how everything works. They don't want to be told; they want to find out on their own. They are scientists. They don't take anything for granted, but rather must prove each hypothesis. Nurture this quality in them!

Infants and toddlers are creative in another sense too. They are creating knowledge (according to Piaget). They don't just take in information and ideas, and they don't just manipulate toys and materials. They are not empty vessels to be filled. They are instead builders of their own understandings. They use a creative construction process to order their experiences. This is an active process, though only half of the action shows—the half during which children creatively explore the world outside themselves. The other half occurs inside, as children use mental processes to make sense of input from the senses.

Although rich and full, Piaget's view of cognitive development concerns itself only with the development of logical thinking. Even though at the infant-toddler level logic is not yet very evident, the progression is toward rational thinking, using reason to understand the world. Piaget was concerned with what is now called "left-brain thinking."

Robert Samples puts forth another view of cognitive development in *The Metaphoric Mind,* which explains what has been called "right-brain thinking." This kind of thinking is intuitive, holistic, and extremely complex, dealing with paradoxes and ambiguities. Of course, the human brain is cleverly designed to use both modes of thinking at the same time, so it's hard to separate one from the other.

Discussing the intuitive mode presents some problems because it doesn't develop in the nice, neat progression of the rational mode. But because the rational mode is so highly valued, the other mode should be at least mentioned, though it isn't given equal space here.

Infants seem to be masters of the "right-brain mode," at least insofar as their thinking is holistic. At first they don't separate themselves from anything—they and universe are one and the same from their perspective. Of course, from the logical point of view, this is pretty immature thinking, but from the point of view taken by Eastern philosophers, this is the highest kind of thinking. Here's what Robert Samples says about infant cognition:

> The sensorimotor repertoire has as its basic quality the quality of invention. Children in the first two years of life are inventing the whole universe that they perceive. . . . From the crib children are totally immersed in sensing all things. The clatter in the kitchen, the warm cooing sounds from parents, the feelings they get from different colors, the warmth, the cold, the feeling of liquids going into their bodies, the feeling of liquids coming out . . . all are of equal importance. Some even suggest that it is not an optical quandary facing children in the first few weeks after birth when they have trouble focusing—it may be a super sensory one. Newborn and early infants probably see the auras of energy associated with our bodies . . . a phenomenon we confuse with their eyes being "out of focus."

Samples is talking about a subjective, holistic mode of cognition.

This chapter has examined the development and fostering of cognition. Two major modes have been mentioned, one briefly, the other at length. Samples's theory, which is holistic and subjective, is a right-brain mode. Piaget's theory is a left-brain mode. Piaget saw cognition as developing in stages, each leading toward more logical, rational, and objective thinking.

Piaget created his theory by observing infants and by talking to toddlers and older children. He discovered that language gives clues to the logic of children's thinking. So we'll move on now to language, the subject of Chapter 9.

Notes

1. Robert Samples, *The Metaphoric Mind* (Menlo Park, Calif.: Addison-Wesley, 1976), p. 103.

For Further Reading

T. G. R. Bower, *Development in Infancy* (San Francisco: W.H. Freeman, 1982).

T. G. R. Bower, *A Primer of Infant Development* (San Francisco: W.H. Freeman, 1977).

C. Kamii and R. DeVries, *Physical Knowledge in Preschool Education* (New York: Prentice-Hall, 1978).

J. Marzolla, *Supertot: Creative Learning Activities for Children One to Three and Sympathetic Advice for Their Parents* (New York: Harper and Row, 1977).

John L. Phillips, Jr., *The Origins of Intellect: Piaget's Theory* (San Francisco: W.H. Freeman, 1969).

Robert Samples, *The Metaphoric Mind* (Menlo Park, Calif.: Addison-Wesley, 1976).

Chapter 9
The Development of Language

Language is communication, but more than that, it is a tool for thinking, a way of organizing experience in order to understand events. Language allows children to label experience, store information, categorize it, abstract from it, and reason with it. This chapter will examine the foundations and progression of language development, bilingualism, and some guidelines for fostering language development.

Progression of Language Development

Foundations of Language: Receptive Qualities

Infants share their pleasure in making sounds with their partner or caregiver. They come to associate language with a social occasion. As they coo and babble, they find that they are responded to, which in turn encourages them to respond to and imitate their partner. They become aware of rhythms, pitches, and sounds of words. Language can become a way to excite or to soothe a baby.

Eventually, babies begin to make connections between sounds or sound patterns and events or objects. They notice, for example, that when they are handed a particular object (such as a teddy bear), the same sound pattern occurs time after time. Their storybooks have the same sounds with the same pictures. They notice that whenever their diapers are changed, they hear some of the same sounds and patterns. What the infant takes in and understands is called receptive language.

From the beginning, of course, infants react to being spoken to, but it is the voice—pitch and tone—rather than the meaning of the words that they respond to. Later, when they begin to respond to the meaning behind the words, this response is true receptive language. Caregivers are sometimes surprised to discover that receptive language is so advanced. I remember the time I said to one of my sons, "Go get your hat," not expecting a response. I was astounded when minutes later he was back, hat in hand. I was later surprised again, when Magda Gerber was giving a demonstration of receptive language, seeing a child just a few months old respond to the statement, "I'm going to pick you up now." You had to look hard to see the response, but it was there—a slight whole body movement toward the adult. When children are spoken to in meaningful ways, they understand what is being said to them much earlier than you might expect.

Learning to Verbalize: Expressive Language

As their early cries and vocalizations are responded to, infants learn to refine them, eventually sending more specialized vocal signals. The more they know that their signals or messages are received, the more skilled they become in sending them. From their partnership with a caregiver or two, they learn to convey a variety of feelings—hunger, discomfort, anger, and pleasure. The key to infants' beginning to connect sounds with meaning is the caregiver's responsiveness. If no one responded to their initial cries and vocalizations, infants would have no reason to strive to make signals.

The actual moment a child utters her first word may be quite a surprise to the adult who is present to hear it. One day a little girl may see a banana on a counter and reach for it, saying "nana." She may be surprised by the reaction—such a flutter and flurry of smiles, hugs, and pats, followed by a piece of banana being placed in her hand. She will probably smile back and say her new word two or three more times. Later on she may be asked to repeat her performance as the late shift of caregivers arrives. Perhaps the caregivers, so pleased with this new accomplishment, will report it to the parent. Or maybe they'll keep their pleasure to themselves and decide not to disappoint the parent, who missed the event, by mentioning it, but will let the parent be the one to report the first word when he or she hears it.

Suppose you observed a child who was just beginning to talk and you wrote down exactly what he or she said. Your notes might look something like this:

> mmmmm mmm (pause) oooo (pause) milk (pause) mimimimim-
> imimi (pause) burrrrrr, burrrrrr, burrrrrrr (pause) ooooooo milk
> eeeeeeee (pause) uhuhu (pause) milk!

Rather meaningless, isn't it, without the context? A description of the whole scene would clarify for you what the child was communicating.

> A caregiver holds out a cup to a baby seated at a low table. "Do you want a drink of milk?" he asks.
>
> The child answers, "mmmmmmm mmm, ooooo, milk!" He reaches for the cup.
>
> The caregiver pours a small amount of milk into the cup. The child lifts it to his lips and takes a sip. Then he says, "mimimimimimi, burrrrrr, burrrrrr, burrrr" into the cup, delighted in the effect of the movement of his lips on the milk. Milk splashes onto his face. The caregiver reaches for a wet washcloth. The child sets the cup down, and it tips over, making a puddle on the table. "ooooooooo milk . . . " says the child, pointing to the puddle.
>
> The caregiver reaches for a sponge with the other hand and puts it on the puddle while wiping the child's face with the washcloth. "Eeeeeeee." Squeals of protest accompany the face cleaning. When all is in order again, the caregiver reaches for the carton, holds it out, and asks, "Do you want more milk?"
>
> The child answers, "Uhuh, milk!" emphatically, with a vigorous shake of his head while shoving the cup away from him.

This child conveyed a variety of meanings through a few sounds and a single word. In a short time, this same scene might include this verbal sequence:

> "Me milk" (meaning "Yes, please, I'd like some milk.")
> "Milk spill" (meaning "Hey there, somebody spilled the milk!")
> "Me, no" (meaning "No thank you, I don't want any more milk.")

By the time this child is a toddler, he will be saying the same thing using longer phrases—something like this:

> "Give me milk." (perhaps with a "please")
> "Oh, oh, Mike, me spill milk."
> "Me no want more."

Without ever being "corrected," this child will eventually say:

> "I want some milk (please)."
> "Oh, oh, Mike. I spilled my milk."
> "I don't want anymore (thank you)."

Children refine their language on their own. They don't need corrections or language lessons. They learn by being part of real conversations —ones that move forward. Sometimes conversations just go around in circles when the adult tries to teach by just repeating everything the child says in a more correct form. If nothing the adult says adds to the content, these merry-go-round conversations are meaningless, and frustrating to the child besides.

Fostering Language Development

Caregivers can foster language development in infants by using language with them from the start. *Talk* to them long before they can talk to you. Use real, adult talk. Include them in conversations with other people. Also *play* with them using sounds. Interact with them—create dialogues. Listen to infants, and encourage them to listen, too. Make sure that you have an infant's attention when you are talking together, and be sure to give him or her yours. It's surprising how responsive even very young infants are to language. The rhythm of their body movements corresponds with the rhythm of language when engaged in one of these early dialogues. Here are some guidelines for fostering language development in infants and toddlers:

1. Engage in dialogue from day one, during caregiving times and during play time (when appropriate). With the younger infants, exchange sounds. This is a natural activity most adults engage in without being told to. They imitate the baby's sounds as well as initiating their own sounds. This kind of dialogue sets the stage for later, when the dialogue on both sides will contain words.

2. Create monologues also. Discuss the present. Describe what is happening as it occurs. Your running commentary will contain the labels children need to learn—labels for people, feelings, actions, objects, and events. When the infant responds, turn the monologue into a dialogue. (It's best always to talk *with* a baby, not *at* him or her.)

3. Discuss the past—remark about what happened just now to infants; with toddlers, you can talk about earlier in the day, yesterday, and last week. The older the child, the farther back you can go.

4. Discuss the future. Knowing what's about to happen helps infants predict events as well as begin to understand labels for things, actions, events, and people. Toddlers can be involved in discussions about the future, including what will happen this afternoon, tomorrow, and next week. The older the child, the farther into the future you can go.

5. Tell stories, sing songs, and recite or create rhymes and poems. Make room in your telling, singing, or reciting for the children's

participation or responses. Don't just entertain them; interact with them. They learn language from using it, from being involved, not just from listening.

6. Play games with sounds and words. If you're not good at this yourself, take lessons from the children. Many young children have an outstanding ability to create playfully with sounds and words. This starts early with those first cooings and babblings and continues, if valued and encouraged, until children are creating their own nonsense rhymes and sound games.

7. Be sure older toddlers have plenty of experiences to talk about. The infants will find enough subject matter in the day-to-day play and caregiving routines, but, as they grow, their world needs to expand a bit. It's up to you to be sure that expansion occurs. Create "happenings" inside and outside. Bring in visitors. If possible, go on short field trips—a walk around the block can provide conversation material for some time.

8. Read books from infancy on. Read individually or to small groups at any appropriate time when there is an interest. Don't make a daily circle time with required attendance for the whole group. Make it a frequent, short, spontaneous activity accompanied by lots of cuddling and snuggles. Stop when interest wanes, and don't require each child to stay and listen to the whole book. Make this an interactive activity rather than an entertainment. Allow children to "read" to you or to other children. Story or book time for infants and toddlers should resemble what parents do at home more than what preschool teachers do at circle time. The purpose is to familiarize infants and toddlers with books and to create a number of pleasurable associations with books, and eventually with reading. The language goals, though important, are secondary.

9. Bring in pictures, novel objects, and bits of science and nature, and carry on extemporaneous discussions when a child's interest is sparked. Again, these should be dialogues, not lectures.

10. Ask questions—questions requiring a choice. Do you want the square cracker or the round one? Do you want to go for a walk before snack or after snack? Ask questions that have no right answer (called open questions). How does the bunny feel to you? Tell me about Grandma's visit. What did you see on your walk? Closed questions (those with one right answer) are fine, too, as long as the child enjoys them and doesn't feel interrogated. (They are often overused in an attempt to teach language.)

11. Encourage children to ask questions. A favorite game of beginning talkers is "What's that?" They like to ask the question as well as answer it, and in doing so, they practice and collect labels for objects.

12. Encourage children to clarify what they don't understand. Some people try to teach children through questioning them. If pressured for correct answers, children can learn to act as if they understand things they don't. If you encourage an inquiry attitude, they'll ask about words they don't know and then practice them on their own without being taught or pushed. An example is one of my sons, who at about three asked about the word "budge" in a story we were reading. That very afternoon he called me for help, explaining the box he was trying to push wouldn't "budge"!

13. Put language into gross motor activities. Don't regard your language curriculum as something that happens during sedentary times. The way children learn about spatial relations and the prepositions that go with them is through experiencing these concepts with their own bodies. When adults add a label, they help the child classify, store, and remember the concept. "Mario is *under* the box. See him hiding?" "Who's going to sit *beside* you at the table? Oh, Emily's going to." "I see you're *on top of* the steps, Jason. Are you going to stay *up* there or are you going *down?*"

14. Really listen when toddlers talk to you. Resist the temptation to rush children or interrupt them. Give them time to say what they want to say.

15. Help children listen to each other. Talk for them or interpret when necessary, but keep the focus *off* yourself *on* the two children who are trying to communicate with each other. "She's trying to tell you she doesn't like you to push her." "Ask her what she wants." "Tell him you want some play dough too."

16. Recognize and respect the parents' ability to understand their own child. Get them to explain or interpret. As you get to know each child's unique method of communicating, you'll need less interpretation, except maybe about events that happened outside of the day-care day.

Cultural Differences in Language Development

All these guidelines are culturally bound (as is everything else in this book). Some cultures view language practices and the language socialization process differently from the way that it has been presented here. They may have different goals for their children regarding language. They may also use different methods from the beginning. You may or may not approve of the cultural approach to language of some of the parents in your program, but you must respect cultural differences and try to understand how values and approaches other than your own may serve the individual in the particular culture.

An example of a cultural difference in language is provided by S. B. Heath, who describes a culture in which babies are made a part of everything that is going on by being held continually but are rarely talked to during the first year. They pick up language by being immersed in it, not by having it directed at them. This shows later in their use of language. They have a holistic view of objects in context. They have difficulty talking about an object out of context, such as sorting out the attributes of that object and comparing them to those of another object out of context. When shown flash card pictures of a red ball and a blue ball and asked, "Is the red ball or the blue ball bigger," children from this culture would have difficulty sorting out the attributes of color and size, though in a real life situation they could determine the larger ball and throw it when asked to do so. This culture, rather than teaching the concepts accepted as important by the mainstream American culture (such as color, shape, and size), values the creative use of language, including metaphors. Their children show great skill at creative verbal play and use of imagery.[1]

Children in child care are influenced by the caregiver's culture. Children who grow up in two cultures and incorporate both are said to be bicultural. Whether or not those two cultures conflict and cause the child to feel torn between them depends on the child, the parents, the caregiver, and the cultures themselves. Sometimes children seem to get caught *between* two cultures and experience a lot of pain in their upbringing.

A child can be bicultural and still be English speaking, as are many children in this country and other parts of the world. However, many bicultural people speak more than one language. The rest of this chapter will concentrate on the language acquisition of the bilingual child.

Bilingualism and Infants and Toddlers

Infants can learn two languages from day one, and by the time they are toddlers, they can be very skilled at switching back and forth between them to different people and in different contexts. My husband was such a child—born in Mexico into a family where both German and Spanish were spoken, he could from his earliest memories use whichever language the situation called for.

Bilingualism is a skill to be valued and nurtured. Day care can provide excellent opportunities for this skill to develop as children of one language background come into contact with caregivers of another. Take advantage of any chance you have to help children become bilingual (with the parents' permission, of course). You can do this by talking to them in your own language (if their family speaks a different one) or another language (if you are bilingual yourself).

A factor to keep in mind is what I call the "language relationship." The language relationship is established without fanfare when two people meet for the first time. For two monolingual English-speaking people, there is no option; the language of their relationship is English, and they never even think about it. But when two bilingual persons meet, the situation is different. There is a choice, and once the choice is made, the two feel most comfortable when they speak the language of their relationship to each other, though both may be fully capable of speaking the second language.

Numerous factors are at work in the establishment of which language will become the language of the relationship. Sometimes the decision is unconscious; other times it is made consciously. Again my husband serves as an example. His parents spoke only German to him—their relationship with him was a German language relationship. It was a conscious decision on their part to teach their children German. They spoke Spanish to each other, which meant *they* had a Spanish language relationship. My husband grew up completely bilingual, using German with his parents and some of his relatives and Spanish with others. Yet even with native ability in Spanish, he reports a peculiar feeling when he spoke Spanish instead of German to his parents. This discomfort relates to the fact that he was stepping out of the language relationship that his parents had established with him at birth.

When a bilingual caregiver meets a young infant, the choice of language is present to some extent because the baby is not yet a full-fledged member of a language community. If bilingualism is a goal, establishing a relationship in the target language from the beginning is quite simple.

Establishing this relationship is a little more difficult with a child who is already partway along in his or her language development because of the difficulty in communicating until the child learns the second language. The strength of the bilingual goal and the extent to which children feel secure and are able to get their needs met should determine whether to establish a language relationship in a language other than the child's own with the primary caregiver. When both caregiver and child are skilled at nonverbal communication, the choice isn't so difficult. Once the language relationship is established, there is a motivation to learn the second language, and it isn't long before verbal communication is established. It is important, however, to remember that, although some children seem to "pick up" language fast, language acquisition doesn't happen overnight. Communication is necessarily weak at the beginning and often for a long time afterward. It's very hard on some older babies and toddlers to be put into situations where they can't understand what is said to them. Just imagine how you would feel being totally dependent on someone who didn't speak your language.

When bilingualism is a strong goal and the child is liable to suffer from the initial lack of communication, it is best to have two caregivers to relate to the child. One can then establish a relationship in the second language while another is present to establish a language relationship in the child's own language. This way the child can become bilingual in a secure situation. This way of ensuring bilingualism is common practice in many families in different parts of the world.

Be careful that you don't ask bilingual or limited English-speaking parents to speak English to their children when their inclination is otherwise. If you do, you are disregarding the language relationship. And you may be impairing the communication between parent and child. Magda Gerber, a bilingual person herself, says that it is natural for parents to speak to their children in the language they themselves were spoken to in infancy and toddlerhood. Even parents who have become proficient in English may find that the words of caring come easier in the language of their own beginnings. Be careful not to hinder parents' ability to communicate caring and tenderness to their children.

As caregivers, you should also be concerned about the quality of verbal communication in your program if bilingualism is a goal. Unless you are proficient in the language you are using to communicate with the child, the goal of bilingualism may get in the way of communication. If your ability to express yourself in the target language is limited, you should weigh communication and the child's language development against the goal of bilingualism.

As already mentioned, a solution to this problem, if there is more than one adult and bilingualism is a goal, is for one to establish relationships in one language and the other to establish them in the second language. In this way, children establish a relationship with someone who is proficient in one language and are assured of good communication while they progress in a second language. Without someone to communicate with who is proficient, the child misses out. With one proficient speaker and one less than proficient one, the child can gain some added benefits without losing out on first language development. This scene shows how bilingualism can work in a family day-care home.

> It's late in the afternoon, and a woman is heating tortillas on the stove. A three year old watches her from the kitchen table. He tells her that he is hungry—in Spanish. She smiles and answers him in Spanish, at the same time handing him a warm, soft, rolled-up tortilla. Another three year old appears at the doorway, requesting a tortilla in English. She obliges with a second tortilla and again answers in Spanish. Both children stand by the table chewing their tortillas, obviously relishing the flavor.
> A man enters the kitchen. "Ummm, something smells good," he comments.
> "Yes," replies the woman. "Guess what?"
> "Tortilla. It's yummy," says the first child, holding his out to show the man.
> "Want a bite?" asks the second child.
> "Here's one for you," says the woman, handing the man his own fresh, hot tortilla.
> All three chew contentedly. Then the man says, "How about Grandma? Go ask her if she wants a tortilla."

The first child runs from the room, calling, "Abuelita, Abuelita, quieres tortilla?"

This child, only three years old, is managing to learn two languages and, further, is learning when to use each one. The other child is getting exposure to a second language and developing his receptive language skills. Depending upon the circumstances, he may begin to use it himself one day. In the meantime, he's in a situation where he can use and be understood in his own language while learning another one.

The skill of using language appropriate to the situation is not limited to children using two languages. All speakers learn early to distinguish between language styles. Listen carefully to the difference between the way two three year olds talk to each other and the way they talk to adults. Listen, for example, to the way children "play house." The one playing the mother talks the way she perceives adults talk; the one playing the baby speaks in a different way altogether. Clearly, they have learned that there is one style for talking to peers and another for talking to adults. Children also distinguish among the adults they speak to. The way they talk to mother may be different from the way they talk to father, caregiver, or a stranger on the street.

Language is culturally bound and influences our lives immeasurably. Infants and toddlers learn to use language in natural settings when they are spoken to, responded to, and listened to. Language influences how they perceive the world, organize their experience, and communicate with others. Language acquisition is truly an awe-inspiring process.

Notes

1. S. B. Heath, *Ways with Words: Language, Life, and Work in Communities and Classrooms* (Cambridge, England: Cambridge University Press, 1983).

For Further Reading

T. G. R. Bower, *A Primer of Infant Development* (San Francisco: W.H. Freeman, 1977).

Roger Brown, *A First Language: The Early Years* (Cambridge, Mass.: Harvard University Press, 1973).

Courtney B. Cazden, ed., *Language in Early Childhood Education* (Washington D.C.: National Association for the Education of Young Children, 1981).

Magda Gerber, "Babies Understanding Words," *Educaring* 3 (4), Fall 1982, pp. 5–6.

Kenji Hakuta, *Mirror of Language, the Debate on Bilingualism* (New York: Basic Books, 1986).

Chapter 10
The Development
of Social Skills

S ocialization connects us to other people, ensuring that individuals will get along with each other as they form into groups and groups into a society. From the socialization process comes tribes, culture, and civilization.

Humans have to learn social skills—they aren't born with them and they don't just unfold in a universal, predesigned pattern as do gross motor and language skills, for example. Social skills are special to the culture from which they come and are learned only from other people.

This chapter looks at the progression of social development from infancy through toddlerhood. It also discusses how caregivers can provide for the skill development so necessary for the future of the society—indeed, of the world. At no time in history has the development of social skills been so important because the stakes are so high. We can't afford to raise a generation to believe that might is right, or we'll blow up the world with our nuclear stockpiles. We need to teach young children how to resolve conflicts without resorting to force. This teaching starts with infants.

Early Social Behaviors

Infants come equipped with a set of social behaviors that start to work right from the beginning to involve the people around them in the socialization process. In fact, just hours after birth you can see babies interact with synchrony by moving their bodies to the rhythm and body movements of anyone who talks to them. The dancelike movements are minute, but they are present, in spite of the fact that the speaker is usually unaware of them. They occur only in response to language (any language, not necessarily that of the baby's family), but do not show up in response to other kinds of rhythms.[1]

Another early social behavior is imitation. Babies' inclination to imitate serves the socialization process well as they copy or model after adult social behavior (which means, of course, the adult must be aware of modeling prosocial behaviors). This imitating behavior starts very early. In the first weeks, babies will imitate such behavior as opening their eyes wide or sticking out their tongue.

Another evidence of early social behavior that seems by nature designed to involve the adult in the socialization process from the beginning is smiling. Whether the first smiles are "real" smiles—social smiles—is still debated. Whether truly social or not, smiles almost always elicit a social response from the adult smiled upon.

By a few months old, most babies are effective at nonverbal communication with the people they are attached to. As they get better and better at communication with particular people, they develop fear when around people who don't know their unique communication systems. This fear, called "stranger anxiety," often appears around the sixth month. It seems to be strongest in babies who have excellent communication with their partner(s). The fear is intensified when the "stranger" tries to communicate with the babies. Often the fear is lessened when the "stranger" remains silent and noncommunicative. If you think of how you would feel when confronted with someone speaking a foreign language who seems most anxious to tell you something, you may understand the infant's upset when faced with a communicative stranger.

By the second year of life, babies are already making communicative social gestures that predict to some extent which of them will be well-liked preschoolers and which will have difficulty with peer relationships. The infants who will probably become well-liked preschoolers already have a number of *friendly* gestures that they exhibit regularly, such as offering toys, clapping hands, and smiling. Infants who regularly use threatening or aggressive gestures or a mixture of friendly and unfriendly gestures to their peers are more likely to grow into less-liked preschoolers.[2]

Attachment is the prime factor in the development of social skills. From a primary relationship come the skills for developing other relationships.

Stages of Psychosocial Development

The theorist who has the most to say about social development is Erik Erikson. In *Childhood and Society*, he describes three stages of what he calls psychosocial development that apply to children under three.

Trust

The first is trust. Sometime during the first year of life, if infants find that their needs are met consistently and gently, they decide that the world is a good place to be. They develop what Erikson calls a "sense of basic trust." If infants' needs are not met consistently, or are met in a harsh manner, they may decide that the world is unfriendly and develop mistrust instead of trust. Such infants can carry this outlook into adulthood if nothing happens to change their view of life.

If infants are in day care, the adults in the program have some responsibility for ensuring that the children in their care come to gain a sense of basic trust. That means that *needs* must be a primary concern of everyone from the director down. There is no way to run an infant program that emphasizes anything but individual needs—infants are not like older children, who can put group needs before their own and wait for lunch or snack or wait an hour to go to the bathroom. Infants cannot be treated as members of a group, but must be responded to as individuals.

The importance of developing a sense of basic trust also means that infants in day care need small groups with consistent caregivers. Stability in programs contributes to the infants' well-being and building sense of trust.

Part of developing trust means coping with separation. As attachment strengthens, so does the pain of being away from the person(s) to whom the child is attached. Day-care workers spend a lot of time and energy helping children manage the feelings separation brings forth. Here is an example of a child experiencing some of those feelings.

A mother enters the room carrying a child who has a tense look on her face. She has both arms around her mother's neck and is hanging on tight. Her mother puts her diaper bag into a cubby by the entrance, then speaks briefly to the caregiver. She bends to remove her shoes, then walks into the play area, stopping on a rug. She bends over to put her daughter down, saying, "I have to go pretty soon, Rebecca. You're going to stay here with Maria. She'll take care of you while I'm gone." Maria has come close to the pair and kneels down, waiting.

The child clings tighter. The mother sits down on the floor, Rebecca still in her arms. They both sit there for several minutes. The child begins to relax a bit. She reaches for the handle of a push toy, which her mother hands her. She runs it back and forth across the rug while still in her mother's arms. Finally, she gets down, and, sitting right next to her mother, Rebecca begins to bang a plastic hammer on a pounding bench. She gets absorbed in her activity and moves slightly away from her mother. With that her mother gets up, looking over to Maria, who is across the room by now. She then leans down, kisses her daughter, and says, "It's time for me to go now. Good-bye." She walks over, slips her shoes on, then moves quickly to the door. Her daughter follows her with a distressed look on her face. At the door her mother turns once briefly, throws her a kiss, turns back, opens the door, and is out it. At the sound of the door closing, Rebecca lets out a wail, then collapses in a heap, sobbing.

She looks up as a hand touches her shoulder. She sees, kneeling beside her, Maria, the caregiver. She moves away from the touch. Maria continues to stay close by her. "I see you're upset that your mom left." Rebecca begins to scream again.

Maria remains close, but silent. Rebecca's screams subside, and she goes back to quiet sobbing. She continues to sob for a while; then she spots her diaper bag where her mother left it in her cubby. She reaches for it; her tear-stained face has a look of expectancy on it. Maria gets it out for her. Rebecca clings to it. Maria reaches inside and pulls out a stuffed bear wrapped in a scarf. Rebecca grabs the bear, hugging it fiercely. She strokes the scarf, holding it to her nose periodically and smelling it. Her face gets more and more relaxed.

Maria moves away from her. Rebecca doesn't seem to notice. Maria comes back with a box of dolls and blankets, which she arranges on the floor near Rebecca. Rebecca crawls over immediately, tips the box over, and crawls inside. The scene closes as Rebecca is wrapping a doll in a blanket and putting it to bed in the box next to her bear, which is covered with the scarf.

Notice how Maria helped Rebecca cope with separation. She stated the situation and the feelings. She was available, but not pushy. She was sensitive to Rebecca's responses to her touch and to her words. She encouraged Rebecca to find solace from familiar belongings. She set up the environment to entice Rebecca to explore when she was ready. She waited a bit, however, so that the enticement did not distract Rebecca from her feelings.

Here are some more ideas about how to help children through the process of temporary separation as they say good-bye to parents.

1. Be honest. State the facts, including the emotional facts. Say something like Maria did or something like this: "Your mom had to go to work, and you're unhappy about being left." If the feeling you perceive is anger, you can state that.
2. Handle the situation with the appropriate degree of seriousness. If the suffering is minor, don't make it more serious than it is. But don't make light of it either. Don't underplay the importance of the relationship of child to parent and the degree of suffering the child may be experiencing. You may think to yourself, "This is nothing—you'll be taken care of—there's nothing to be afraid of here." But the child doesn't know that, and in spite of your reas-

surance may not believe it. It will take time for the child to discover that is the situation—there really is nothing to be afraid of. In the meantime, if the child is terrified, accept that fact.

3. Provide a balance of kindly concern and matter-of-fact confidence. Somehow convey the attitude that it hurts now, but you'll survive it—and grow from it. Be careful about being overreassuring. If you make promises, the child may begin to wonder if you're really positive that his or her parent will return.

4. Offer support and help with coping. Physical closeness may help. Some infants and toddlers do better with an adult close by; others move from parent to a toy or interesting material put out to be enticing. Sometimes children will play out their feelings with a toy.

5. Welcome things from home. Some children find comfort in a link to home provided by a familiar object. This may be some special attachment object such as a blanket or stuffed animal, or it may be something that has no emotional significance other than the fact that it came from home. One toddler felt great comfort in the fact that his mother left her purse (an empty purse) by his diaper bag. It seemed that he wasn't sure she would come back for him, but he *knew* that she would come back for her purse!

6. Allow children individual ways of feeling comforted. Some children refuse to remove a sweater, a hat, or other piece of clothing. Something about wearing it seems to make them feel more secure when away from home. Or maybe it has to do with feeling the stay is only temporary as long as they don't take off the piece of clothing—something like the message adults give when they enter a room and keep their car keys in their hands the whole time they are there.

It's hard to be attached and dependent and be away from home. Can you remember feeling small, helpless, and separated from the person you were attached to? Think about what it was, in your experience, that helped you cope with being apart from the people you were attached to? Has another person been helpful to you during a difficult separation? If so, can you remember what it was that person said or did? Use your own experience to help you promote coping skills in infants and toddlers.

It is important to deal with separation even with a child who is not creating a big fuss. Coping with loss and separation is a lifetime task, not something we get over when we are babies after the first separation from parent(s). All our lives we lose those we are close to as friends and family grow away from us (or we from them), move to another city, or die. The coping skills we develop in our first years serve us for the rest of our lives. When children learn to cope with fears of loss and separation, they get feelings of mastery. When they don't learn to cope, they feel failure and mistrust.

Sometimes it is difficult for adults to deal with infants' and toddlers' feelings about separation because of their own experiences. They may have old issues around separation—unfinished business, so to speak, that they aren't ready to deal with. So they may prefer not to reopen old wounds. In that case, they may feel uncomfortable around children who are suffering a sense of loss. Instead of trying to understand the feelings and help the children cope, they wish the feelings would just go away. They may distract children from their feelings, hoping they will forget the pain. But the pain doesn't just "go away." Children need to learn to cope with the feelings. Separation skills are a competency infants and toddlers build; they don't usually arrive in a program already competent. So when separation is an issue, separation is the curriculum, and that's where the adult focus should be.

Recognizing the range of feelings that comes with separation can be helpful for caregivers. The feelings of loss may range from mild discomfort and anxiety to sadness, even grief. Fear and anger are other reactions common to a separation situation. A feeling of loneliness is another reaction. A child may be feeling all of these at once or may feel just one. All of these feeling words have been used by adults to describe their reactions to a loss that came from being apart, temporarily or permanently, from someone they were attached to. Though infants and toddlers aren't necessarily competent at describing feelings, it is easy to detect that they feel the same range as adults feel.

An additional issue that caregivers often have to face is that of parental behavior around separation. It is common to hear caregivers complain that parents magnify separation problems and even create additional ones. This happens when parents have as much (or more) pain at leaving their children as their children have at leaving them. Because of these feelings, parents may act in ways you don't approve of. Some prefer to sneak away because they can't stand saying good-bye. Others prolong the good-byes until everyone is in pain, though the child has already shown he or she is better off with a quick, uncomplicated departure. Some parents suffer because the child cries when they leave; others suffer because he or she *doesn't*. Be sensitive to parent feelings, and realize that separation is hard on them too. The parents' difficulties may be compounded by a sense of guilt at leaving their children. Give them all the support and help you can. There's more on this subject in Chapter 14.

An additional factor when looking at separation in infant-toddler day care is that of attachment to caregivers. As shifts change, personnel changes, and adults come and go, infants and toddlers may have to deal with separation from a beloved caregiver before they say hello once again to a beloved parent. In fact, a day in a day-care center may be full of hellos and good-byes because of breaks, lunches, and assorted responsibilities that may call a particular caregiver out of the room. These comings and goings are usually less of a problem for infants and toddlers in a family day-care home.

Autonomy

Erikson's second stage, autonomy, occurs as the growing infant reaches the second year and begins to move around in the environment. When infants become toddlers, they begin to perceive themselves as separate individuals—not just a part of the person(s) they are attached to. They discover the power they possess, and they push toward independence. At the same time, their developing capabilities allow them to do more for themselves. They learn self-help skills.

Readiness for toilet training, discussed in Chapter 3, is an example of the coming together of increased capabilities and the push for independence. The necessary capabilities lie in three separate domains—the physical (control), the cognitive (understanding), and the emotional (willingness). The trick is to get the movement toward independence working for you and not against you. If you get too demanding or pushy, you may find yourself in a power struggle over toilet training, and then the child, in the name of independence, feels the need to oppose you. Independence becomes linked in the child's mind with diapers or "accidents." Far better if the child sees you as a support and an aid rather than an obstacle to his or her own developing capabilities and independence.

Language provides clues about another area of autonomy. The "NO!" for which toddlers are so famous is a further clue to the push for separateness and independence. They differentiate themselves from others by what seems to be contrariness. If you want them to go in, they want to stay out. If you want them to stop, they want to start. If you're serving milk, they want juice.

Granted, caregivers don't usually see as much of this kind of behavior as parents do. The tie between parent and child is a much stronger, more passionate one. And many children feel more secure and therefore free to express themselves in words and actions at home than they do in day care. It is important not to make parents feel they are doing something wrong because more defiant and rebellious behavior comes out when they are present. Rejecting behaviors are normal—even good—for toddlers to exhibit. They show that the child's growing sense of autonomy and separateness is strong.

The strength with which rejecting behaviors can come forth when a child feels attached and secure can be surprising. I once observed a toddler program where the staff was proud of how "well behaved" the children were. That was bad news for me because I was looking for examples of rejecting behavior. Needless to say, I was finding very few examples as I observed all these "well-behaved" toddlers. After spending an hour or so there, I was about to give up and look elsewhere when a new child walked in the door. She obviously was not new to the program because she acted right at home from the first minute. Very soon she was filling up my notepad with examples of rejecting behaviors. I was delighted, but mystified. Not being familiar with the program or the people in it, I didn't discover the answer right away. But eventually I realized that her mother was one of the caregivers in the program. I should have guessed. She was obviously the only child who felt strongly attached to someone on site, and she felt comfortable enough to push right and left. Of course, I was the only one present, I'm sure, who was glad to see her behaviors. But I've worried ever since about toddlers who are "good" all day, five days a week, and go into a rejecting mode only on evenings and weekends. Are they getting what they need in day care? What does it do to their relationship with their parents if they have to concentrate all their rejecting behaviors into the few hours they spend with them?

Language provides further clues about other areas of autonomy that are part of the toddler period. "Me do it!" shows the drive for independence. By capitalizing on this drive, you can promote the development of self-help skills. When children want to "do it," set up the situation so they *can*.

Another language clue shows up when toddlers shout, "Me—Mine!" at each other and you. This development shows that they have begun to see themselves not only as individuals, but as individuals with possessions. It takes some time for this concept to be complete, often beyond the toddler years.

Because we want children to grow up being cooperative and sharing individuals, we sometimes push them to share before they are ready. Children who have no sense of possession can't understand the concept of sharing. Children who have some sense of possession still may not be ready to share. Some take a long time to develop a feeling that something *belongs to them*. If they spend most of their waking hours in an environment where everything belongs to everybody or to the program, it may take a good deal longer.

Sometimes, in the name of fairness, children are constantly asked to give up a turn or a toy before they are finished with it. When this occurs in an environment where there are no private possessions, rather than learning to be a sharing person, some learn just not to care. It doesn't matter to them whether they play with this toy or that or for how long. They learn to stay uninvolved rather than face the pain of being constantly interrupted and sidetracked. Think what it would be like to be a child who never gets a chance to play out a fantasy or an interest or reach a point of satisfaction by being allowed to have a toy or material in your possession until you are really through with it. How would this situation affect attention span? Do some children learn to have short attention spans because some caregivers over-stress sharing?

Initiative

Erikson's term for the stage of older toddlers as they approach pre-school age is initiative. The focus on autonomy eventually passes. The energy that has previously gone into separating and striving for independence, and which often resulted in defiance and rebellion, is now available for new themes. This energy pushes children to create, invent, and explore as they seek out new activities. At this new stage, toddlers become the initiators of what happens in their lives and gain enthusiasm from their newfound power.

The caregiver should respond to this need to initiate by providing information, resources, freedom, and encouragement. Although the older toddler still very much needs limits, the caregiver can set and keep the limits in such a way that toddlers don't feel guilty about this powerful push they feel to take initiative. People with initiative make valuable citizens. They gain this quality early in life when the people around them encourage them to be *explorers, thinkers, and doers.*

Guidance and Discipline

The socialization process in infants comes about as adults meet their needs. Infants require no guidance or discipline. Limits come naturally from their own limitations. Control may be a minor issue at times. Usually, meeting a specific need will take care of their lack of control, or they may need to be held close and tight. An example of providing control when an infant needs it is when newborns cry in distress that is not hunger. Sometimes they quiet down when wrapped tightly in a blanket. The blanket seems to provide the control that they do not have as their legs and arms hang free under loose covers.

This same theme, tightness providing control the infant lacks, looks different in the toddler stage. Toddlers may also appreciate a "feeling of tightness" when control comes from the outside, in situations when their own underdeveloped ability to control themselves gives way. Holding out-of-control toddlers tightly usually enables them to regain inner control.

Toddlers need to feel that there are limits even when they do not need the tightness of outside control. Think of limits—rules of behavior—as invisible fences or boundaries. Because they can't see these boundaries, children need to test in order to discover them. And they have little faith in words alone. Just as most of us are compelled to touch the surface behind the "wet paint" sign, so are toddlers compelled to bump up against a limit to see if it is really there and to make sure it will hold. Some children will do more testing than others, but all children need to know that there are limits. The fact that limits are there provides a sense of security, just as the tight blanket does for the newborn.

To illustrate the security that limits provide, think of yourself driving across a high bridge. You probably have done that more than once in your life. The limits on the bridge are the rails on the sides. Can you imagine yourself driving across that bridge if the rails were removed? You don't physically need those rails, you know. After all, how often have you actually bumped the rails while driving across a bridge? I never have. Yet the thought of the bridge without the rails is terrifying. The rails provide a sense of security, just as the limits set for toddlers provide security in their lives.

Any discussion of limits, guidance, and discipline in toddlers quickly brings forth a discussion of what to do about such behaviors as biting, hitting, throwing things, and negativism. No single answer covers all behaviors in all situations with all children. The only single answer that applies is "It depends. . . . "

Let's look at biting. Start by asking, "Why is this child biting? What is behind the behavior?" If children are very young, they may be biting out of love. Sometimes when adults model playful nibbling, chewing, or "eating up" as a way of demonstrating affection, infants imitate their actions by biting those they love. This is not hard to understand if you relate to feelings implied in the expression "to sink your teeth into something." Mouths are expressive organs, and when a child is too small to convey the intensity of a feeling with words, biting may do it.

Of course, not all biting is done for love; some is done for power. When a child is small, physical power is minimal. But the jaws have powerful muscles, and little teeth are sharp. Even a very young child can do real damage with a bite. Some children learn this as a means of getting their own way with children who are bigger than they are.

Some biting may be done out of curiosity. Just as infants mouth and bite objects, so may they mouth and bite people. They do this with no malice intended—they are merely exploring.

Some biting is done as an expression of anger. Adults clench their jaws and grind their teeth; infants and toddlers sink their teeth into any available arm.

Some biting may be a means of gaining attention. Imagine yourself a toddler in a program where adults are available but are spread thin, and you get focused attention from one of them rarely and then only briefly. Or imagine that you do get focused attention, but the adult tends to be warm and rather vacant. There's more of a shell than a real person. No matter what you do, you can't seem to tap the real person inside the shell. Then one day you discover that by merely putting your teeth into a child's leg, you can get an adult to come over and touch you—even pick you up, hold you tight, look you right in the eye, and talk at length to you. This adult who was all fluff before becomes hard and real as the exchange provides passion and intensity. The message is that you finally did something that *mattered!*

Some young children need this kind of strong interaction. It tells them that you care what they do, that their behavior matters to you. If they can't provoke an intense interaction any other way, they may continue to bite, just to get it.

The way to stop biting is to prevent it, not try to deal with it after it happens. Biting is too powerful a behavior to allow to continue. It's too painful for the person bitten, and it's too frightening for the biter to have that much power to do harm. When biters can't control their own behavior, it's up to you to control it. A useful technique after waylaying the biting is to redirect the urge. Give these children something to bite on that is made for biting—teething rings, cloth, or rubber or plastic objects. Offer these as choices, saying something like, "I can't let you bite Craig, but you can bite the plastic ring or this wet washcloth." Don't do this in a punitive way.

What else you do besides control the behavior and offer biting alternatives depends on the origins of the biting. If it is being modeled, try to cut off the modeling. If it is an expression of a feeling (love, frustration, or anger), teach alternative means of expression. Help children redirect their energy into positive ways of expressing the feelings. Redirecting the biting to objects is a start, but go beyond that. If a power issue is involved, teach children other techniques for getting what they need and want. If it is an attention issue, find ways to give children the attention—the intense interactions they need—without biting being the trigger. None of these is an easy solution, and it may take a good deal of brainstorming, discussion, cooperation, and teamwork even to identify the origins of the behavior and the appropriate approach.

Biting is an example of an aggressive behavior. Other aggressive behaviors that cause toddler caregivers problems are hitting, kicking, shoving, hair pulling, throwing objects, and destroying toys and materials. To figure out what to do about these behaviors, you must go through a problem-solving process, looking at the particular child, the possible origins of the behavior, the message behind the behavior, the way the environment may contribute to the behavior, the way adult behavior may trigger the aggression, and the resources the child has for expressing feelings. Beware of advice that advocates any one simple solution. Behavior is complex, as are children. No one approach is right for everyone all the time.

Another category of difficult behaviors caregivers of toddlers deal with is negativism. A continual complaint I hear from my beginning student teachers who work with toddlers is, "They won't do what I say." Part of the problem may be that toddlers can't always translate word messages into physical control, even when they understand what you want. But another part of the problem is that, when toddlers are faced with demands or commands, they often do the opposite.

The secret to dealing with negativism is to stop issuing challenges. Stay out of power struggles. Try not to be boldly confronting. If you approach a toddler who is outside a limit, say a girl climbing on a table, start by being calm and matter-of-fact rather than confrontive. Don't issue a challenge (such as "get off the table"). State the limit in positive terms, such as "The ramp is for climbing" or "Feet belong on the floor." One particularly talented teacher simply says, "You can put your feet right here," patting the appropriate place. Nine times out of ten the feet go directly to where they belong! Something about the way she says it conveys such a confident and positive attitude that there is no challenge issued.[3]

Teaching Prosocial Behavior

There is another half to discipline and guidance besides setting limits—that is developing prosocial behavior. Prosocial behavior doesn't just automatically occur by putting infants and toddlers in groups and setting limits. You have to plan for it to happen. You have to *make* it happen.

Some children have natural inclinations toward kindness and compassion from the early years, but most have to be taught. We used to think that the egocentricity of preschool age children kept them from seeing another person's perspective. We know now this is not true. Even infants cry in empathy for other infants, and many toddlers will offer a toy or a pat to a child in pain, obviously trying to comfort or help. Here are some ideas about how to promote and teach prosocial skills.

1. Whenever you set a limit, explain *why*. Let children know the effects of their behavior on others—that hitting hurts, that grabbing toys causes unhappiness.

2. Notice children who show they care about other children. Mention the behaviors. You can even make a big fuss, if appropriate. Call attention to the behaviors you wish to occur more often. Use such simple statements as, "I see how you are being very careful with the doll," "I liked the way you gave Chelsea her blanket when she was crying," "I noticed you tried to help Joanie solve that problem," or "I bet you feel good about giving that toy to Sammy when he asked you for it." Remark about specific behaviors rather than making global judgments (such as "good girl!").

3. Model prosocial behavior yourself. Say thank-you when someone shares something with you. Be kind and considerate not only to the children you work with, but to other adults they see you with.

4. Take a problem-solving view rather than a power stance when there is a conflict. Not only model conflict resolution with other adults, but help the children in their dealings with one another. Encourage them to talk to one another rather than to you. Give them the words to use if they need them: "Tell Jesse you don't like it when he takes the toy away from you." Then turn and see what Jesse says back. Help him make himself understood if he needs help. Help the children see one another's points of view and come to some kind of conclusion. Don't solve their conflicts for them; teach them to solve them themselves.

5. Encourage cooperation. Have cooperative activities where children do things together rather than separately. Instead of individual art projects, try taping butcher paper to a table, making felt pens or crayons available, and letting children create a group picture.

6. Pay special attention to children who are constantly picked on or rejected by their peers. They need extra help with social skills.

Both aggressor and victim need your extra attention (but not when they are aggressing or being victimized). Teach aggressors other ways of getting what they need or want, and teach victims how to stand up for themselves.

7. Avoid punishment. Punishment may work to curb antisocial behaviors, but it works against teaching prosocial ones.

Promoting social development and teaching social skills is not easy. Often you end up undoing what you've been trying to do. Some undesirable behaviors are impossible to ignore, but by paying attention to them, you ensure they will continue. You're also bound to model behavior you don't want the child to pick up. "Never do that," I used to say after making some questionable maneuver to my daughter, who as a beginning driver was watching my every driving move. I don't advocate that method. The message is far stronger if you model the behavior you're after. But as human beings, we can't be perfect, which in itself is an important message to infants and toddlers. As you forgive your own less than perfect social skills, so, perhaps, can you forgive theirs.

This chapter has examined early social behaviors and discussed Erik Erikson's stages of trust, autonomy, and initiative. The practical applications of Erikson's theory have been outlined in the sections on discipline, limits, and teaching prosocial behavior. The next chapter follows in logical progression and discusses how infants and toddlers learn to cope with and express feelings as they develop a sense of self.

Notes

1. T. G. R. Bower, *Development in Infancy,* 2nd ed. (San Francisco: W. H. Freeman, 1982), p. 256.
2. Jaipaul L. Roopnarine and Alice S. Honig, "The Unpopular Child," *Young Children,* September 1985, p. 61.
3. Doyleen McMurtry, Ed. D., early childhood instructor, Solano College, Suisun, California.

For Further Reading

T. G. R. Bower, *Development in Infancy* (San Francisco: W. H. Freeman, 1982).
Erik H. Erikson, *Childhood and Society,* 2nd ed. (New York: W. W. Norton, 1963).
Alice Sterling Honig, "Compliance, Control and Discipline," *Young Children,* January 1985, pp. 50–58.
Cheri Sterman Miller, "Building Self-Control, Discipline for Young Children," *Young Children,* November 1984, pp. 15–19.

Chapter 11
The Development of Feelings and a Sense of Self

What are emotions or feelings? Where do they come from? The word "emotion" comes from a Latin word meaning to move, stir up, agitate, or excite. Emotions come from within the individual, though they may be triggered by an external event. The external event may be real and immediate, or it may be a memory from the past, an anticipation of a future event, or even an entirely imaginary occurrence. Whether or not the *event* is, or ever was, real, the *feelings* are real.

The point is that we own our feelings—they are ours. They may be triggered from the outside (for example, by someone else), but the feelings themselves belong to the person experiencing them. Also, one should never discount another's feelings. A young child may be in distress over something you consider very minor. But his or her feeling is real and should be acknowledged and accepted.

Caregivers can help infants and toddlers recognize, accept, and value their feelings. They can also encourage them to discover ways to sooth their feelings through self-calming devices. Eventually, children learn how and when to express their feelings. They also learn to determine when it is appropriate to act on certain feelings and what constitutes sociably acceptable actions. As caregivers help children discover and learn about their feelings, they are contributing to the child's inner sense of self-direction. That's what this chapter is all about.

The Progression of the Development of Feelings

Feelings develop. Newborns' emotions are related to immediate experiences and sensations. Newborns' emotional responses are not very defined, but are rather a general stirred up or calmed down response. Refined responses depend on development that occurs after birth. Memory and ability to understand and anticipate are examples of how emotional expression evolves through the cognitive development that occurs gradually during the first two years.

That newborn infants do have emotions from the first moments of life is a concern of the gentle birth advocates, such as Dr. Leboyer, the French obstetrician. Until Dr. Leboyer advertised his gentle birth techniques, it was widely believed that babies do not feel much at birth. If they have sensations, the possibility that they have emotional responses was discounted. We know now that infants do have the use of their senses at birth; consequently, researchers and caregivers are now questioning the emotional aspects of what infants feel. Although infants cannot talk about what they experience emotionally at birth, we can see physical reactions. Evidence exists that they react to harsh stimulation with tenseness. We once thought that the panicky birth cry and the tightly clenched fists were normal and even necessary. Now that Leboyer and others have demonstrated what happens when you reduce such harsh stimuli as bright lights, loud noises, and abrupt changes in temperature, we know that a newborn can be relaxed and peaceful. Some babies born under Leboyer's method even smile right after birth.[1]

In the first weeks of life, infants' emotional responses are not very refined. Very young infants are either in a stirred up state or they are not. They may cry with great intensity, but it is hard to put any labels on what they are feeling. As they mature, however, the stirred up states begin to become differentiated into familiar adultlike emotions—pleasure, fear, and anger. By the second year, you can see most of the finer variations of these basic emotions.

Sometimes people want to divide feelings into two categories—good and bad. However, all feelings are good; they carry energy, have purpose, and can provide us with messages that are important to our sense of self-direction. A better way to divide them is into "yes!" feelings and "no!" feelings.

Some examples of "yes!" feelings are joy, pleasure, delight, contentment, satisfaction, and power. Infants and toddlers should experience plenty of these kinds of feelings. Power is a feeling you might not expect to find in a list of "yes!" feelings in infants and toddlers; yet it is vital to very young children. Power comes as they discover they can make things happen in their world—they can influence the objects and, most especially, the people around them. Attachment is one means of ensuring a sense of power in infants. Day-care programs should be very aware of whether each child is feeling powerful and take steps to remedy the situation if some are not.

The "no!" feelings, especially fear and anger, are the ones that command the most attention, and they will be discussed here at length.

Helping Infants and Toddlers Cope with Fears

The scene that follows shows a child who is afraid.

A baby is sitting on the floor playing with a soft rubber ball. She stops playing for a moment and looks around the room, searching. She finds her mother close by, a look of relief passes over her face, she gives a big smile, and she continues to play. She hears a door open and sounds coming from the other room. Two people enter. The baby freezes. One of the people approaches her enthusiastically—holding out her arms, talking warmly and excitedly. The baby stiffens. As the person moves nearer, the baby's whole body attitude is one of moving back, away. She remains in suspended animation until the moment the person's face arrives close to hers. She then lets out an enormous howl. She continues to scream and stiffen even though the person talks soothingly and moves away slightly. She stops only when the caregiver moves away and her mother comes in close to soothe and comfort her. She clings to her mother, swallowing her last sobs while keeping a suspicious eye on the stranger.

"I'm sorry I scared you," says the caregiver, gently keeping her distance. "I see that you are really afraid of me." She continues to talk in a quiet, calm, reassuring voice.

This child is obviously attached and experiencing strong feelings of fear that result from her cognitive ability to distinguish her mother from strangers. Stranger anxiety, which was discussed in Chapter 10, is a common and perfectly normal fear.

The caregiver in this scene found it effective to back off from the infant. Next time she will probably approach more cautiously and slowly, allowing the child time to "warm up to her." And she will discover what it takes for this particular child to accept her. Some children will allow a direct approach; others do better when the stranger ignores them but remains near enough so that the child can decide to approach, when he or she is ready to do so.

The causes of fear change as infants grow into toddlers. After the first year or two, the fears of noise, strange objects, and unfamiliar people, pain, falling, and sudden movements decrease; but new sources of fear take their place (for instance, imaginary creatures, the dark, animals, and the threat of physical harm). Notice that the movement is away from immediate events and sensations alone to more internal events, imagined, remembered, or predicted. This change is related to the child's growing ability to think and consequently to understand potential dangers. Consider the caregiver's response in this scene.

> The toddler room is full of activity. A jack-o-lantern on the shelf gives a clue to the time of year. Three children are on a low loft in a dramatic play area putting on hats and shawls and other dress-up clothes. A child enters the room, holding onto his father's hand. He is wearing a mask. He sees the three children in the loft and immediately comes up to join them. Two children go about their business, but the third one takes one look at the mask and begins to cry quietly. He backs off and tries to hide behind the box of dress-up clothes. He keeps his eyes on the masked face. A caregiver, seeing his distress, approaches quickly.
>
> She speaks matter-of-factly to the masked child. "Kevin, Josh doesn't like your mask. He needs to see your face." She takes the mask off Kevin and holds it out toward Josh. "See, Josh, it's Kevin. He had a mask on. That's what scared you." Josh still looks nervous as he glances from the mask in the caregiver's hand to Kevin's face and back to the mask. "Here, do you want to see it?" she offers to hand it to him. Kevin protests, grabs the mask, and puts it back on. Josh looks terrified again. The teacher firmly removes the mask. "I won't let you wear that, Kevin, because Josh is scared." She hands the mask to another caregiver and asks him to put it away. Kevin protests mildly and then gets occupied trying on a furry hat and admiring himself in the mirror. Josh then crawls out from behind the box, watches the mask disappear across the room, and looks at Kevin's face. Then he picks a hard hat out of the box, puts it on, and goes to stand by Kevin to look in the mirror. The caregiver, seeing the situation is over, leaves to mop up a spill at the drinking fountain.

This caregiver, like the first one, understood and accepted the child's fear. Acceptance is vital if children are to come eventually to recognize, identify, and accept their own feelings.

Compare the following two responses to a crying, fearful infant:

> "I know you're afraid right now. I will be here if you need me to help you."
> "Oh, poor baby . . . don't be afraid . . . I'll make everything all right. . . . "

By saying, "Don't be afraid," the caregiver in the second example is telling the baby that his feelings are not all right or appropriate. Instead of offering security and helping the infant find his own ways of coping, the caregiver in the second quote is "saving" the baby, teaching him that he cannot manage on his own. Comforting should be done in a way that leads children to learn to comfort themselves and to know when to ask for help.

Sometimes it helps if an infant can "relearn" a situation that was once frightening. (This relearning is called conditioning.) For example, a particular object or activity that provokes fear can be proved harmless if it is presented along with something that is pleasant or if a loved person is present to explain the situation. It may take several introductions. Stop if the child seems highly anxious and try again in a few months.

Here is a summary of tips on how to help infants and toddlers cope with their fears:

1. Accept all fears as real and valid. Do not minimize the child's feeling, even though the incident that provoked it may seem insignificant to you. Acknowledge the fear.
2. Give the child support, and show confidence that he or she can find ways to cope.
3. Use foresight to prevent fearful situations when possible. The caregiver in the first scene could have approached more carefully. The caregiver in the last scene could have met Kevin at the door and taken the mask. (In a toddler program, there is sure to be at least one child who is afraid of masks.)
4. Prepare toddlers for potentially frightening situations. Tell them what to expect.
5. Break frightening situations into manageable parts.
6. Couple the unfamiliar with the familiar. A comforting person or object can help a child cope with a new, potentially frightening situation.
7. Give young children time to adjust to something new.

Think about how you deal with your own fears. Do you use withdrawal and avoidance techniques as well as seeking comfort and security? Do you find that expressing your fears helps you cope with them? Perhaps you can discover something about your own coping devices that will help you in responding to a fearful child.

Consider the following situations. Would knowledge of your own coping techniques help you respond to these children?

A nine month old child has just been left in the center by his mother, who is late to work. Although she did stay with her son a few minutes before handing him over to the caregiver, who happens to be a substitute and new, he started screaming when she hastily said good-bye to him and hurried out the door. He is now sitting on the floor, terrified, alternately screaming and sobbing. How would you respond if you were the substitute?

A two year old is looking through a stack of books lying near at hand. She is on a soft cushion looking very relaxed. Next to her is a caregiver, who is holding another child who is also holding a book, looking at the pictures. The child on the cushion picks a book and flips through it. She comes to a picture of a clown, slams the book shut, and sits looking terrified. How would you respond if you were the caregiver?

A two and a half year old is making an enclosure out of large plastic blocks. She stands inside looking very proud of herself, saying, "Look at my house, teacher." A siren screams outside in the street. She freezes. Then she races to the stack of cots and crawls under the bottom one, squeezing her body almost out of sight. How would you respond if you were the caregiver?

In your responses, did you acknowledge the children's feelings? Did you have the urge to rescue them, or could you find ways to give them some help in discovering their own methods for relieving their feelings? Can you see what purpose the fear might serve in each of these situations?

In general, fear protects the individual from danger. In infants, it is fairly easy to see how fear functions because infants react to falling, to harsh assaults on their senses, and to being separated from the person primarily responsible for their well-being. Fear can protect them from danger. Toddlers have more complex fears because their cognitive development allows more to go on inside. Both infants and toddlers often protect themselves when frightened by withdrawing, as contrasted to angry infants and toddlers, who more often lash out.

Helping Infants and Toddlers Cope with Anger

Anger, like fear, may make life hard for caregivers. Look at the following example.

The scene is a family day-care home. A two year old is taking the toys off a low shelf and putting them in a cardboard box. She wanders off from this activity and stops briefly to look out the window—touching her tongue to the cold glass. Then she meanders over to a three month old who is lying on a blanket beside a caregiver. Dropping down heavily, she reaches for the baby's head. The caregiver reaches out and touches the toddler's head softly, saying, "Gently, gently. You may touch, but you have to be gentle." Her abrupt motion turns into a light touch, and she strokes the infant for a minute the way she has just been stroked. But then she gets more energetic, and her stroking becomes a heavy pat. Her hand is held back by the caregiver, who once more says, "Gently, gently," as she strokes her head again and holds her hand. But this time the child's response is different, and she lifts her free hand to hit the infant, an expression of determination crossing her face. She is prevented by the firm grasp of the adult. Thwarted in her desires, she turns on the adult, eyes flashing, and begins to struggle. At the same time, she starts to make protesting noises. The scene ends with a very angry little girl being removed from the vicinity of the helpless infant. The last thing you hear is the caregiver's calm voice saying, "I know you're angry, but I can't let you hurt little Trung."

Notice that the adult dealt respectfully with both children. She protected the infant, but in doing so made the other child angry. Nevertheless, she treated her anger with respect by accepting the fact that she was angry and by acknowledging the fact to her. She did not allow her to act on her anger by hurting Trung.

Although the cause of this toddler's anger seemed to be being thwarted, causes are sometimes not related to the immediate situation and come from some deeper place. It is harder to accept an infant's or toddler's feelings as real and valid when *you* do not see any good reason for them. When the cause for anger is not as obvious, or considered by adults as not valid, they tend to make remarks like, "Oh, that's nothing to get mad about" or "Oh, come on now, you're not really mad." But feelings are real even when the cause isn't obvious or doesn't seem valid. Respectful caregivers treat them as such. They do not contradict the feelings an infant or toddler expresses, even if their own experience is otherwise. They pay attention and try to reflect what they perceive coming from the child. They neither tease nor distract the child by changing the subject. This approach says to the child, "What you feel is important." Nothing is done to discount or minimize the importance of recognizing and accepting feelings. One should not have to justify feelings—that they are there is enough.

To accept and reflect feelings, caregivers must manage somehow to be serene, tolerant, and self-controlled. They must be able to be empathetic. But, at the same time, they must not deny their own feelings. Just as was stated in the sixth principle in Chapter 1, caregivers should be honest about how they feel and be able to decide when it is appropriate to express their feelings. Good caregivers also learn how to set aside their own feelings when appropriate in order to understand what a child is feeling. This is the empathetic relationship. It is important in helping children recognize, accept, and then cope with their own feelings.

In addition to responding by accepting a child's feelings and expressing their own when appropriate (which teaches by modeling), caregivers can deal with infants' and toddlers' anger in several other ways. Prevention is sometimes possible. Be sure that infants and toddlers do not confront too many frustrating problems during their day. For example, toys should be age appropriate. They should also be in good repair. Toys that don't work or have missing parts can be frustrating. Don't remove all sources of frustration, of course, because that eliminates problem solving.

Provide for infants' and toddlers' physical needs. A tired or hungry child is more easily angered than one who is rested and full. Short tempers hinder problem solving because the child gives up in unproductive anger.

Think about how you deal with your own anger. You might even list the ways you express and cope with it. Are you satisfied with how you cope? Can you teach infants and toddlers to cope with their anger in some of the same ways? Do you find that you often do not express anger when you feel it—especially when you cannot act upon it? A difficulty arises when the built-in responses for emotions are inappropriate and one cannot use the energy that rises with the anger. Then the feelings, and the energy, are blocked. That energy is released through action or expression. Some adult ways of directly expressing anger are through words and actions. Some indirect ways are physical activity, such as jogging or chopping wood, or some artistic pursuit, such as painting, music, or writing poetry.

Young infants have limited resources for expression. Crying may be all they are capable of. However, crying is a good release valve for infants because it involves both sound and physical activity. The early crying can later become refined physical activity and words as infants grow in their ability to use their body and language. Caregivers who allow infants to cry in anger are also able to direct angry toddlers' energy to pounding clay, throwing beanbags, and telling people how they feel. This way neither infants nor toddlers learn to deny or cover up their anger in an unhealthy way.

Look at the following situations and think about how the caregiver might respond. Here's a situation with an angry two year old:

> The boy is playing with a plastic rake next to a low fence in the yard of an infant-toddler center. He sticks the rake through the fence and twists it. When he tries to pull it out again, he finds it is stuck. He pulls and twists, but the rake doesn't come loose. He shows frustration on his face. His little knuckles are white from holding onto the rake handle. His face is getting red with anger. He kicks the fence, then sits down and cries.

> Here is another two year old—angry for a different reason:
> The girl is dragged into the center, screaming and kicking. Her exasperated mother gives the unwilling little hand to a caregiver, tells her daughter good-bye, and walks briskly out the door. The child runs after her mother, begging her not to go. As the door shuts, she grabs the handle and tries to open it. When she finds she cannot, she lies on the floor right in front of it, screaming and kicking.

Sometimes anger mobilizes extra energy for problem solving or gives motivation to keep on trying. Not all problems have satisfactory solutions, of course, and in such a case the anger can be used only as an expression of the frustration felt. This expression can be seen as an aspect of asserting independence.

A caution—some cultures have different ideas about expressing anger and do not see independence as a goal. It is important to take into consideration what each parent wants for his or her child.

Self-Calming Techniques

Most infants discover ways to calm themselves and use these devices into toddlerhood and beyond. It is important that children not rely solely on others to settle their emotional upsets. Most infants are born with varying degrees of abilities to do this. These abilities are called self-calming devices. At first the techniques are quite simple, just as the infants' emotions are also simple (though intense). The most commonly seen self-calming device is thumb sucking, which may start at birth (or even before). As infants' emotions become more complicated, so do their abilities to deal with them. The variety of self-calming behaviors seen in an infant-toddler child care setting will give you an idea of how these behaviors work.

Twelve children are engaged in various activities. Two infants are asleep in their cribs in a blocked-off corner of the room. One six month old is on the lap of a caregiver, taking her bottle. Two three month olds are lying on their backs in a fenced-off corner of the room watching two toddlers who are poking toys through the slats of the fence. These children are being watched by one adult, who also has her eye on a toddler who is headed for the door, apparently intent on some outdoor activity. In another corner of the room, four toddlers are eating a snack, seated at a table with another adult. Suddenly, a loud bang from the next room interrupts all activity.

One infant wakes up, starts to cry, then finds her thumb, turns her head down into the blanket, and goes back to sleep. The other sleeping infant startles without waking up, twists around slightly, and goes back to sleep.

The six month old taking her bottle stops, looks intensely at the caregiver, gropes with her free hand for something to hang onto, and hangs on tight.

The two infants on their backs start to cry. One struggles to change his position, gets involved in his effort, and stops crying. The other continues to cry.

The two toddlers who have been watching them stop their activity. One sits down and starts twisting her hair. The other heads for his cubby, where he knows he will find his special blanket. The child who was headed to the door runs to the caregiver, picking up a doll on the way. He stands by the caregiver, stroking the smooth satin dress of the doll.

Of the children who were having a snack, one cries and cannot comfort himself until the caregiver's voice soothes him saying, "Yes, that was a loud noise, and it scared you." One cries for more food, one cries for mommy, and one climbs under the table, whimpering.

Some self-calming behaviors are learned; others, like thumb sucking, appear to be innate. A newborn who is tired or frustrated will suck even when no nipple is present. When children are a bit older, thumb or finger sucking still serves in times of stress. Knowing that someone they trust is nearby and checking in with them by glancing toward them or calling to them helps children calm themselves.

This growth of self-calming behaviors, from one as simple as sucking to one as complex as sharing important feelings, is a process influenced and supported by social relationships.

What do you do to settle yourself down when you are upset? Are you aware of your own self-calming devices? How are your self-calming behaviors similar to or different from those of the infants and toddlers in the previous scene?

Developing Self-Direction

Emotions, and the resultant attempts at self-calming, are related to a sense of self-direction. Each of us has within us a force that provides the natural thrust toward maturity, guides growth, and gives direction to our life (both in the long term and from day to day). This force guides growth toward health and wholeness, the integration of all aspects of development.

C. G. Jung described this force as "an inner guiding factor that is different from the conscious personality. . . . It is a regulating center that brings about a constant extension and maturing of the personality."[2]

Abraham Maslow also recognized this self-directing force. He saw it as a process and called it "self-actualization." He argued that healthy people are always in the process of self-actualizing. That means they are aware of their potential and, at least at times, make choices that move them toward it instead of away from it.

What are the characteristics of self-actualizing people? Maslow says they perceive reality clearly, are open to experience, tend to be spontaneous and expressive, have a sense of aliveness, function well, are able to be objective and detached, tend to be creative, have the ability to love, and, above all, have a firm identity, autonomy, uniqueness—a strong sense of self.[3] (More about helping children develop a sense of self and self-concept is in Chapter 13.)

Maslow makes it very clear that people come to have these characteristics only when their physical, emotional, and intellectual needs are met.

He sets out five levels of needs (see Figure 11.1). Only when the needs of one level are satisfied can a person move on to deal with those on the next level.

What are the implications for caregivers in Maslow's levels of needs? Levels 1 and 2 are of primary concern in an infant-toddler child care program. The needs of those levels are usually regulated by licensing requirements (in states that have licensing requirements). Levels 3, 4, and 5 are more often left up to the staff of the center or the caregiver(s) in a family day-care home. This book has taken as its primary focus the top three levels. A look at the principles in Chapter 1 shows little focus on the physical needs of infants, but rather assumes that caregivers will provide for these needs first. They are, after all, the obvious needs. The aim here has been to bring out the needs that must be met after the basic ones have been satisfied. The aim in Chapter 2 was to show how to serve physical needs in ways that respond to higher needs at the same time.

While Maslow stresses the importance of meeting needs, he also points out that overindulgence is not good. That means if most of the time children's needs are met promptly, sometimes they can wait a bit. He says, "The young child needs not only gratification; he needs also to learn the limitations that the physical world puts upon his gratifications. . . . This means control, delay, limits, renunciation, frustration-tolerance, and discipline."[4]

All creatures have a need for stress, for problems. A lack of problems creates deficiencies. *Optimum* (not maximum or minimum) stress gives children an opportunity to try out their own powers, to develop their strength and will by pushing against something. Problems, obstacles, even pain and grief, can be looked upon as beneficial for development of a sense of self-direction. What else can caregivers do to help a child develop a sense of self-direction? Here are some suggestions. First, help children pay attention to what their perceptions, feelings, and bodies tell them. As stated earlier, don't contradict their perceptions with statements like, "That soup is not hot!" or "That didn't hurt, now did it?"

Second, don't interrupt when children are obviously deeply involved in something. When you break in, you are asking them to pay attention to *you*. Children have the ability to get the most out of whatever it is they experience, so let them fully experience it. And be sure to allow periods without stimulation. Let children have peace and quiet so that they can hear their inner music, feel their inner urges, and see their inner images.

Third, don't push development. Provide a prepared environment and good relationships, and then trust that children's sense of self-direction will ensure that they will do what they need to do when it comes to conquering developmental tasks like crawling, walking, or talking. When they have very thoroughly done what they need to do at one stage, they will become bored and will move on. When pushed, children lose touch with their own inner sense of direction.

Fourth, give choices. Maslow says, "In the normal development of the healthy child, it is now believed that, much of the time, if he is given a really

FIGURE 11.1
Maslow's hierarchy of physical, emotional,
and intellectual needs

LEVEL 5
Self-Actualization
(needs that relate
to achievement and self-
expression, to realize one's
potential)

LEVEL 4
Esteem   Self-Esteem
(needs that relate to maintaining satisfying
relationships with others—to be valued,
accepted, and appreciated, and to have status)

LEVEL 3
Love   Closeness
(needs that relate to love, affection, care,
attention, and emotional support by another)

LEVEL 2
Safety   Security   Protection
(needs that relate to physical safety to avoid external
dangers or anything that might harm the individual)

LEVEL 1
Sex   Activity   Exploration   Manipulation   Novelty
Food   Air   Water   Temperature   Elimination   Rest
(needs that are essential body needs—to have access to food,
water, air, sexual gratification, warmth, etc.)

Source: Abraham H. Maslow, *Motivation and Personality* (New York: Harper and Row, 1970), p. 72.

free choice, he will choose what is good for his growth. This he does because it tastes good, feels good, gives pleasure or *delight*. This implies that he 'knows' better than anyone else what is good for him."[5]

Fifth, encourage children to develop independence and become self-sufficient. Growing means letting go. One learns to walk only when one is willing to let go, to take risks. Caregivers can help children let go by allowing them to take reasonable risks and by providing warmth, confidence, reasonable safety, and a home base. The choice of when to let go is up to the child.

You may notice that these suggestions are related to and in some cases restatements of the principles of caregiving listed in Chapter 1. All of them involve respecting the child, which is what the principles are based on. The child's sense of self-direction is nourished by the respectful child-adult relationship that these principles promote.

Are you in touch with your own inner sense of direction? Are you good at determining your needs? Do you take care of them? How do you move from something safe and familiar to something new and unknown? How do you arrange to have quiet, unstimulating periods to be alone with yourself? Are you aware of your own feelings? Do you know how to pay attention to what goes on inside you and make decisions about when to act on inner messages? Do you promote your own growth? What better model for a child than an adult with a well-developed sense of self-direction?

Sometimes people who work in child care do not feel respected by others. Your self-respect is as valuable as your attitude toward the children you care for. Valuing and getting to know yourself better is a worthy goal for children and for all of us. Here's what Kahlil Gibran says about getting to know yourself:

> Your hearts know in silence the secrets
> of the days and the nights.
> But your ears thirst for the sound of
> your heart's knowledge.
> You would know in words that which
> you have always known in thought.
> You would touch with your fingers the
> naked body of your dreams.
>
> And it is well you should.
> The hidden well-spring of your soul must
> needs rise and run murmuring to the sea;
> And the treasure of your infinite depths
> would be revealed to your eyes.
> But let there be no scales to weigh your
> unknown treasure;

And seek not the depths of your knowledge
with staff or sounding line.
For self is a sea boundless and measureless.

Say not, "I have found the truth," but
rather, "I have found a truth."
Say not, "I have found the path of the soul,"
say rather, "I have met the soul walking upon my path."
For the soul walks upon all paths.
The soul walks not upon a line, neither
does it grow like a reed.
The soul unfolds itself, like a lotus
of countless petals.[6]

This chapter has examined the progression of the development of feelings as well as how to help infants and toddlers cope with their feelings of fear and anger. A look at self-calming techniques takes the chapter into a discussion of a sense of self. This discussion focuses on Maslow's theory of self-actualizing. Tips are given on helping children develop a sense of self. This chapter concludes the section that focuses on child development information and implications for caregivers. The next section focuses on program issues.

Notes

1. Frederick Leboyer, *Birth Without Violence* (New York: Random House, 1978).
2. M. L. von Franz, "The Process of Individuation," in C. G. Jung et al., *Man and His Symbols* (New York: Doubleday, 1964), p. 162.
3. Abraham H. Maslow, *Toward a Psychology of Being*, 2nd ed. (New York: D. van Nostrand, 1968), p. 157. Copyright 1968 by Litton Educational Publishing, Inc.
4. Ibid., pp. 163–64.
5. Ibid., p. 198.
6. Kahlil Gibran, *The Prophet* (New York: Alfred A. Knopf, 1923). Reprinted with permission of the publisher. Copyright 1923 by Kahlil Gibran; renewed copyright 1951 by Administrators C. T. A. of Kahlil Gibran Estate and Mary G. Gibran.

For Further Reading

Magda Gerber, "Helping Baby Feel Secure, Self-Confident and Relaxed," *Educaring* 1 (4), Fall 1980, p. 4.
Frederick Leboyer, *Birth Without Violence* (New York: Random House, 1978).
Dorothy Lee, *Valuing the Self* (Englewood Cliffs, N.J.: Prentice-Hall, 1976).
Romayne Sternad, "Separation," *Educaring* 1 (3), Summer 1980, pp. 1–2.

Part 3
Focus on the Program

Chapter 12
Physical
Environment

The environment as it relates to play was discussed briefly in Chapter 4. This chapter will cover the total environment, including an expanded look at setting it up for free play for infants and toddlers. Much of what is discussed applies to family day-care settings as well as centers.

The child development associate assessment process defines quality settings for infant and toddler care as those that are safe, healthy, learning environments. I'll look at each of those components in turn and end with a set of dimensions for a general assessment of the environment for infants and toddlers in programs or in family day care.

A Safe Environment

Safety is a first consideration for planning for infants and toddlers. Here is a checklist:

- Cover all electrical outlets.
- Cover all heaters so children are kept well away from them.
- Protect children from all windows and mirrors that aren't shatter-proof.
- Remove or tie up all drapery cords. (Long strings, cords, and ties of any kind should be eliminated to prevent strangling.)
- Get rid of all slippery throw rugs.

- Get instructions from your local fire department on how to put together a plan in case of fire. Consider number and location of fire extinguishers, easy exit, and methods for carrying children who can't walk. Then schedule periodic fire drills.
- Make sure there are no poisonous plants in the environment. (Many common house and garden plants are deadly poison. If you don't know which ones are, find out!)
- Make sure all furniture is stable and in good repair.
- Remove lids from toy storage boxes to prevent accidents.
- Make sure all cribs and other baby furniture meet consumer protection safety standards—that is, slats close together so babies can't get their heads stuck. Crib mattresses must fit tight so babies can't get wedged between mattress and side and smother.
- Keep all medicines and cleaning materials well out of reach of children at all times.
- Beware of toys with small parts that can come loose and go into mouths (such as button eyes on stuffed animals).
- Remove all broken, damaged toys and materials.
- Be sure no toys or materials are painted with or contain toxic substances.
- Know first aid and CPR.
- Keep a first aid kit at hand.
- Keep emergency numbers handy by the phone along with parent emergency information. Update parent emergency numbers frequently.
- Make sure the equipment you have is appropriate for the age group served. For example, climbing structures should be scaled down for toddlers.
- Supervise children well, and allow them to take only minor risks but not risks where consequences are grave. (Don't differentiate between boys and girls on the degree of risk you allow.)

Healthy Environment

A healthy environment is as important as a safe one. Good light, comfortable air temperature, and ventilation contribute to the health and well-being of the infants and toddlers in the environment. Here is a checklist of health and sanitary practices:

- Wash hands often. Hand washing is the best way to keep infections from spreading. Wash after coughing, sneezing, wiping noses, and changing diapers and before preparing food. Use dispenser soap instead of bar, paper towels instead of cloth ones. Avoid touching faucets and waste receptacles after washing. (Foot-controlled faucets and trash cans with a foot control lid opener are great.)

- Wash children's hands regularly also—especially before eating.
- Do not allow children to share washcloths or any other personal item.
- Clean toys and play equipment daily for any group of children who are young enough to mouth objects.
- Wear socks or slippers rather than street shoes in areas where infants lie on the floor.
- Vacuum rugs and mop floors regularly.
- Be sure each child has his or her own bed, cot, or pad, and change sheets regularly.
- Take routine precautions in changing diapers to prevent spread of illness. Provide a clean surface for each changing by washing down waterproof diaper changing area with disinfectant solution, and/or provide fresh paper each time. Wash hands carefully after each changing.
- Take routine precautions in food preparation, serving, and cleaning up. Wash hands before handling food. Store food and bottles in refrigerator until right before using. To wash dishes and bottles, use extra hot water. (Dishwashers with hot water heater turned to high work to eliminate germs.) Use a weak bleach solution if you don't have a dishwasher. Date all stored food. Clean out refrigerator regularly and throw away old food.
- Be sure all children in your care are up to date on their immunizations.
- Learn to recognize the signs of common illnesses.
- Make clear policies about which symptoms indicate when a child is too sick to be in your program. Parents' and caregivers' ideas and needs often differ when it comes to this subject.
- Require permission slips before you administer any medicine, and then be sure to give prescriptions only to the child with his or her name on the bottle.

Although you do not want to compromise health practices, be aware that cultural differences may arise concerning health matters. Try to be sensitive to parents who have different ideas from accepted practice about the paths to good health.

Offer good individualized infant nutrition, or ask the parents to provide nutritional food and bottles. Some guidelines agreed upon by most pediatricians are to wait on solids for three to six months, then introduce them slowly, one at a time, working up from a spoonful to a reasonable sized infant helping. Most pediatricians have a favorite order in which they advise introducing solids, starting with cereal. Most advise waiting to introduce those solids that may trigger allergies, such as egg white and orange juice. Stay away from mixtures (like casseroles) that contain several foods, in case one causes an allergic reaction (you won't know which one). Stay away from all additives—salt, sugar, and artificial colors and flavors. Infants need pure, natural, unseasoned food. Don't serve infants under a year old honey because it may contain a certain kind of spores that give them a food poisoning to which only infants are susceptible. Avoid foods infants can choke on.

Nutrition for toddlers follows many of the same guidelines. Choose food that is pure and natural—not processed with additives. Toddlers (and infants too) enjoy finger food. They need a break from purees and cereals. Give fruit or vegetable snacks rather than cookies or highly salted crackers. Give apple slices and carrot sticks (and then be cautious of apple peels) only when they have enough teeth and ability to chew them. Avoid such foods as popcorn, nuts, peanut butter, hotdog rounds, and other foods on which toddlers might choke.

Learning Environment

Much of the structure of an infant-toddler program comes from a well-planned environment. Research shows that behavior is influenced by environment.[1] A structured environment gives us clues about how to behave in it. You know that yourself. Just compare the library with the workout room in the gym. Or think of how the grocery store communicates what's expected, with carts at the door and open shelves and checkout stands, compared to a jewelry store, where you sit at a glass counter and someone offers you things from behind lock and key.

Infants and toddlers too get messages from the environment if it is well planned and consistent. In fact, learning to receive those messages is an important part of their socialization process as they learn about expectations for various behavior settings.[2]

Although much learning goes on in the play area of the infant-toddler environment, it is not confined to that area. The whole environment, including caregiving areas, is the learning environment in an infant-toddler program.

Layout

There are some general rules for setting up an environment for infant-toddler care, whether in a center or family day-care home. You should have a designated place for arrivals and departures. Near this area should be storage for children's belongings. The sleeping area should be apart from the play area and should be subdued in atmosphere—restful colors, quiet, nonstimulating. The eating area also should be somewhat separate from the play area, though the two may overlap at times, as you use eating tables for various other kinds of activities. The eating area should, of course, be close to a kitchen or other warming or cooking facility. The diaper area should be away from the eating area and close to a bathroom, or at least a sink. The indoor play area should be cheerful, well lighted, and invite exploration. There should also be an outdoor play area that is equally inviting to explore. (It's appealing to some to have eating and sleeping areas outdoors also.) Storage and office space (and least a desk and phone) are also usually part of the environment. Infants and toddlers come to learn what is expected in each space if the spaces are distinctive from one another.

The furniture, equipment, and materials for caregiving activities vary somewhat with the philosophy and goals of the program. The following corresponds to the philosophy of this book.

Eating

Refrigerator and provision for warming food either in the room or nearby are essential. Sink and counter are also essential. A dishwasher is handy. Tools and utensils for food preparation are needed, as are unbreakable dishes, cups, spoons, in addition to bottles and nipples (which the parents may send with the children). The eating and food preparation area needs storage for food, dishes, and utensils. Small, low tables and chairs that children can get in and out of themselves add to their feeling of independence. (Some children eat better in smaller groups because they are less stimulating, which is something to consider when choosing tables.) Some programs feel high chairs are a necessity, but other programs find they can get along without them. It takes some training on the part of the caregivers to get the children to eat at the table if they have a choice to leave. If provision is made for adults to eat in comfort—whether in the room or somewhere else—it makes them feel more at home than if they always have to stand at a counter or squat in tiny chairs.

Sleeping

The sleeping furniture depends on the age of the children. The youngest infants are more secure in bassinets or cradles; the older infants need cribs. Toddlers can sleep on cots or pads on the floor. Children should not share cribs, cots, or bedding, but each should have his or her own.

Diapering

This area needs counters or tables to change diapers, with storage of all equipment right at hand. Equipment includes diapers, cleaning supplies

for disinfecting the changing surface after each diapering, and sanitary
storage or disposal for soiled diapers.

Toileting

Toddlers need child-size toilets and sinks with soap and paper towels
(or a sanitary way to use cloth towels). This area should be convenient to play
space, both indoors and outdoors.

Age Appropriateness

The most important factor in a learning environment is that it be
developmentally appropriate for the age group. Infants are not served in an
environment planned only for toddlers, just as toddlers do not behave the
same in an environment designed solely for infants or for preschoolers.
Developmental appropriateness is vital.

You often have to be extremely flexible when you have infants and
toddlers in the same room, as we do at the Napa Valley College Lab School
Infant Center. Although the older toddlers (two to three) are not in the
infant center, but in their own program in a separate room, the younger
toddlers are with the infants. The age range in the infant center is from six
months to two years. The distribution of ages within that parameter changes
from semester to semester. One semester the enrollment reflects a wide
range of ages—with a few younger infants but most of them almost two year
olds. The next semester we'll find ourselves with mostly nine to ten month
olds. The environment not only has to respond to the needs of the particular
age constellation from semester to semester, but also the changes as the
children grow and develop within a given semester.

Jim Greenman illustrates this notion of flexibility in an interview in
Child Care Information Exchange.

> Flexibility comes from rethinking the usual, like a couch. For infants, a
> couch provides a perfect space for two caregivers to sit and hold babies. As
> children learn to crawl, the couch can be moved out from the wall to create
> an interesting path. When children want to practice walking, the same
> couch provides a soft walking rail. Once toddlers become fascinated by
> more complex kinds of spatial games like hide-and-seek, the couch can
> become the base for a slide or for tunnels made from blankets. This process
> of designing and redesigning an environment creates a caring and a work-
> ing space which keeps pace with changes in the children.[3]

Another example of flexibility is what Maggie Cole, head of the
Napa Valley College Infant Center, did with a set of shelves that holds toys.
She found the children constantly dumping the toys on the floor and trying
to climb up the empty shelves, so she laid the unit down on its back, and it
became a piece of gross motor equipment as children crawled in and out,

curled up between the shelves, and "drove" in it like a truck. You could just see their imaginations at work when involved with this supine bookcase.

How is the environment different for the infant and for the toddler? Partly it is size. The younger the child, the smaller the group and the space around should be. For the newborn, space can be frightening, and very confined space is appropriate—like a bassinet. Older immobile babies need expanded space, but not enormous space. They need to be on the floor, but protected from walking feet that appear as if they might step on or trip over the helpless infants. This is the age that playpens are most appropriate. As babies begin to move around, either by rolling or crawling, they need even more space. The playpen is too small. When they first get upright, they need support for cruising—rails or furniture to hang on. In a home environment, coffee tables, end tables, chairs, and couches provide this support. In an infant center, other provisions must be made. (The *outside* of the playpen will work for this purpose.)

A word about cribs: cribs are not good learning environments; they are good sleeping environments. When the message is consistent about what cribs are for, some babies learn early to associate them with sleeping and have less difficulty going to sleep when put down. But if the crib is lined with toys and hung with mobiles, music boxes, and bags of goldfish, a mixed message is given. The environment is stimulating, not conducive to sleep. Better to give the message that playing happens outside the crib. They're too small for all but the youngest babies to play in anyway. Better to use them only to confine tired children, not alert, awake ones. Awake ones need a different environment.

Toddlers, of course, need even more space and gross motor challenges appropriate to their age level. They also need an environment that encourages independence—steps up to the sink so they can wash their hands, swings they can get in and out of themselves, pitchers to pour their own milk and juice, sponges so they can wipe up their own spills, a dishpan at hand so they can bus their own dishes.

Toddlers also need an environment that invites them to explore using gross and fine motor skills and all their senses. The play space should contain a variety of age-appropriate toys and equipment that encourage active, creative, whole-body play as well as manipulative skills. It should suit the mood of all children at any given time on any given day—those who feel energetic, those who feel mellow, those who want to be alone, and those who feel sociable.

As to what should be in the play environment (toys, equipment, and materials), age appropriateness is again the key (see Appendix B). Newborns and very young infants need little, maybe a few things to look at. The most interesting object in their environment is the live human face. Recognize that fact, and don't try to replace it with toys, pictures, or even television. They need responsive people more than they need any animate or inanimate object. (They also need lots of peace and quiet and minimal stimulation.)

As infants get older, they need a limited variety of soft, washable, bright colored toys to be looked at or sucked on. Bright scarves and soft beach balls are easy to grip and wave around. Rattles, squeeze toys, plastic keys, and large plastic beads are interesting to babies who are learning reaching and grabbing skills. Toys that are responsive and make noise encourage babies to try different kinds of manipulations.

By nine months of age, infants enjoy a wide variety of objects, including cloth or cardboard books, a variety of hats and other head gear, dolls, plastic or wooden cars and trucks, play or real telephones, and nesting toys. They also like objects from the adult world—wooden spoons, pots and pans, and real telephones. Crawlers are very interested in exploring, manipulating, and testing the world of objects.

Beginning walkers enjoy push and pull toys in addition to all the things already mentioned. They spend more time walking around carrying and dropping toys than manipulating them at this stage, when they are practicing their walking skills. Large, very light weight blocks are a hit. They enjoy hauling them around, stacking them, and building enclosures.

By eighteen months of age, toddlers are still enjoying all the above in addition to play with more dress-up clothes (besides hats) and using available objects for dramatic play. By making available such things as housekeeping tools and equipment, toy stoves, brooms, plastic dishes, dolls, and steering wheels, you encourage their dramatic play.

Two year olds are even more sophisticated in dramatic play and need a larger variety of objects to encourage it. They also enjoy small figures, doll houses, snapping blocks, and beads to string. Two year olds also enjoy books and can use real ones as well as "baby-proof" ones. Simple puzzles, lock and latch boxes, button and zipper boards, and other manipulative devices appeal to them. The closer to three the child is, the more the environment can resemble a typical preschool.

The list of appropriate toys and materials in the environment can be almost endless. Practically anything you can think of that is safe and interesting can become a learning tool for infants and toddlers. Here is a general list of things for the inside environment you might not have thought of that Maggie Cole used at Napa Valley College Lab School Infant Center.

- Bean bags. They can be hauled around, put in things, dumped, and thrown. They don't fall off when stacked. (They do sprout when sucked on.)
- Plastic margarine tubs with damp sponges cut in different shapes.
- Blocks of all sizes—especially large, light weight, plastic-covered foam ones that allow even the youngest toddlers to build, stack, and produce structures and enclosures with them.
- Shoe boxes with lids. Infants and toddlers love to take lids off and put them on again. You can put a surprise inside—bubble packing or a piece of white tissue paper.

- Scarves, scarves, scarves. These are fun for all ages, even the very youngest.
- Books, books, books. Baby-proof ones are needed for the youngest children, regular ones for older toddlers.
- Muffin pans with a ball in each cup (a beginner's "puzzle" that even the very youngest can be successful with).
- Water. The possibilities are endless—scooping, pouring, straining, floating objects (soap, sponges), and washing dolls are a few ways to use water as a learning medium.
- Flannel boards with felt pieces. Make them available to toddlers, and watch them explore, experiment, and talk as they move the pieces around.
- Paper to tear. Toddlers have very long attention spans when paper tearing is an activity.

The outside environment should give infants a feeling of being safe and should give toddlers plenty to do. Younger infants need a shaded, grassy, protected place to lie on a blanket. Crawlers need safe spaces to crawl and explore with textures to feel that don't hurt their knees. They need safe objects to manipulate and mouth. Beginning walkers need smooth surfaces that aren't too challenging as well as push and pull toys. Wheel toys are good for this age group too.

Some ideas of what to have in the outside environment for toddlers come from Molly Sullivan, a family day-care provider in Berkeley, California.

- Truck inner tube. These are usually free. Don't inflate them fully. They make great bouncers.
- Knotted ropes to swing on.
- Trapezes made of a dowel suspended from ropes. Wrap the ends of the dowel with duct tape.
- Sling swings for the children to swing on belly down.
- Milk crates, big wooden boxes, thick planks, saw horses, and ladders to make whatever climbing structure strikes your fancy.
- Wheel toys, including riding toys, push toys, and wheelbarrows and wagons to haul things around.
- Slides they can go down head first.
- Various elevations—especially a hill. The hill is always fairly dry, even after a rain, and it's a challenge to walk up and down it. If you can get grass to grow on the hill, it makes a good place to roll.
- Rocking toys that children can get off and on by themselves.
- Sandbox with all sorts of containers, shovels, and funnels, big and small.
- Water in all sorts of containers—little plastic swimming pools, big saucers, cement mixing pans, baby bath tubs. Make available containers, funnels, hoses, sponges, cloths, and paint brushes. Painting with water is always a favorite.

• Straw provides additional softness for outside. Children can jump into it and haul it around.

Assessing the Quality of an Infant-Toddler Environment

Besides looking at age appropriateness, there are other ways of assessing the quality of a learning environment. I will consider several here.

Elizabeth Jones and Elizabeth Prescott in *Dimensions of Teaching-Learning Environments, II. Focus on Day Care* defined five dimensions of a learning environment: soft-hard, intrusion-seclusion, high mobility-low mobility, open-closed, simple-complex.[4]

The soft-hard dimension is fairly self-explanatory. The question to ask when assessing an infant-toddler environment is: is the learning environment full of softness? Infants and toddlers need thick rugs, soft blankets, stuffed animals, cozy furniture, mattresses, pads, cushions, and laps inside. Outside they need grass, sand, water, soft balls, pads, and laps. A soft environment is *responsive*. Many centers tend to have less softness than infants and toddlers need—partly because it is more difficult to clean soft materials and surfaces and partly because they tend to wear out. Day-care homes usually do better than centers on the softness dimension.

Is there also some hardness, or is every inch of floor carpeted, every inch of the yard in lawn? Hard floors and smooth cement present a different feel to the crawler, are sometimes easier for the beginning walker to walk on, and make nice noises for the older toddler. Some hard surfaces and hard toys and materials belong in infant-toddler care, but the emphasis should be on softness.

The environment should provide for both optimum intrusion and seclusion. Desirable intrusion comes as the outdoor environment moves inside, providing interest and novelty. Low windows allow children to see what is happening in back or on the street but protect them from the dangers and noise. Desirable intrusion also occurs as outsiders come into the infants' and toddlers' environment—the telephone repair person, parents picking up children, visitors. Caregivers should maintain an optimum level of intrusion. For example, at the Napa Valley College Lab School Infant Center, observers are scheduled so that the children are not exposed to more than one or two unknown people at a time.

Seclusion should be provided so children who need to be alone or with one other child can find spaces to do that. Of course, supervision must always be a concern, but there are ways to make private spaces that adults can still see into. One simple way is to move a couch out from the wall. One center has a series of topless wooden boxes against one wall with holes to crawl into. The sides screen the crawlers and toddlers from the rest of the room, but adults can see into them.

High mobility and low mobility both should be encouraged in an environment for infants and toddlers. Children who are old enough should be able to move around freely. Children should not have to wait for outdoor time to engage in vigorous movement. That means, of course, that group size must be on the small side. Twelve is big enough for an infant-toddler group. Two to three year olds can manage in a slightly larger group if the environment is well planned.

The open-closed dimension has to do with choices. An example of openness in the environment is low open shelves with toys displayed to choose from. Closed storage is also appropriate to regulate or reduce choices and to get rid of a cluttered atmosphere.

Openness also has to do with arrangement of furniture and dividers. A good arrangement is to have openness from your waist up, so you can supervise, but some feeling of closed space below so that infants and toddlers aren't overwhelmed by large expanses of space.

The open-closed dimension also has to do with whether a toy or material has one right way to do it (like a puzzle, form board, or graduated stacking rings) or whether it encourages all kinds of exploration. A stuffed animal and play dough are both open, as is water play. Children under three need many more open materials and toys than closed ones. Older toddlers may enjoy some closed materials and tasks, but younger ones and infants disregard their intended use and make everything open. They find ways to use all toys and materials (closed ones as well as open ones) that adults never dreamed of. For an infant, the concept of the wrong way to use a toy doesn't exist.

The simple-complex dimension is more of a concern to caregivers with older toddlers. The more complex a material or toy (or combination of materials and toys), the more things toddlers can think of to do with them. Sand, water, and tools to use in them present lots more possibilities for action than any one of the three by itself. Caregivers who explore this dimension find attention span increased when complexity is introduced into the environment.

Jim Greenman in "Designing Infant/Toddler Environments" has some additional dimensions to consider when planning learning environments for infants and toddlers.[5]

Scale

Greenman points out that, just as adults feel small in environments designed to promote that feeling (such as courtrooms or cathedrals), so infants and toddlers feel small in any environment designed for other age groups. Even a preschool environment will add to infants' and toddlers' feelings of smallness. When they sit in chairs that leave their feet dangling, swing in swings they can't get into or out of, or play at chest-high tables, they feel smaller than they need to feel. Infants and toddlers need rooms, ceil-

ings, furniture, and spaces scaled down for them. You want them to feel big
and capable, not small and inadequate. The physical environment can make
a difference in their self-concept.

Aesthetics

Infants and toddlers should spend their time in a place that is visually appealing. Lighting is an important factor in visual appeal. If possible,
avoid the overlit and even effect of fluorescent lighting. Natural and incan-
descent lighting give variety and add warmth. Color and its different emotional qualities should be considered, as should visual noise. In most infant-
toddler environments, there is so much going on—so much to see—that the
background should be calm, warm, and neutral. Greenman suggests avoid-
ing the usual riots of color and design when planning walls, surfaces, curtains, and other fabrics. With a neutral backdrop, the people, toys, and
materials stand out better, allowing children to find them and focus on them.
The children are less distracted.

Acoustics

Noise can be a real problem where infants and toddlers are together
in a group. Every effort should be made to lower the noise level and to
protect the children who need quiet from those who are shouting, crying, or
engaging in noisy activities. Group size has a lot to do with noise level, which
is an important reason to keep groups small. Dividing the space helps too,
as does providing plenty of softness to absorb sound (carpets, stuffed furniture, pads and cushions, curtains, and acoustical ceilings). Be aware of
background noises and their effect on the children and adults as a group and
individually. Some lights emit a high pitched sound that irritates sensitive
ears. Noise from fans or other machinery can be soothing or irritating,
depending on the sound and the room.

Order

Relating to both aesthetics and acoustics is a sense of order. Because
infants and toddlers create constant disorder as they spread toys and materials around, pull things apart, dump, and rearrange everything they can get
their hands on, the environment needs to provide a sense of basic order that
is a contrast to the constant mess on the floor. Room arrangement should
contribute to the sense of order. Using furniture, shelves, and screens to
divide play space into small modules just large enough for two or three
children (or slightly more for older toddlers) helps them focus and cuts down
on noise (visual as well as auditory). Clear pathways should lead to these play
spaces, and each space should contain shelves of toys. In addition, if en-

trances to spaces offer some motor challenge, such as stepping up or crawling through, children spend less time wandering.

Of course, the divided room need occur only below the three-foot level so that the whole room is in view at the adult level. That's an important point to make—that there are two environments in the room: below three feet and above three feet. To fully understand the children's environment, you need to get down at their level. When you're down there, you'll discover things like baseboards, of which you are probably usually unaware. It is good to get low and take the children's perspective regularly when planning and maintaining an environment for them.

The environment is never determined once and for all. Planning, arranging, evaluating, and rearranging is an ongoing process as caregivers strive for quality and find what works best for them and for the children.

This chapter has examined the layout of the physical environment as well as three factors that influence the quality of the setting: safety, health, and learning. The last part of the chapter focused on planning a learning environment, looking at a variety of factors, including toys and materials. The physical environment is only part of what makes for quality in programs. Equally important is the social environment, the subject of the next chapter.

Notes

1. Elizabeth Prescott, "The Physical Environment—Powerful Regulator of Experience," *Child Care Information Exchange,* Reprint No. 4, C-44, Redmond, Wash., 98052.
2. Roger G. Barker, *Ecological Psychology: Concepts and Methods for Studying the Environment of Human Behavior* (Stanford, Calif.: Stanford University Press, 1968).
3. Dennie Wolf, "An Interview with Jim Greenman," *Child Care Information Exchange,* September 1987, p. 19.
4. Elizabeth Jones and Elizabeth Prescott, *Dimensions of Teaching-Learning Environments, II. Focus on Day Care* (Pasadena, Calif.: Pacific Oaks, 1978).
5. Jim Greenman, "Designing Infant/Toddler Environments," in Robert Lurie and Roger Neugebauer, eds., *Caring for Infants and Toddlers: What Works, What Doesn't,* vol. 2 (Redmond, Wash.: Child Care Information Exchange, 1982).

For Further Reading

Jerry Ferguson, "Creative Growth-Producing Environments for Infants and Toddlers," in Elizabeth Jones, ed., *Supporting the Growth of Infants, Toddlers and Parents* (Pasadena, Calif.: Pacific Oaks, 1979).

Magda Gerber and Andrea King, "Modifying the Environment to Respond to the Changing Needs of the Child," *Educaring* 6 (1), Winter 1985, pp. 1–2.

Jim Greenman, "Designing Infant/Toddler Environments" and "Furnishing the Infant/Toddler Environment," in Robert Lurie and Roger Neugebauer, eds., *Caring for Infants and Toddlers: What Works, What Doesn't, vol. 2* (Redmond, Wash.: Child Care Information Exchange, 1982).

Elizabeth Jones and Elizabeth Prescott, *Dimensions of Teaching-Learning Environments, II. Focus on Day Care* (Pasadena, Calif.: Pacific Oaks, 1978).

Elizabeth Prescott, "The Physical Environment—Powerful Regulator of Experience," *Child Care Information Exchange*, Reprint No. 4, C-44, Redmond, Wash., 98052.

Karen West, ed., *Family Day-to-Day Care* (Mound, Minn.: Quality Child Care, 1979).

Dennie Wolf, "An Interview with Jim Greenman," *Child Care Information Exchange*, September 1987, p. 19.

Chapter 13
Social Environment

The social environment is harder to talk about than the physical environment because it is far less visible. You can stand and look around the physical environment to evaluate it. But you have to catch behaviors as they happen in order to see the social environment.

A good deal of Part 1 and some of Part 2 focus on the social environment without calling it that. The environmental chart in Appendix B outlines the social environment. This chapter focuses on the aspects of the social environment that haven't yet been discussed.

Self-Concept

An important goal of the social environment is that each child in it develop a good self-concept. The self-concept, which relates to attachment, is made up of the child's feelings about him or herself in general as well as feelings and perceptions of body image and cultural and gender identification. The social environment, the way the child is treated by adults and children, affects this self-concept and influences the degree of self-esteem.

Attachment

The prerequisite for high self-esteem in infants and toddlers is attachment. From attachment comes the feeling "I matter to somebody. Who

I am and what I do is important because somebody cares." All the self-esteem activities in the world won't make a difference if the child's basic attitude is "Nobody really cares about me."

"Caring" in the sense of attachment has to happen at home, but it is important in day care too. It seems as though "caring" is what infant-toddler programs are all about because of all the caregiving focus. But "caring" the feeling is different from "caring" the action (taking care of). You can care for a child, wash his bottom, feed his face, without really caring for him. And you can't *make* yourself care for him (in the feeling sense). You can make yourself respect the child, and that may help the caring feeling come. Respecting the child will help you deal with all of him, not treating him as a bottom or a face, and in turn he may feel better about himself and reveal more of himself to you. That may help the caring feeling come.

But what can you do if you are respectful, and you still find a child doesn't "matter to you"? First of all, don't blame yourself, and don't work up a good case of guilt. Perhaps you and the child just don't hit it off—you have personality differences, you clash. If you're in a center, it's possible that another caregiver has a different feeling about this child, and that's all that's needed. Someone cares about him. It doesn't have to be you, as long as you continue to be respectful.

If you're the only caregiver of a child you don't care about, that's a real problem, but it's not insolvable. Here are a couple of ideas of what to do that might work.

Observe the child. Step back and really pay attention to her every move. Try to understand her. See if you can view the world from her perspective. Do a "child study" in which you make a series of short observations over a period of time and then put them together and examine them for evidence of growth. Carry a notebook around in your pocket, and every chance you get make notes about what you see this child doing. Be very detailed and specific. Note body posture, quality of movement, facial expressions, and tone of vocalizations. Try hard to be very objective—don't judge, just observe. If you get good at stepping into and out of an "observation mode," you can do it quickly and effectively many times during the course of a day. In addition, at the end of the day, write some anecdotal records—notes about what you remember about the child that day and what you remember about your interactions with her. These reflection records as well as on-the-spot observations will provide you with material for your child study in the course of a few months. The observations alone may help your feeling for this child grow.

Observation can have powerful effects. I do an exercise in my child development classes where I ask each student to examine an orange or other piece of fruit for a short time. I tell them to "really get to know" their orange, and then introduce their orange and all its uniqueness to someone else in the class. Then I collect all the oranges in a basket. When I pass the basket around again, each student is able to identify his or her "own" orange. An outcome of this activity for some people is attachment. They have a personal feeling for "their" orange. If five minutes of observation attaches you to a piece of fruit, think of what a few hours spread over several months can do to your feeling for a child.

A friend of mine, required to do an extensive child study for a class once, chose a child she didn't like very much. She said it was the best choice she could have made because, after she really got to know him and began to understand him better, her feeling for him changed.

Studying a child is a very rational approach to take—a left-brain way of tackling the problem. That idea may leave you cold, in which case, here's another idea—a right-brain approach—to help you increase your ability to care about a particular child. Use visualization. Spend some quiet time each day visualizing yourself interacting with this child in a truly caring mode. If he has behaviors that get in your way, try imagining the child without those behaviors. See him as he could be. Here's a sample of how a visualization can work:

> You work with a two and a half year old who doesn't appeal to you at all. She is very verbal, and she has a loud, piercing voice, which is even louder when she is angry, which is ninety percent of the time. She is bossy to the other children and reports every little misdeed to any nearby adult. When you ask her to do something, she's very likely to say no. If you try to persuade her, she stands with her feet apart and screams, "You can't make me." All of those behaviors bother you, and the more you try to change them, the worse they get. The days she is absent are a big relief. You notice not only a difference in you, but in the other children.
>
> One day you decide you have to do something about your feelings toward this child. You've heard about visualization—a form of meditation. You're dubious, but at this point you'll try anything. It can't hurt.
>
> You take ten minutes before bedtime to sit quietly, in a relaxed position, and clear your mind. As a person who is used to meditating, you find this part easy. But then it gets harder.
>
> First you try to visualize the child without the behaviors that bother you so much, but nothing comes. You just can't seem to disconnect her from the way she behaves. So you try a different tack. You decide if you can't even *imagine* her different, you'd better work on yourself first.
>
> So you spend your ten minutes imagining the little girl as she behaves every day, but you visualize yourself not reacting to her. It's hard. At first you are like a statue, standing still and cold. You don't like that image very much. After a short time of cold silence, you notice that your image has become more like a wooden puppet. In your mind's eye you watch as the child screams, tattles,

defies you, and bosses, and you just dangle from your strings with a blank smile on your face. You don't like that image very much either, but you continue to let your visualization lead where it will. You watch in surprise as the wooden puppet changes before your eyes to a strong, sturdy tree. Now you're in a comfortable image (though it seems a little weird to you). You feel good as you respond to the wind of the little girl's voice—your leaves rustle, your branches bend, but it doesn't affect you. She tries harder to affect you. She seems to want to blow you over, but your roots are deep, and your trunk is strong. You bend slightly, but you come back upright as soon as she stops. She tries harder. She gives up and walks away. You end the visualization.

For the next few nights you try the same visualization. You're a tree and she's herself. You practice withstanding her onslaught without getting caught up in it. You do nothing different during the day, but for some reason her behavior isn't bothering you so much. You wonder if it is changing or if you just feel it less.

One night after you have been doing this for a few days ten minutes at a time, a change in your visualization surprises you. The child has been frantically trying to get to you, trying to do damage, but all is in vain. She is kicking your trunk (which you can't feel because of your thick bark) when suddenly she throws her arms around your trunk, slides to the ground, and lies there sobbing pathetically, one little hand clutching at an exposed root. The little girl who rises off the ground is a different child, though she looks the same. Now at last you can imagine her without the behaviors that were so a part of her before. You change out of your tree shape, melting and twisting and ending up in your own shape. You sit down on the ground and hold her.

The next time your visualization is very different. You can now imagine yourself interacting with her during the day, and the behaviors are gone. Sometimes it's hard to see her, but other times the images come quite easily. You notice that she is very insecure at times, and other times she seems to need attention badly. At one point you are astounded to take a close look at her face and discover your own!

Meanwhile, during the day, you've gained a deeper understanding of her behavior, seeing the scared, uncertain, powerless feeling little girl who's behind the defiant, bossy one. Her behavior hasn't changed much, but yours has. No longer do you react so strongly. No longer do you dislike her so intensely.

Eventually, you begin to find ways to help her both gain social skills and feel better about herself. You've learned something about this child—and something about yourself too. You give up the visualization, satisfied that it has done its job.

Of course, visualization doesn't work for everyone, but it is worth noting that we all carry around in our heads unconscious images that influence our expectations of others as well as our own behavior toward them. These images can be very powerful, and visualization is one way of clarifying them in order to change them.

Self-Image

Children are influenced not only by the images of them that adults carry around, but also by the image they have of themselves. Part of self-concept is one's own perception of oneself that relates to body image and awareness. Body awareness is a major task of infants and toddlers and grows as their motor skills develop. As they learn what capabilities their bodies have, they develop an image of themselves. You can watch a nine month old backing down off a couch he has crawled up on and get an idea of his body awareness. The child with good body awareness knows where he is in space and how far to back before putting his feet over the edge of the couch. He can guess how far it is to the floor, so he is able to slide off and remain in control.

As children develop competency, their self-concept expands. They take pride in each accomplishment. Thus the thrust for independence and the development of self-help skills relate to the growth of self-concept.

Cultural Identity

Cultural identity is also a part of self-concept. The culture we come from influences every detail of every action of our lives, including how close we stand to people, where we touch them, what gestures we make, what we eat, and how we talk, think, and regard time and space—how we look at the world. You bring your culture to your work with infants and toddlers. You are teaching them your culture every day in everything you do. In a program where the children and caregivers are of the same culture, there is real consistency. Those children don't think about culture—it's so much a part of them.

In fact, few of us think about culture until we encounter someone who comes from a different one. This can happen to infants and toddlers quite early when they go into day care. The question is how exposure to two cultures affects infants and toddlers. What do they do with a second set of cultural messages? This is no new phenomenon: throughout history, members of one culture have been involved in raising the children of another. A modern example, outside of day care programs, is the au pair system popular among some well-off American families. A young woman, the au pair, comes from another country to live with the family and be a nanny. Her culture may be similar or very different from that of the parents.

One theory is that children who are raised biculturally or multi-
culturally have a greater understanding and acceptance of differences in
people. They may also be more willing to see beyond cultural differences
and relate to people as individuals, regardless of their cultural differences.
This is the theory behind the present push for multicultural education. The
goal in multicultural education is to help children appreciate both their own
culture and cultural differences. The advocates of multicultural education
see it as a way to fight prejudice of all kinds and racism in particular.

But what is a multicultural curriculum in an infant-toddler center?
It is easier to talk about what it is not than what it is. It is not pictures stuck
on walls, rotating ethnic foods, or celebrations of holidays. Infants and toddlers do not gain much understanding of culture from those devices, though
you may choose to include such components in your program for various-
reasons, including your own enjoyment and satisfaction or that of the parents.

A more meaningful multicultural approach comes from learning
from parents how their culture differs from yours. Some of this you may be
able to just observe. It helps to ask. By asking, you might open up a dialogue
about cultural differences. All of this may turn out to be interesting and
valuable to you.

However, none of this makes a real difference to the infants and
toddlers in your care. What does make a difference when you care for
children of a culture different from your own is your listening to what their
parents want for them in their day-to-day care. This means discussion of
caregiving practices. It also means potential conflict when your beliefs and
values clash with those of the parents. For example, take a parent who does
not understand your goals for each child to become independent. She may
insist on spoon feeding the child way beyond an age you feel is appropriate.
Or take a parent who stresses independence beyond your own goals. She
may ask you to allow a toddler to sleep or eat whenever or wherever he wants
without regard to any kind of schedule. Or a parent may want to keep
siblings together even though the age difference makes your environment
inappropriate for one or the other. Or a parent may ask you to help her toilet
train her child even though the child is far younger than you think appropriate. Or a parent may ask you to dress or not to dress her child in a certain
way or in certain kinds of clothes you don't approve of. All of these can be
cultural issues.

A true multicultural infant-toddler approach in such cases would be
to invite parent input and then figure out what to do with it. Some requests
are easy to respond to immediately; others take more talking, clarifying,
understanding, and perhaps negotiating. Still others go against your deeply
held values and beliefs, and no amount of talking or negotiating will con-
vince you to comply with the parent's wishes. Sometimes when a serious
conflict like this occurs, the parent has other choices for child care, in which
case he or she may find someone who is more able to comply. But often the
parent has no other choice, so difficulties arise. One way some caregivers get

around these difficulties is to stop discussing the issue, pretend to go along with the parent just to keep peace, and then keep doing what they believe in when the parent leaves. However, it is much better to work continually toward resolving the conflict. It's good practice for all of us to open up and expand our cultural awareness by being persistent in solving these difficult kinds of dilemmas.

Gender Identity

Part of self-concept is gender identity. Most children are aware quite early whether they are a boy or a girl, and their feelings about their gender influence how they perceive themselves.

Throughout this book mention has been made, mostly in the form of questions, about your awareness of sex role stereotyping. Children can grow up with a severely limited view of their capabilities and potentials by being taught narrow sex roles. These teachings start early. Even at birth, the expectations can be different for a boy baby than for a girl baby. Those expectations influence a child's self-concept. If you expect boys to grow to be strong, brave, unemotional, and capable, you act differently toward them than you do toward girls. If you expect girls to be sweet, kind, attractive, emotional, and not too smart, they are likely to live up to your expectations.

You can see for yourself how people treat boys differently from girls with a simple observation. Just keep track of what adults, especially strangers, say to very young children. They are much more likely to comment to girls on appearance and clothes. Boys are noticed for their deeds and less often for appearance. Perhaps things have changed since the last time I paid attention to adult comments to children, and I hope you'll do this little observation and prove me wrong.

Children learn about what is expected of their gender by such simple, innocent remarks. They also learn from the clothes they are given to wear. (It's hard to crawl and climb in a dress.) Toys give messages too. When boys are encouraged to play with tools, construction sets, and doctors' kits, they get one message. When girls are given dolls, play dishes, and makeup kits, they get another message. Children learn about expected gender roles from television, books, and, above all, role models. If the family day-care provider waits until her husband gets home to fix the screen door and makes it clear that she never touches tools, she is giving a message. When centers leave their tricycles unrepaired until a man comes on the scene, they too are giving a message.

If current trends continue, the children in infant and toddler programs today will grow up into a world of a variety of job opportunities for both sexes. The days men were restricted from some jobs and women from others are in the past. Yet, if children grow up with a limited view of their capabilities because of the narrow sex roles taught them, their freedom to qualify for these jobs will be limited.

Here are four ideas about how to offer both the boys and the girls you work with a broad view of their gender roles. First, be aware of treating boys and girls differently. Do you offer more support and sympathy to girls when they get hurt and expect boys to "tough it out"? Do you help girls when they need it and wait for boys to figure it out on their own? Do you offer girls dolls and boys blocks, or do you encourage and support both sexes to play with all the toys? Do you touch girls more than boys (or vice versa)? Do you talk to girls more than boys (or vice versa)?

Second, model expanded gender roles. If you're a woman, how often have you tried to fix something, or do you just put it aside, convinced you don't know how? Can you check your own oil? (Learn—it's easy.) If you're a man and you're reading this book, you've already expanded your gender role. Can you think of ways to expand it further?

Thirdly, avoid exposing children to media messages that teach narrow gender roles. Hopefully, the infants and toddlers in your program aren't watching any television, so you don't need to worry about that medium. Find books that show strong, capable women as well as nurturing men in a variety of occupational roles.

Finally, avoid linking occupations to gender—say police officer rather than policeman, fire fighter rather than fireman. These are simple changes, but they make a difference.

Discipline

The way you guide and control behavior can influence a child's ideas of and feelings about him or herself. The discussion here will center around ways to discipline that don't tear down self-esteem.

Much of what is appropriate discipline for infants and toddlers comes about naturally through meeting individual needs in a timely fashion and through setting up an environment that is appropriate to their age level. If they can't get to hot stoves, they won't touch them. If they can't reach radio knobs, they won't turn them. If they have no access to steep stairs, you don't have to find ways to prevent them from climbing them. To a great extent, the environment sets the limits.

However, you do have to protect them from hurting each other, and sometimes you have to prevent them from ruining toys and furniture by banging, chewing, and throwing. You can do this by firmly but gently restraining the child physically (if a word won't do it) and removing the object or the child if he or she threatens to continue this behavior. If you remain calm and gently persistent, you won't be as apt to trigger rebellion as you would if you issue sharp warnings or commands. You do need persistence because older infants and young toddlers continually test limits. That's how they find out about you and the world they live in. Once they're satisfied you really mean it, the test is over—until the next situation anyway. The way to preserve their good feelings about themselves, as well as their sense of power, while enforcing the limits is to avoid shaming, belittling, blaming, or criticizing them.

Punishment, scolding, and anger have no place in the discipline of infants and toddlers. You may, of course, feel and express anger at times when you are not able to control the behavior of the children you care for. That's normal and doesn't hurt anything. However, recognize that the anger is personal. Don't blame the children for it, and don't use anger to control their behavior. Find other ways to get the effect you want from them. Using anger to get your way will quickly be picked up by the children, and you'll find them trying it on you.

Punishment damages self-esteem. There are other ways to change undesirable behavior that not only leave self-esteem intact, but actually enhance self-concept as children learn to control their own behavior and feel good about getting attention for staying within the limits and exhibiting prosocial behavior.

Before you consider ways of changing behavior, you must define what is undesirable behavior. The child's age will influence your definition. For example, the screams of a young infant are not undesirable behavior; they are communication and must be attended to. Touching and mouthing objects are not undesirable behaviors in older infants; they have a need to touch and mouth. Experimentation and exploration are not undesirable behaviors in toddlers; they're how they learn about the world.

When considering alternatives to punishment, you have to realize that no one approach works for all the children all the time. What works depends on the child, the situation, and the origins of the behavior. For example, if a certain toddler behavior has in the past been rewarded by adult attention, it has been learned. Therefore, the approach is to "unlearn" it by removing the reward. At the same time, you must be sure to replace the attention the child has been receiving when you remove it from its connection with a particular behavior. Sometimes adults forget that there must be two parts to this approach of removing the reward from undesirable behavior. The children *need* the attention you're denying them. Find other ways to give it to them. Also be sure before you try this approach to determine whether this behavior is communicating some other unfulfilled need. If that is the case, don't ignore the behavior; regard it as communication, and fulfill the need.

Some behaviors are expression of feelings. Accept the feelings. Help the child learn to express them in sociably acceptable ways. What is acceptable expression of feelings varies with the culture. Some people see screaming in anger as healthy; others find screaming unacceptable.

Here is a summary of six approaches to changing undesirable behavior in toddlers:

1. Ignore the behavior you want to see change. Often it is being done for your benefit. (But of course don't ignore behavior that

threatens safety or communicates a need. A hungry, crying baby needs to be fed, not ignored.)

2. Pay attention to behavior that is socially acceptable. Praise children publicly for being gentle with one another, for taking care of toys and equipment. Make a big fuss over desirable behavior (not undesirable behavior).

3. Restructure the situation. Perhaps there are too many choices of things to do, or not enough. Either situation can cause infants and toddlers to act in less than desirable ways. Maybe two children need to be separated for awhile.

4. Prevent harmful behavior from happening. Stop the hitting before it occurs. Catch the biting before the teeth sink in. The strong reaction children get from the children they hurt can be very rewarding. That reward is cut off when the action is not allowed to happen. Such behaviors will decrease if you stay on your toes instead of letting them happen and then dealing with them afterward.

5. Redirect the energy when appropriate. When you must restrict a child, give several other choices of things he or she can do. ("I won't let you throw the block, but you can throw the pillow or the soft ball." "I won't let you bite Maria, but you can bite this washcloth or this plastic ring.")

6. Teach them socially acceptable behavior. Modeling is one of your most effective teaching methods. Children naturally pick up your behavior; make sure it is the behavior you want to teach.

A word about time out. A 1987 California law pertaining to children under two in child care reads, "Confinement to cribs, high chairs, playpens or other similar furniture or equipment shall not be permitted as a form of discipline or punishment."[1] Time out, which is touted as nonpunitive, is obviously seen as harmful by California lawmakers. Time out has become an alternative to spanking because corporal punishment is illegal in California child care facilities. It is used as a blanket approach by caregivers and teachers who have limited knowledge of other means of discipline, and it ends up being quite punitive, which must be the reason for the California law.

However, time out is not punitive, ineffective, or illegal when it meets the needs of a particular child at a particular time. Sometimes toddlers are out of control because of being overstimulated. They need to get out of the situation. Removing out-of-control toddlers to a quieter place for a short time helps them regain composure and control. Confining children, even by making them sit in a chair, as a punishment for a rule infraction is not the same as helping them gain control when they need to.

Once you perceive that children have this need occasionally, you can help them learn to judge the situation and make the decision to leave on their own. The ultimate goal of discipline, after all, is to turn it over to the individual. Your approaches to discipline should lead eventually to self-discipline—the establishment of inner controls.

Modeling Self-Esteem by Taking Care of Yourself

It may seem strange to find a section on taking care of yourself in a book that focuses on caring for infants and toddlers. But many caregivers are poor models for the children they work with. The job demands sacrifice, it is true, and you need to put your own needs last quite often. But the job also demands high self-esteem. Children need to be around adults who see themselves as worthy, who respect and care for themselves. The opposite of the worthy adult is the adult whom everyone tramples on—the children, the parents, and the coworkers.

I can't tell you how to increase your worth in your own eyes, but I can give you advice on how to take care of yourself. First, take care of your needs. You have the same range of needs that the children have (that is, physical, intellectual, emotional, and social needs). Don't neglect yourself. Eat right, exercise, pamper your body regularly with a swim, a hot bath, a walk, whatever it enjoys most. Take regular breaks at work, even if that's hard to arrange. Find a way. Stimulate your mind with a good book, a class, a game of chess. People who work with children sometimes feel as if their minds are decaying. Don't let that happen to you. Feel your feelings; don't ignore them. Learn to express them in healthy (for you and the children) ways. Find ways to use anger to help you solve problems or gather needed energy for making changes. Nurture your social life. Build relationships. Build a broad base of support. Don't depend on just one person to support and nurture you—spread out that function to several people. The more choices you have, the less chance that you'll be let down. And don't hide your relationships from the children. It's good for the children to be with an adult who relates to other adults.

Second, learn to be assertive. Say no when appropriate. Family day-care providers are especially famous for saying yes, yes, yes, until everyone in their lives is taking advantage of them. Don't let that happen to you.

Third, learn conflict management. Negotiation and mediation skills are important, not only in working with children, but also with adults.

Fourth, learn time management. This set of skills helps you immeasurably by teaching you to use the time you have in ways that benefit you most.

Fifth, find ways to explain the importance of your job so that you can be proud of it. Don't apologize for what you do. The first years are the most important ones. The high school teacher or the college professor touches lives minimally and makes little difference compared to you. The people who rear America's children (that is, you and the parents) are the people responsible for the future of this country.

And finally, play. Adults need to play just as children need to play. You may even be able to find a way to play at work and do your job at the same time. Play renews energy and brings out a creative spirit.

This chapter has covered a lot of territory, from *caring about* each child that you *care for* (and how to work toward that goal if it doesn't happen naturally) to taking care of yourself, with stops along the way to look at self-concept from the view of culture, gender, and discipline. The social environment is made up of all these factors and more. The next chapter examines another programmatic issue: adult relationships. Although it is in a chapter by itself, it is nevertheless a part of the social environment.

Notes

1. California State Health and Safety Code, Title 22 Child Care Facility Licensing Subchapter 2. Infant Care Centers. Section 101423.1, Infant Care Discipline.

For Further Reading

Edward T. Hall, *The Hidden Dimension* (New York: Anchor Books, Doubleday, 1966).

Elizabeth Jones, *Teaching Adults: An Active Learning Approach* (Washington, D.C.: National Association for the Education of Young Children, 1986).

Dorothy Lee, *Freedom and Culture* (Englewood Cliffs, N.J.: Prentice-Hall, 1959).

Dorothy Lee, *Valuing the Self* (Englewood Cliffs, N.J.: Prentice-Hall, 1976).

Judith Leipzig, "Helping Whole Children Grow: Non-Sexist Childrearing for Infants and Toddlers," in Bonnie Neugebauer, ed., *Alike and Different: Exploring Our Humanity with Young Children* (Redmond, Wash.: Exchange Press, 1987).

Letty Cottin Pogrebin, *Growing up Free: Raising Your Kinds in the 80's* (New York: McGraw-Hill, 1980).

Mike Samuels and Nancy Samuels, *Seeing with the Mind's Eye* (New York: Random House, 1975).

Mike Samuels and Nancy Samuels, *The Well Baby Book* (New York: Summit Books, 1979).

Chapter 14
Adult Relations: Parent and Staff

Although left until the end, the subject of parent-caregiver relations is very important. Every professional who provides a service to others must develop a relationship with his or her clients. in the field of infant-toddler care, this relationship with the client (that is, the parent[s]) is vital because it affects the relationship of the children to the caregiver.

Parent-Caregiver Relations

Sometimes caregivers forget that their client is the parent(s) and not the child alone. They make their own decisions about what to do for the child without consulting parents as to their goals and desires. They may even have feelings of competition with the parent. If these competitive feelings are strong enough, they result in what I call the "savior complex," when caregivers see their role as rescuing children from their parents. The savior complex is a stage many of us go through when we first find ourselves in charge of someone else's children.

I remember well my own savior period. I was not only going to save each child in my care from his parents (with a few exceptions, of course), but I was going to save the whole world through what I was doing with children! I didn't recognize this phenomenon until a few years later, when a friend of mine entered stage one and rode around on her high horse for a year or so. I had come down off of mine by then.

Most people move out of that stage when they realize that their charge is only part time and is temporary. They may influence children for part of the day while they are in child care, but the parents are the predominant and permanent force in children's lives. Parents give children a sense of connection with the past and a view of the future. About the same time caregivers come to see the importance of parents in their children's lives, they also begin to see individual parents' points of view. Caregivers in this second stage have more understanding about what influences the parents' child-raising practices.

During the second stage, caregivers come to see parents as clients. Although still in the glow of the savior complex, caregivers work to change parents—to educate them. The difference between stage one and stage two caregivers is the perception of who the client is. The savior effect is still in operation as caregivers see themselves as superior substitutes for parents.

The final stage comes when caregivers see themselves as partners— as supplements and supports to parents rather than as substitutes. The parent and caregiver *share* in the care of the child. This stage brings on a mutual relationship in which the caregiver and parent communicate openly, even when conflicts arise. In this stage, the caregiver is clear about how important it is to do nothing that weakens children's sense of belonging to their own family. I don't know if these stages are universal, but they occurred in my own development, and I've seen them in my students.

Being a support, a surrogate, a supplement doesn't make you any less professional. Look at architects. Their job is not to impose ideas on the client, but rather to take clients' ideas and needs and, using professional expertise, come up with something that pleases the clients. Communication is an important part of the process.

The architect's responsibility is considerably less than that of caregivers. The goal of the architect's process is merely a structure; the caregiver is dealing with human lives.

The California state regulations governing licensing of infant-toddler facilities obviously place value on communication between client and professional—between parent and caregiver. They mandate cooperation in planning for infant care in centers. Licensing requires written plans for care developed mutually by the caregiver and parent and signed by the parent. The law reads:

> Prior to the infant's first day at the center, the infant care center director or assistant director shall complete a needs and services plan. Such plan shall be completed with the assistance of the infant's parent at the personal interview specified in Section 101219.1. The parent's or guardian's participation in the preparation of the plan shall be verified by the parent's or guardian's signature on the plan. The needs and services plan shall be in writing and shall include the following:
>
> 1. The individual feeding plan.
> 2. The individual toilet training plan if applicable.

3. Any services needed by the child which are different from those provided by the center's normal program.
4. A plan for subsequent personal interviews with the parent or guardian.

Of course, mandated communication (such as the state of California imposes) is not nearly as successful as communication that occurs because both parties want it to.

What kinds of information should be discussed in the development of a needs and services plan? Parents should make caregivers aware of their children's habits, special needs, ways of communicating, and daily routines. Such information should include when and how much sleep, how the child goes to sleep, eating habits, needs, likes and dislikes, bowel function, liquid intake and output, cuddling needs, comfort devices, and so on. These should be talked over when the child enters the program and on a daily basis thereafter. It may be hard to find "talking time," and shift changes may mean the child's caregiver is not present when the parent arrives, but simple written records give the information that may be of great importance to the parent. (Did he just have a snack, or is he crying because he is hungry? How long did he sleep? Can I expect him to go right to sleep when we get home, or did he just wake up from a nap? Did he move his bowels?) Older children can express their needs. Younger children can't, and parents need all the information they can get to help determine just what children need when they get them home.

Although difficult to find time to do it, writing down anecdotes is also useful because some parents appreciate hearing about what went on that day. But be careful about leaving a parent feeling guilty about the child's behavior. It's up to you to guide and control behavior while you are with the child. If you had a hard time that day, don't blame the parent for it. Also be careful when you're relating positive anecdotes that you don't make parents feel left out because of all the cute things the child did that they missed. If the child took a first step that day, you want to weigh your own excitement with the parents' possible disappointment of not having been there to see it.

Be sure that while you're conveying information you are also listening. You need information too—about what happens in the other part of the child's life. Is she particularly fussy this week because something is going on at home? Is he tired today because he didn't sleep much last night, or might he be coming down with something? Are her bowels loose because of something she ate that didn't agree with her, or might she have picked up an infection? Listening is half of communicating.

Sometimes it's hard to listen when you are angry with a parent. The source of your anger can be something as simple as a personality conflict or as deep as a basic attitude toward parents who leave their children to go off to work—especially when there seems to be no financial reason to do so. Ironically, some caregivers feel ambivalent about child care and whether or not it is good for children. I have known family day-care providers who

decided it was better for them to stay home with their children than go out
to work, so they went into the business of caring for children of other
mothers who did leave home to work. If a woman who made this choice sees
it as a sacrifice, she may resent a mother who arrives in the morning well
dressed, happy, and about to embark on what the caregiver perceives as a
more socially or intellectually stimulating day. This is an unfortunate situation and can cause hard feelings between caregivers and parents. A first
step to solving this problem is the caregiver facing such feelings squarely,
recognizing that anger or annoyance over child or parent behavior really
springs from this source. What to do about it will become clearer once the
feelings are acknowledged.

Sometimes it's hard to listen because a parent is angry. Parental
anger is often misplaced, centering on some minor issue instead of the real
source. Parents may cover their insecurities, their conflicting feelings, or
their feelings of guilt and stress with anger. Parents may sense uncomfortable
competition—real or not—between themselves and the caregiver. Parents
often feel threatened by competent caregivers. They worry that they are
losing their children as they see them express affection for the caregiver.
Parents who feel insecure about parenting skills may hide that insecurity
by acting extra wise or knowledgeable—even pushy. If you listen carefully
enough, you may be able to detect the real message behind the words. Just
as when children feel insecure you try to bolster their confidence in themselves, point out their strengths and competencies, and steer them toward
successes, so you can take the same approach with an insecure parent.

Some parents actually need parenting themselves. They look to you
as wise and capable and lean on you for support. You have to decide how
much of this need you can fulfill. You can't be everything to everyone, and
this parent's needs may be one burden too many for you. Then you have to
decide whether you can put the energy into supporting the parent while you
help him or her become self-sufficient, whether you have to redirect the
parent to someone else, or whether you have to just set a limit and say no.
Sometimes you can get parents together with one another, and they will
form a mutual support system.

Sometimes it's hard to listen when you feel you're being attacked.
You end up defending yourself instead of allowing the other person to really
express what is on his or her mind. For example, a parent may say that all her
child does is play in your program and she wishes he were learning something. If you get defensive, show anger, and close down communication, you
may never have a chance to create the kind of dialogue in which you can
listen to each others' points of view. But if you are able to listen, eventually
you'll have a chance to point out all the child is learning through the caregiving and free play.

You can open the communication by letting parents know you heard
them. This can be done as simply as restating their own words, which allows
them to correct you or explain further. As you establish a dialogue, you'll be

able to get a better picture of what parents want and explain your approach and what you believe in.

Besides day-to-day communication, periodic informal conferences can be helpful to gain insights and set long-range goals. It is important to help parents feel secure about such a conference. They may perceive themselves as being in the "hot seat." Some parents arrive at conferences with all the old feelings left from report card sessions in their elementary or high school days. In such situations, you need to do all you can to relax them and make them feel comfortable so you have real communication.

Start by looking at the environment in which you will conduct the conference. If you sit behind a desk with a file folder in front of you and a wall of reference books behind you, that sets a certain tone to the proceedings in which you are an expert, removed from the amateurs—the parents. Any insecurities they arrive with will be magnified in this setting.

Because you are on your own territory, it is especially important that you make the parents feel welcome and at home. If you know educational, psychological, or developmental jargon, try not to use it. That gets harder as you begin to see yourself as a professional. After all, professionals have their own way of talking that sets them apart. But just think how you appreciate the doctor who can explain your symptoms without sending you off to a medical encyclopedia. At the same time, don't talk down to parents. It's hard to communicate openly when one party is being patronizing.

If you have a specific goal for the conference, state it at the beginning. If it is to be just an informal give and take, state that. Don't leave parents wondering why they have been asked to this conference. Use conferences to examine issues between you, explore problems and questions concerning the child, decide on ways to approach behavior that needs changing, exchange information, and develop goals. If the child is present at the conference, don't talk around him or her. Include the child in the conversation (even babies).

Sometimes parents and caregivers have disparate needs or differences of opinion that put them in conflict with one another. Just listening isn't enough; what is needed is some problem-solving or conflict resolution approach. When this happens, it is important to both listen and express your own feelings and position. When you have defined the problem, then brainstorm potential solutions. Try to keep out of a blaming mode and in a problem-solving mode. Here is an example of that process in a not so unusual day-care situation:

> A mother arrives, obviously in a hurry. She greets the caregiver, grabs a diaper bag from a shelf, and enters the room to pick up her daughter. Her daughter runs toward her, arms outstretched. The mother starts to smile, then takes a look at the knees of her little pink pants, which are bright green with grass stains. A big

frown takes over the mother's face. She picks her daughter up a little brusquely. Muttering to herself, she strides over to the nearest caregiver.

"How did this happen?" Her voice sounds strained. The caregiver looks concerned and seems to be weighing her words before she responds.

"We were outside this morning—it must have happened then. I'm sorry. I can see that you're pretty upset about it."

"You bet I am!" the mother spits back at her.

"It's going to be hard to get out," the caregiver says understandingly.

"Yes, it is." There is a pause in the conversation. The caregiver waits, still attentive to the mother. She seems to be waiting to see if the mother wants to say more. Then she adds, "You must be pretty mad at us."

At that the mother explodes. The words rush out on top of one another, first about her anger, and then about how she is going to meet her fiance's mother and it's important that her daughter look her very best. She talks about how insecure she feels around the new family that she's about to become a part of. When she's finished, she looks a lot better. The frown is gone, replaced by a slightly nervous look.

"Do you have time to sit down for a minute?" the caregiver asks kindly.

"Not really," replies the mother, sitting down anyway. She's holding her daughter with tenderness now, and the child plays with her hair.

"I'm just wondering how we could keep this from happening next time," says the caregiver tentatively.

"You could keep her inside," says the mother immediately.

"I hate to do that," says the caregiver. "She loves to be outside."

"Yes, I know," admits the mother.

"Besides," continues the caregiver, "there are times when we are all outside, and there's no one inside to watch her."

"Well," says the mother hesitantly, "I suppose I could send her in jeans. But she looks so cute in her little outfits. . . . When I'm going someplace after work, like today, I want her to look nice." She thinks for a minute. "I guess it makes more sense to dress her up when I pick her up than to expect her to keep an outfit nice all day."

"It would sure make us feel better to have her in jeans instead of trying to keep her from getting her clothes dirty."

"Yes, I guess I can understand that. Well," she says, standing up, "I really do have to go. Thanks for listening to me."

This problem was resolved quickly and easily by the caregiver listening and not getting defensive and angry herself. This particular problem of clothes is not always solved so easily. Some parents do not want their children to be away from home in anything but good clothes. They won't be persuaded so easily that it's better for everybody if the child arrives in play clothes with sturdy knees. Sometimes this reflects a cultural attitude about "school" and has to do with the family wishing to retain a certain image. A cross-cultural conflict like that would take a lot more talking, brainstorming, and problem solving.

Communicating with parents whose culture is different from yours may be difficult; yet it is important that you accept the parents' ways of doing things as much as possible and try to carry out their wishes. That is easy to do when the ways and the wishes don't tread on your theories of what is good for children. It's much harder when what the parents want conflicts with what you think is right. The problem is that theories are culturally bound—there is no one right answer, no one truth. I forget that now and then when I get carried away telling people what is good for babies. I have to remember to listen to their ideas rather than just selling mine. The danger in writing a book like this is that it is culturally bound; even the experience and research behind it is culturally bound. For that reason, when you are deciding what is good for babies and toddlers, you have to take culture into consideration.

And while you're looking at culture, you have to look at generation as a determinant of perspective. The generation gap is real. If you're a grandmother and the parents of the children in your care are much younger, they may well have a different way of looking at what's good for children, even if they are of the same culture you are. The experience differential doesn't explain all the differences; you have to consider the times in which the person grew up. Or if you're twenty and many of the parents are twice your age, you have to recognize that they may have a different view. One isn't right and one isn't wrong; they are just different.

A gender gap may also get in the way of communication. The way a father perceives his child may be different from the way a mother does. Male caregivers' responses, reactions, and understandings of children may differ, because of their gender, from those of female caregivers.

Whether communication comes easily or not because of age, gender or cultural differences, or just individual differences, there are some ways that you can facilitate it. Here are some tips for opening and maintaining lines of communication with parents.

- Regard communication as a two-way process. If you're having problems with a child's behavior, the parent probably is too. Make it easy to exchange information.
- Develop your listening skills. Learn to listen for the feelings behind the words, and discover ways to encourage parents to express those feelings without offending you.

- Develop a problem-solving attitude, and learn techniques of communication, mediation, and negotiation to use during conflict management and resolution.
- Keep records so you can report specifics.
- Make time available when it is apparent that a parent needs to talk. It helps to have a comfortable place to sit.
- Try to talk to each parent every day at arrival and pickup, even if you're busy.
- Try to make parents feel welcome whenever they are around— even if they pop in and disturb your program. I visited a teen parent program on a high school campus where the mothers came by between classes. It was hard on some of the children for awhile because they had to learn to handle the continual hellos and good-byes. But the staff was understanding about these parents' needs even though it made their job harder.

Parent Education

Your job is not only infant and toddler education, but parent education as well. Education involves not just knowledge, but knowledge along with attitudes and skills. If you build a relationship, parents will be influenced by you in all these areas. But if you set yourself up as an expert and try to teach them directly, you're bound to run into trouble. Knowledge alone doesn't change attitudes. They change over time with exposure to different people's values, ideas, methods, and attitudes. Most parents leave a program knowing more and feeling different from when they first enrolled, even if they never attend any kind of formal lecture on parenting or child development. Over time they will pick up knowledge of child development by watching other children and seeing what is common behavior, by reading what you make available, and by asking questions and getting into discussions with you. You may set up discussion groups or even have parent meetings with guest speakers to augment this knowledge building that happens naturally when parents spend any time around a center—even just short drop-off and pick-up sessions.

Most parents are eager to learn more if they don't feel threatened or pushed. An invitation to observe or participate either occasionally or regularly is welcomed by many parents and is a further means to parent education. A warm memory I have of a family day-care home involves a father who stayed an extra half-hour in the afternoon once or twice a week. He would sit and play the piano and interact with the children who approached him. He not only contributed to the program, but he gained knowledge.

Skill building comes gradually too. Parents come to you with varying degrees of parenting skills. Most will gain more by being exposed to professional caregivers. However, a danger lurks when caregivers present themselves as models for parents. The parent role is different from your role as a professional caregiver, though it may look similar at times. You don't have the parent's involvement or commitment. You don't have the shared history, nor will you be part of the child's future. You don't have the intensity of interest that brings about passionate exchanges. If the child "behaves just fine" with you and becomes a tyrant when the parent arrives, don't brag or feel superior. The explanation for the contrast is more likely to center around the normal parent-child relationship and strong attachment than it is your seemingly superior competence.

Children need competent caregivers, but they also need totally human, emotional, and connected parents. What you see as poor handling of a situation is more likely a parental handling than a professional handling. The two are different—though each should have many elements of the other. Parents operate (and should operate) from the gut level, reacting emotionally rather than responding reasonably. Of course, parents should also use their heads, should be objective now and then, and should build some of the competencies you have (which will happen to some extent through observing you). They should also gather information about child development and caregiving so they can *think* about what they are doing. But they should still parent mostly from gut reactions rather than from thought-out approaches. Parents should be far more human than competent. Caregivers should also be human, should step out of competency now and then and interact intensely and passionately with children; but they should mostly be fairly objective and thoughtful in goals and reactions.

If you are both a parent and a caregiver, you can probably understand what I'm talking about when you think about those times you handled things differently as a parent of your own child than you would have as the caregiver of someone else's. Perhaps at the time you felt guilty—I know I have. But if you look at role differences, you can be glad that you are a normal parent. Your children deserve a real parent, not a professional caregiver. And other people's children deserve professional caregivers, not more parents.

That doesn't mean that a professional caregiver should be cold and detached. If you've read this far in this book, you know that the message throughout has been to be real, to get connected, to feel your feelings. The point is balance. The balance swings more to feelings and spontaneity in the parenting role and more to thoughtfulness, objectivity, and planning in the caregiver role.

Sometimes, in spite of all your efforts in the parent relations and parent education department, you may have a child in your care who isn't doing well. He or she may be disrupting your whole program, taking a large portion of your time so that you have to worry about neglecting the other children. If you're in a center, the first step is to talk to other staff members (and the director). If you're in a family day-care home, you may not have such a clearly defined problem-solving support group with which to discuss issues like this, but it is important that you find somebody—another day-care provider perhaps.

You'll also want to talk to the parent(s)—not to place blame, but to get additional perspectives on the problem and further ideas for strategies to find ways to meet this child's needs. Teamwork and cooperation at home and in the program may work.

Or nothing may work. After trying and assessing various strategies, you may find that the child's behavior is still causing considerable turmoil. You'll probably also conclude that the situation isn't good for you, the other children, *or* the child. It is hard to realize that you can't meet every child's needs to the fullest extent. You may resist the idea that you can't be everything this particular family needs.

The next step is a referral. Perhaps some outside source can help this family. That often works. With specialized help the situation becomes tolerable, and you find you can meet the child's needs. But sometimes you have to realize you've done all you can for a particular child, and it's time to ask the family to find care elsewhere. This is an extremely painful process for all concerned, but a necessary one sometimes.

Caregiver Relations

Staff relations are of extreme importance in a job as demanding as day care. In a family day-care home, you don't have staff relations; instead, the issue is family relations, which is somewhat different. I'll deal briefly with that subject before discussing center staffs.

Getting support is valuable if you are a family day-care provider. But if the rest of your family is resentful, it may be hard to get their support. One family day-care provider sat down and wrote out a contract with her family—husband and two preteen children—before she went into business. She felt it was important to be clear about the use of the house, which belonged to all four, and about what was or was not expected of each family member regarding the children in care. This contract was not something she forced them into; it was an agreement that they built together, considering everyone's ideas and feelings. In this family the children were old enough to understand the contract, their rights, and their obligations. The contract saved the family a good deal of conflict.

In many day-care families, conflict is the name of the game. If the children are younger, it's hard for them to understand why they have to share room, toys, even "mommy." Usually the agreements are less clear than a written and negotiated contract. As a result, a good deal of resentment, tension, and friction can arise. Some friction is, of course, normal but may be unexpected when a provider first goes into business. But in most families the advantages outweigh the disadvantages, and the friction falls into place with the other ordinary family conflicts.

Family day-care providers should also look for support outside their own families. It is hard because you're tied to your home all day every weekday, but if you look, you can find other family day-care providers to talk to. The provider who worked out the contract found another family day-care provider in her own neighborhood through attending local support meetings. The two met regularly at the park with their children (it's a short walk) so they have adult company as well as an outing for the children. No one can listen with more understanding to a family day-care provider than another family day-care provider. Find someone to talk to if you haven't already.

In a center setting, staff relations are different because you work together and are not related to one another. It's a strange situation to be around adults all day but seldom focus on them. That can create problems because you have little time to sit down and talk things out. Most day-care staffs have staggered schedules, so the only time all the staff is there together is during the busiest time of the day, when the adults have little time to relate to one another. Some staffs working with older children are able to get together during nap time, but that won't work for most infant center staffs. In many centers even breaks are staggered so that no two staff members are off the floor at the same time.

If day care were like other fields, there would be built-in time for staff meetings, for staff training, even provisions for staff renewal. But for most programs those are expensive luxuries they can't regularly afford.

Obviously, staff members can seldom get off and talk to one another without the children around. And they need to talk to establish relationships, settle conflicts, share information on children and families, set goals, evaluate, and share resources. Most of all they need adult contact to alleviate the isolation that adults who spend many hours a day with children commonly feel.

When I first entered the field of day care, I was surprised to see adults standing around or sitting around talking while the children played. I was quite critical for a long time because my own training made it sacrilege to focus on anything but the children when you were working (except on break). But over the years I've come to realize that those talks are important to staff members who work all day every day with very young children. And they are important to the children. How else are children to see adults relating to adults if their daily contact consists only of adults who focus on them and ignore the other adults present? Children need to see adults exhibit a wider range of behavior than what they see when the adults relate only to children.

In a three-hour program, I'd still prefer to see adults concentrate mostly on the children, but that expectation is neither realistic nor desirable in all-day care. Of course I'm not condoning focusing on adult relationships to the exclusion of the children and to the point of neglecting their needs. But if each child gets plenty of "wants-nothing" quality time, when the caregiver is available to him or her during free play, as well as "wants-something" quality time during caregiving activities when the focus is on the individual child, the adult can relate to other adults while the children are present without neglecting the children.

This chapter has been about adult relations and their importance to the children in day care. Children need to see their caregivers as full human beings, and they can't if they don't see them in relation to other adults—their parents as well as other staff members.

For Further Reading

Gail Bjorklund and Christine Burger, "Making Conferences Work for Parents, Teachers and Children," *Young Children,* January 1987, pp. 26–31.

T. Berry Brazelton, *Working and Caring* (Reading, Mass.: Addison Wesley, 1987).

California State Health and Safety Code, Title 22 Child Care Facility Licensing Subchapter 2. Infant Care Centers. Section 101423.1, Infant Care Discipline.

Janet Gonzalez-Mena, "Mrs. Godzilla Takes on the Child Development Experts: Perspectives on Parent Education," *Child Care Information Exchange,* September 1987, pp. 25–26.

Joel Gordon, "Childcare Professionalism and the Family," *Child Care Information Exchange,* July 1986, pp. 19–23.

Joel Gordon, "Separation Anxiety: How to Ask a Family to Leave Your Center," *Child Care Information Exchange,* January 1988, pp. 13–15.

Elizabeth Jones, ed., *Supporting the Growth of Infants, Toddlers and Parents* (Pasadena, Calif.: Pacific Oaks, 1979).

Elizabeth Jones, *Teaching Adults: An Active Learning Approach* (Washington, D.C.: National Association for the Education of Young Children, 1986).

Joanne Curry O'Connell, "Children of Working Mothers: What the Research Tells Us," *Young Children,* January 1983, pp. 63–70.

Conclusion

"**I**'m not a babysitter" is the plaintive cry heard over and over from caregivers as they explain time and again that they're professionals in the early childhood education field. This is not a message the general public is able to hear. The U.S. Department of Labor ranks the status of child care workers on the same level as parking lot attendants. It doesn't really matter who takes care of your car while you are gone, but it matters a great deal who takes care of your child. If that fact weren't immediately obvious, it is also backed up by research. According to the National Day Care Study, the training of the adults is what determines the quality of the program.[1] The way they relate to and interact with the children is of primary importance in outcome.

Caregiving as a profession needs a boost up the status ladder. By 1995, it is estimated that seventy-five percent of the children in this country will have working mothers. That means caregiving is an *important* profession. People in whose hands the lives of our children and the future of America lie need to be recognized for what they do.

More than one group is working on improving the quality of child care and the status of its workers through professionalization. Some states require training and certification of child care workers, though requirements vary greatly from state to state. At best they mandate only minimum standards.

The largest professional group working nationally to improve the quality of care and status of workers is the National Association for the Education of Young Children (NAEYC). The Child Development Associate

(CDA) credentialing process, supported by the NAEYC, has resulted in a number of child care workers nationally, including those who work with infants and toddlers, being trained and credentialed through a field-based assessment of their competencies. Recently, NAEYC has developed an assessment process for programs that allows programs to voluntarily become accredited. The accreditation process sets high standards—above the minimum ones of state licensing regulations.

NAEYC has also developed a code of ethics and continues to examine it. A code of ethics is a must for a profession, which by its very definition regulates itself and its members.

These are changing times for the field of early childhood education in general and for child care in particular. Just what the future will bring is not clear. What is clear is that the responsibility for the next generation lies not just with parents alone, but with all of us. In Hawaii, there is a concept called "Ohana," which means the community taking responsibility for children in an extended family kind of way. It's time now for the nation to incorporate the Hawaiian concept of Ohana. We cannot, as a nation, afford to leave parents feeling isolated, alone, and burdened in their responsibility for their children.

I see the answer as choices. Parents need options to choose from regarding their child care needs. They need to have available quality programs both in centers and in homes, staffed with well-trained personnel, who earn decent salaries and enjoy reasonable benefits. Backing up these programs should be the support services so vital to keeping America's families strong—access to pediatricians, social workers, physical therapists, speech therapists, neurologists, and child and family psychotherapists.

Infant-toddler care, the newest star in the child care constellation, is getting a good deal of attention at present. This book is an attempt to direct that attention along a path of healthy development to ensure a quality approach to infant-toddler caregiving.

Notes

1. R. Ruopp, J. Travers, F. Glantz, and C. Coelen, *Children at the Center,* final report of the National Day Care Study, vol. 1 (Washington, D.C.: Office of Human Development, Department of Health, Education and Welfare, 1979).

For Further Reading

Nina Gunzenhauser and Bettye M. Caldwell, eds., *Group Care for Young Children* (Johnson and Johnson Baby Products Company pediatric round table series, no. 12, 1986).
Robert Lurie and Roger Neugebauer, eds., *Caring for Infants and Toddlers: What Works, What Doesn't,* vol. 2 (Redmond, Wash.: Child Care Information Exchange, 1982).

Appendix A
Quality in Infant-Toddler Programs: A Checklist

1. Look for evidence of a *safe* environment:
   - ☐ no obvious safety hazards, such as electric cords, open sockets, broken equipment, toys with small parts, cleaning supplies within children's reach, unsecured doorways
   - ☐ no hidden safety hazards, such as toxic paint or toys stuffed with toxic materials
   - ☐ fire and disaster plan that includes how adults will get babies outside
   - ☐ emergency numbers posted by telephone
   - ☐ parents' emergency cards on file indicating what to do when the parents can't be reached in an emergency
   - ☐ safe ratios maintained at all times (California law reads no more than four infants [children under two] to one adult.)
   - ☐ children allowed optimum risk-taking opportunities (Optimum means failure involves learning but not injury.)
   - ☐ interaction allowed but children protected from hurting materials or one another

2. Look for evidence of a *healthy* environment:
   - ☐ sanitary diaper changing process
   - ☐ consistent hand washing after diapering and before eating
   - ☐ proper food preparation and storage
   - ☐ staff recognizes symptoms of common illness
   - ☐ health policies that indicate when children are to be excluded from the program because of illness

☐ health records, maintained on all children, showing evidence that their immunizations are up to date

☐ regular washing of sheets and toys

☐ staff knowledge of infant and toddler nutritional needs

☐ food allergies posted prominently

3. Look for evidence of a *learning* environment:

☐ optimum amount of age-appropriate toys, materials, and equipment available for children to choose from

☐ caregivers consider caregiving times as "learning times"

☐ free play valued above exercises, adult-directed play activities, group times

☐ environment includes plenty of softness, some seclusion, provisions for high mobility

☐ environment developmentally appropriate for all children present any given day

4. Look for evidence that the staff's goal is to advance physical and intellectual competence:

☐ staff's ability to explain how the environment, the free play, the caregiving activities, and the staff's relationship with the children comprise the curriculum

☐ staff's ability to explain how the curriculum promotes development of fine and gross motor skills, cognitive skills, including problem solving, communication skills

5. Look for evidence that the program supports social and emotional development and that the staff provides positive guidance and discipline:

☐ staff encourages children to develop a sense of themselves through body awareness, using their name, through promoting cultural identification

☐ staff recognizes and accepts children's feelings and encourages appropriate expression

☐ staff controls and guides behavior without using either physical or verbal punishment

☐ staff encourages creative social problem solving when children conflict

☐ staff teaches respect by showing respect

6. Look for evidence that the program strives to establish positive and productive relationships with families:

☐ regular and ongoing communication with parents at pickup and drop-off times emphasizing an *exchange* of information

☐ friendly atmosphere

☐ conferences and parent meetings

☐ mutual problem-solving approach to conflicts

7. Look for evidence that the program is well run, purposeful, and responds to participants' needs:
   ☐ record keeping
   ☐ attention to infants' individual needs
   ☐ attention to parents' needs
   ☐ responsible program management
8. Look for evidence that the staff is professional:
   ☐ well trained
   ☐ respect confidentiality

Appendix B
Environmental Chart

This chart shows how to set up both the physical and the social environment to promote development. Remember that rates of development vary a great deal among normal children. These age guides may not fit individual children, but the chart as a whole does reflect the *sequence of development.*

Level I: The Beginning of Life

Area of Development	Physical Environment	Social Environment
PHYSICAL	APPROPRIATE TOYS AND EQUIPMENT	ADULT ROLE
Large Muscles	• crib or bassinet, a place to feel secure while sleeping	• use sensitive observation to determine infants' needs
Infants' primary task is head control	• mat, rug, or blanket in a safe space to lie unencumbered: room to move around	• provide a feeling of security when necessary (wrap infants in a blanket and place in a small enclosed space)
• lifts head briefly	• few toys needed yet because environment is stimulating enough	• let infants experience wide open space, like the floor, at times
• can turn head to clear nose for breathing	• faces are interesting and so is a bright	
• Most arm and leg movements are reflexive and are not under infants' conscious control		
Small Muscles		

- cannot control hands—often keep them clenched
- grasp whatever is put into hands because of reflexive action
- stare at objects, especially faces; begin to coordinate eyes

EMOTIONAL/SOCIAL

Feelings and Self-Awareness

- infants show only satisfaction or dissatisfaction
- infants do not differentiate selves from the rest of the world

Social

- may smile
- make eye contact
- are soothed by faces
- respond to being held

INTELLECTUAL

- can coordinate eyes and follow objects or faces as they move
- respond to faces or objects they see
- suck and gum objects that come near the mouth

- display reflexes that are the beginnings of the sensory skills, which in turn provide the basis for the development of intellectual skills

colored scarf
- don't put rattles or toys into hands because they can't let go of them

- infants need to be where safe and secure and needs can be easily met
- large pen provides safety from more mobile toddlers (should be large enough to hold both adults and children)

- infants need an interesting yet safe environment with a limited variety of soft, washable, colorful toys to be looked at or sucked on (be sure there are no small parts to come off and be swallowed)
- allow space for infants to move freely (though they can't yet go anywhere)
- don't prop in infant seat or other restrictive device

- provide peace and quiet and a minimal amount of stimulation— people infants associate with (caregiver and other children) provide enough stimulation
- put infants in a safe spot where they can be part of the center but not overstimulated
- call infants by name
- encourage infants to focus on caregiving tasks
- respond to infants' messages and try to determine real needs (remember that dissatisfaction is not always due to hunger)
- provide for attachment needs by having a consistent caregiver
- hold during feeding
- provide for infant-to-infant contact
- minimum adult interference: infants should be free to develop at their own rates
- give them faces to look at (especially that of the primary caregiver) and opportunities to see, touch, and gum objects
- don't force anything on them
- place on their back so they can have a broader view, both ears can hear, and they can use their hands

LANGUAGE

- listen
- cry
- respond to voices

- at this level people are more important for language development than is physical environment
- set up environment so that infants' needs are easily met and they don't have to wait for long periods of time

- listen to infants
- try to interpret their cries
- talk to infants, especially during caregiving times; tell them what will happen; give time for a response; tell them what is happening as it happens

Level II: Month 3

Area of Development	Physical Environment	Social Environment
PHYSICAL	APPROPRIATE TOYS AND EQUIPMENT	ADULT ROLE
Large Muscles	• large playpen—big enough for caregivers and several infants	• sit with children periodically and watch attentively
• beginning to lose reflexes and have voluntary control of arms and legs	• variety of washable objects within reach of infants for them to look at and stretch for	• respond when called for
• can lift head and control it better when held in upright position	• rug or mat for infants to lie on	• don't continually distract with unnecessary noise or talk; entertainment isn't necessary
	• avoid restrictive devices	• allow infants freedom to explore through looking, sucking, stretching, and reaching
Small Muscles	• same as above	• same as above
• grasp reflex no longer takes over hands all the time		
• reach for objects with both arms, but with hands fisted		
• swipe and miss		
EMOTIONAL/SOCIAL		
Feelings and Self-Awareness	• people are more important than objects	• provide for attachment needs because infants need to develop a primary relationship
• show wider variety of feelings and use voice to express them		• recognize and respect infants' feelings: talk about what infants seem to be expressing, especially during caregiving
• begin to see hands and feet belong to them and begin to explore them, as well as face, eyes, and mouth, with hands		
• begin to recognize primary caregiver		
• respond differently to different people		
• coo and babble when talked to		

INTELLECTUAL

- respond to what they see
- attend longer than at first
- look from one object to another
- can hold object on their own and manipulate to some extent
- give signs of remembering
- when they hear a noise, they look for the source
- look and suck at the same time, but have to stop sucking to listen

- some interesting toys and objects for infants at this level of development include bright scarves, soft balls, rattles, squeeze toys, plastic keys, and large plastic beads

- encourage exploration and curiosity by providing a variety of objects of different textures, shapes, and sizes
- allow children freedom and peace to explore by putting them on their back in a safe area large enough for them to move freely
- provide for interaction with other infants

LANGUAGE

- listen attentively
- coo, whimper, gurgle, and make a variety of other sounds
- cry less often
- "talk" to themselves as well as to others, particularly primary caregiver

- people are still more important than equipment or objects for language development
- some toys do give auditory experiences—let them try making noise with bells, rattles, and squeaky toys

- talk to infants, especially during caregiving routines—prepare them ahead of time for what is going to happen
- respond to babbling and cooing: play sound games with infants

Level III: Month 6

Area of Development	Physical Environment	Social Environment
PHYSICAL	APPROPRIATE TOYS AND EQUIPMENT	ADULT ROLE

PHYSICAL

Large Muscles

- have control of head
- turn from back to stomach and stomach to back
- may move from place to place by rolling
- may creep or inch forward or backward
- may almost get to sitting while rolling over

Small Muscles

- reach with one arm and can grasp at will
- hold objects and manipulate them
- can grasp with thumb and forefinger but not well yet
- change objects from one hand to the other

APPROPRIATE TOYS AND EQUIPMENT

- need more open space and freedom than before
- need a variety of textures under their body—hard floor, rugs, grass, wooden deck, etc.
- need a variety of interesting objects to move and reach toward

ADULT ROLE

- place objects far enough from them so that infants must work to get them
- provide plenty of room and motivation for moving around as well as manipulating and grasping objects
- provide for interaction with other infants
- keep infants in positions they can get in by themselves

EMOTIONAL/SOCIAL

Feelings and Self-Awareness

- display a wider variety of feelings
- becoming aware of body parts
- see difference between self and rest of the world
- respond to name
- have taste preferences
- may want to start self-feeding

- space large enough for exploration and social interactions will promote relationships

- talk to infants, especially during caregiving; place special emphasis on naming body parts
- call children by name
- encourage children to take over self-help skills as they are able

Social

- may respond with fear to strangers
- call to primary caregiver for help
- enjoy games with people (peek-a-boo)

- provide for attachment needs and let children use primary caregiver to provide security in presence of stranger
- play games like peek-a-boo

INTELLECTUAL

- visually alert a good part of waking hours
- recognize familiar objects
- can see and reach for objects they want
- can pick up and manipulate objects
- look for dropped objects
- can use several senses at once
- memory is developing

- infants continue to enjoy all the toys and objects listed in Level II under Intellectual Development
- can now appreciate a wider variety of objects at once
- place objects around a safe area so that infants have reason to move around and reach for them

- allow children freedom to explore
- change or rearrange objects in the environment periodically
- provide for interaction with other infants

LANGUAGE

- respond to different voice tones and inflections
- more control over sounds produced
- use a variety of sounds to express feelings
- imitate tones and inflections

- cloth or cardboard books

- respond to children's communication
- talk to children, especially during caregiving routines
- during play times, comment on what children are doing if appropriate (be careful not to interrupt so the words get in the way of the experience)

Level IV: Month 9

Area of Development

PHYSICAL

Large Muscles

- crawl
- may crawl stiff legged
- may crawl while holding object in hand
- pull to stand on furniture
- may stand alone
- may or may not be able to get back down from standing
- get into sitting position
- may move along holding onto furniture

Small Muscles

- can pick up small objects easily with thumb and forefinger
- explore and manipulate with forefinger
- growing in eye-hand coordination

EMOTIONAL/SOCIAL

Feelings and Self-Awareness

- clearly attached to primary caregiver and may fear separation
- reject things they don't want

Social

- feed selves biscuit
- drink from cup holding handle
- usually a willing performer if asked
- becoming sensitive to and interested in the moods and activities of others
- tease
- anticipate events

Physical Environment

APPROPRIATE TOYS AND EQUIPMENT

- infants need more room to explore—a greater variety of objects, textures, experiences, toys
- plastic or wooden cars and trucks, play or real telephones, blocks, dolls, balls of different sizes, nesting toys
- pillows and low platforms (or steps) can be added to the environment to provide a variety of levels for children to explore
- rails or low furniture needed for standing or cruising

- need the tools for self-help skills, such as cup and spoon

Social Environment

ADULT ROLE

- watch for children who stand up but can't sit back down; help when they indicate they are stuck
- be sensible about helping children who get stuck: don't rescue; but promote problem solving
- provide open spaces and safe climbing opportunities
- allow children to explore with little adult interference
- encourage infants to use manipulative skills, such as pulling off socks, opening doors, taking apart nesting toys, etc.

- provide enough of a schedule for infants to come to anticipate the sequence of events
- allow opportunities for uninterrupted concentration
- encourage problem solving
- don't help until they're really stuck
- allow them to discover the consequences of their behavior whenever it is safe to do so

INTELLECTUAL

- remember games and toys from previous days
- anticipate people's return
- can concentrate and not get interrupted
- pull cover off toy they have seen hidden
- enjoy taking things out of container and putting them back
- solve simple manipulative problems
- interested in discovering the consequences of their behavior

- the objects and toys listed under Physical Development are also appropriate for promoting intellectual development
- also provide interesting and safe objects from the adult world: pots, pans, wooden spoons, and junk such as discarded boxes, both big and little (infants appreciate real objects as much as toys)

- provide the opportunity for infants to become self-assertive
- help children interpret the effect of their actions on others
- give plenty of opportunities for children to develop self-help skills
- help children express separation fears, accept them, and help them deal with them
- provide for attachment to primary caregiver
- provide good models for children (adults who express honest feelings, neither minimized nor exaggerated)

LANGUAGE

- pay attention to conversations
- may respond to words other than own name
- may carry out simple commands
- use words such as "mama" and "dada"
- have intonation
- may repeat a sequence of sounds
- yell

- appreciate a greater variety of picture books

- include infants in conversations
- don't talk about them if they're present unless you include them (especially important at this stage)
- promote interactions with other infants
- respond to infants' sounds
- encourage use of words
- ask questions infants can respond to

Level V: Year 1

Area of Development	**Physical Environment**	**Social Environment**
PHYSICAL	APPROPRIATE TOYS AND EQUIPMENT	ADULT ROLE
Large Muscles	• need lots of space both indoors and outdoors to enjoy crawling and practice walking	• provide for safety and plenty of movement
• can stand without holding on	• need lots of objects to manipulate, explore, experiment with, and carry around	• don't push children to walk: allow them to decide when they are finished with crawling
• may walk but probably prefer to crawl		
• climb up and down stairs		
• may climb out of crib		
Small Muscles		
• may use both hands at the same time for different things		
• use thumb well		
• show preference for one hand		
• may undress self or untie shoes		
EMOTIONAL/SOCIAL		
Feelings and Self-Awareness		
• show wide variety of emotions and respond to those of others	• provide an environment that encourages and facilitates self-help skills	• provide for self-help skills
• fear strangers and new places		• acknowledge infants' possessions and help protect them
• show affection		• give approval
• show moods and preferences		• set reasonable limits
• may know difference between their possessions and others'		• accept uncooperative behavior as a sign of self-assertion
		• give choices
		• give and return affection
		• accept and help infants deal with fears and frustrations
Social		
• feed self	• provide needed tools and equipment for self-help skills	• encourage self-help skills
• help dress self		
• obey commands		
• seek approval but are not always cooperative		

INTELLECTUAL

- good at finding hidden objects
- increased memory
- solve problems
- use trial and error method effectively
- explore new approaches to problems
- think about actions before doing them (sometimes)
- imitate people who are not present

LANGUAGE

- know words stand for objects
- begin to sound like they speak the language of their parents (use same sounds and intonations)
- use gestures to express self
- may say two to eight words

- children at this level enjoy most of the toys and household objects already mentioned but use them in more sophisticated ways
- also enjoy large beads to string, large Lego blocks, small building blocks, stacking cones, wooden snap trains, etc.

- toy telephones, dolls, and books promote language development at this level
- any toy can become a reason to talk as children play
- music promotes language development

- promote active problem solving
- provide for interaction with other children
- set up environment so children see new and more complex ways to use toys and equipment

- promote interaction among children; children learn to talk from adults, but they practice as they play with other children
- give simple instructions
- play games with children
- sing songs and do finger plays
- encourage expression of feelings
- fill in missing words and expand utterance for children when responding

Level VI: Month 18

Area of Development	Physical Environment	Social Environment
PHYSICAL	**APPROPRIATE TOYS AND EQUIPMENT**	**ADULT ROLE**
Large Muscles		• keep the environment full and interesting; may need to change arrangement periodically and introduce new toys
• walk fast and well	• need room to walk and run	
• fall seldom	• enjoy taking walks if adult isn't too goal oriented	• promote interactions among children
• run, but awkwardly		
• walk up stairs holding a hand	• enjoy plenty of sensory experiences such as water play and sand	• allow for enough physical exercise
Small Muscles		
• can use crayon to scribble as well as imitate marks		
• better control at self-feeding		
EMOTIONAL/SOCIAL		
• imitate adults in dramatic play	• provide the tools for dramatic play such as dress-up clothes, dolls, housekeeping equipment, dishes, etc.	• allow children to help as they are able
• interested in helping with chores		• set limits and gently but firmly enforce them
• interested in dressing process; can undress to some extent		• encourage self-help skills
• may be beginning to get some bladder and bowel control		• help children with their interaction and talk them through aggressive situations
INTELLECTUAL		
• can begin to solve problems in their head	• provide a variety of toys available on low shelves for children to choose: small people, animals, doll houses, containers filled with small objects, measuring cups, spoons, etc.	• provide a number of choices
• rapid increase of language development		• help children work on a problem uninterrupted
• beginning of ability to fantasize and role-play		• encourage use of language
LANGUAGE		
• may use words to gain attention	• books with clear, simple pictures	• provide a variety of experiences and help children put language to them
• can use words to indicate wants		• ask questions and encourage children to ask them too
• may know ten words		• read aloud
• enjoy picture books		

Level VII: Month 24

Area of Development	Physical Environment	Social Environment
PHYSICAL	**APPROPRIATE TOYS AND EQUIPMENT**	**ADULT ROLE**

PHYSICAL

Large Muscles

- run headlong, have trouble stopping and turning
- walk up and down stairs (may hold on)
- throw a ball
- kick a ball forward

APPROPRIATE TOYS AND EQUIPMENT

- low climbers and slides
- large balls, both lightweight and heavier
- low three- and four-wheeled, steerable, well-balanced vehicles both with pedals and without
- swings children can get into and out from themselves
- hills, ramps, low stairs
- space to run
- large, lightweight blocks
- wooden puzzles with two to four large pieces
- pegboards
- stacking toys
- big beads to string
- construction sets (easy to put together)
- play dough
- rhythm instruments
- texture matching games
- feely boxes
- sand and water and toys to play with in them
- dolls to dress and mostly *undress*
- books
- felt pens, crayons, finger paint

ADULT ROLE

- encourage freedom to move in any way they like (within limits, of course)
- allow for plenty of physical and sensory experiences
- encourage children to find new ways to combine and use familiar toys and equipment
- offer choices
- allow loving chases or loving wrestles
- play circle games and sing songs with movements (but not with the whole group as a circle time compulsory activity)
- encourage small muscle use by offering a wide variety of choices
- offer a number of sensory activities
- allow children to use toys and materials in creative ways (within limits, of course)
- allow children to combine materials and toys in unique ways (within limits, of course)
- facilitate problem solving when children get stuck

Small Muscles

- put on some easy clothing
- hold spoon, fork, cup, but may still spill
- can use a paint brush but don't control drips
- can turn the pages of a book

EMOTIONAL/SOCIAL

- may understand personal property concepts ("That's mine—that's Daddy's")
- may tend to hoard

- provide space for personal possessions (cubbies or boxes)
- provide duplicates of favorite toys so sharing

- respect children's need to hold onto their possessions
- model sharing rather than require it

possessions—may resist sharing
• assert independence ("Me do it!")
• take pride in accomplishments
• may say "no" even to things they want

isn't such an issue
• provide plenty of things to do so sharing isn't such an issue
• hand puppets sometimes allow children to express their feelings
• art, music, and dramatic play experiences (listed under Small Muscles) allow children to express their feelings
• large muscle experiences also allow children to express their feelings

• allow children to try things by themselves, even when you know you can do it better or faster
• help them have accomplishments they can take pride in

INTELLECTUAL

• can identify parts of a doll—hair, ears, etc.
• can fit forms into a form board
• can solve many problems on their own
• can work simple puzzles

• provide books, puzzles, records, in addition to toys listed above, that allow choices and provide opportunities for concept development and for problem solving

• provide a variety of choices of materials to use and ways to spend time
• give freedom to use materials in creative ways
• encourage problem solving
• allow exploration

LANGUAGE

• use personal pronouns (I, me, you), but not always correctly
• refer to themselves by name
• use two- and three-word sentences
• may know as many as fifty to two hundred words
• talk about what they are doing

• provide a good variety of books (children can use them carefully now)
• pictures at child's eye level around the room, changed often, give children something to talk about
• allow and set up "happenings," experiences that give children something to talk about
• provide for music experiences

• encourage conversation both between children and between child and adult
• help children speculate ("I wonder what would happen if . . . ")
• go places and talk about what you do and see
• encourage verbalization of feelings and wants
• help children begin to talk out differences instead of relying on hitting, kicking, and other negative physical behaviors

Level VIII: Month 36

Area of Development	Physical Environment	Social Environment
PHYSICAL	**APPROPRIATE TOYS AND EQUIPMENT**	**ADULT ROLE**

PHYSICAL

Large Muscles

- walk, run with control, climb well, throw a ball with aim
- jump in place
- balance on one foot for a second or two
- may pedal tricycle

APPROPRIATE TOYS AND EQUIPMENT

Need all the toys and equipment listed for the twenty-four month old, but larger versions that provide more challenges. The thirty-six month old can begin to use the equipment designed for preschoolers and is probably ready to move on from the toddler program

- may enjoy some large wooden blocks, balance boards, planks, boxes, ladders for building
- unit blocks and accessories to go with them
- construction sets with more and smaller pieces
- small wheeled vehicles to go with blocks
- sensory table
- puzzles
- objects to sort
- flannel board and figures
- small beads to string
- wide range of art materials, including paint, collage, scissors, glue, crayons, feltpens, chalk
- dolls and accessories
- doll house
- extensive dramatic play equipment
- puppets

ADULT ROLE

- offer choices
- can move gross motor equipment outside for this age group and expect them to be slightly more restrained inside
- be careful about encouraging gross motor experiences in boys more than in girls (They should get equal encouragement; indeed, girls should get extra encouragement if they are reluctant.)
- allow plenty of choices
- encourage children to use toys and materials in creative ways
- find ways that older children can become involved in small muscle, manipulative activities without being interrupted by younger children who want to dump rather than build
- keep small parts from younger children, who might put them in their mouths
- encourage fine motor activities in both boys and girls (If boys are less interested, find materials that entice them.)

Small Muscles

- put on shoes but don't tie laces
- put on clothing except for buttoning
- feed self alone and well
- scribbles with more control
- can draw or copy a circle
- can use paintbrush and control drips
- use construction toys imaginatively
- exercise bowel and bladder control

EMOTIONAL/SOCIAL

- may show regard for people or possessions

- provide space for personal possessions
- provide plenty of

- begin to encourage sharing and cooperative play

- play with sustained interest
- play and interact with another child
- willing to use toilet
- can conform to group for short periods

materials to allow children to share feelings and to role-play, such as dramatic play equipment, dress-up clothes, puppets, dolls, small figures, musical instruments and experiences, art materials
- books that children can identify with also help them express their feelings
- have toilet readily available

- help children get involved and stay involved in play activities by preventing interruptions by other children
- can expect children to participate in short active group times, such as circle time
- encourage interaction among children

INTELLECTUAL

- may count to two or three
- may draw face or very simple figure
- can work simple puzzles
- more sophisticated problem solving
- calls self "I" and other people "you"
- knows he is a boy or she is a girl
- know most of the parts of the body
- compare sizes

- the variety of construction materials, manipulative toys, dramatic play, and art materials listed above all contribute to intellectual development
- objects to sort
- plenty of puzzles
- parquetry blocks
- simple games such as lotto
- simple, hands-on science displays and experiments

- provide plenty of choices
- encourage peer interaction during problem solving
- encourage absorption, involvement with materials, activities, and people
- encourage an inquiring attitude
- encourage creative thinking
- encourage children to think about past experiences as well as future ones
- encourage development of number concepts in a natural context
- encourage comparisons of size, weight, etc., of objects in a natural context

LANGUAGE

- use plurals
- converse in short sentences, answer questions, give information, use language to convey simple ideas
- name pictures and label actions
- may have nine hundred word vocabulary
- articulation fairly clear

- setting up the environment for gross motor, fine motor, social, emotional, and intellectual experiences should provide plenty for the children to talk about
- add to variety and complexity of books and pictures provided for two year olds
- music experience
- simple hands-on science displays and experiments

- read books, tell stories, sing songs
- embed language in all experiences
- encourage questioning
- encourage conversation
- encourage speculation
- encourage verbal conflict resolution
- encourage verbalization of feelings
- help children listen to one another
- play language games such as lotto

References

Chapter 1

Garcia, R. *Home Centered Care: Designing a Family Day Care Program. A Guide for Caregivers and Parents.* San Francisco: Children's Council of San Francisco, 1985.

Gerber, M. "Respecting Infants: The Loczy Model of Infant Care." In *Supporting the Growth of Infants, Toddlers and Parents,* edited by E. Jones. Pasadena, Calif.: Pacific Oaks, 1979.

Gerber, M., ed. *Resources for Infant Educarers.* Los Angeles: Resources for Infant Educarers, 1979.

Klass, C. S. "Childrearing Interactions Within Developmental Home- or Center-Based Early Education." *Young Children,* March 1987, pp. 9–13.

Chapter 2

Bower, T. G. R. *Development in Infancy.* San Francisco: W. H. Freeman, 1982.

Gerber, M. "Conflict Resolution with Infants." *Educaring* 4(4), Fall 1983, p. 3.

Gibran, K. *The Prophet.* New York: Alfred A. Knopf, 1965.

Goffin, S. G., with Tull, C. "Problem Solving: Encouraging Active Learning." *Young Children,* March 1985, pp. 28–32.

Levine, S. "Stimulation in Infancy." *Scientific American,* May 1960, pp. 436, 624.

Maslow, A. H. *Toward a Psychology of Being,* 2nd ed. New York: D. van Nostrand, 1968.

Chapter 3

Gerber, M., ed. *Resources for Infant Educarers.* Los Angeles: Resources for Infant Educarers, 1979.

Gerber, M. "Respecting Infants: The Loczy Model of Infant Care." In *Supporting the Growth of Infants, Toddlers and Parents,* edited by E. Jones. Pasadena, Calif.: Pacific Oaks, 1979.

Lindbergh, A. M. *Gift from the Sea*. New York: Pantheon, 1955.

Chapter 4

Feeney, S., and Magarick, M. "Choosing Good Toys for Young Children." *Young Children*, November 1984, pp. 21–25.

Ferguson, J. "Creating Growth-Producing Environments for Infants and Toddlers." In *Supporting the Growth of Infants, Toddlers and Parents*, edited by E. Jones. Pasadena, Calif.: Pacific Oaks, 1979.

Gerber, M. "Good Play Objects for Babies." *Educaring* 7(3), Spring 1986, pp. 4–6.

Hunt, J. McVicker *Intelligence and Experience*. New York: Ronald Press, 1961.

Maslow, A. H. *Toward a Psychology of Being*, 2nd ed. New York: D. van Nostrand, 1968.

Papert, S. *Mindstorms: Children, Computers, and Powerful Ideas*. New York: Basic Books, 1980.

Tardos, A. "Facilitating the Play of Children at Loczy." *Educaring*, Summer 1985, pp. 1–7.

Tonge, M. J. "Hanging Out with Babies at Play: Vignettes from a Participant-Observer." In *Supporting the Growth of Infants, Toddlers and Parents*, edited by E. Jones. Pasadena, Calif.: Pacific Oaks, 1979.

Williams, C. K., and Kamii, C. "How Do Children Learn by Handling Objects?" *Young Children*, November 1986, pp. 23–26.

Chapter 5

Ainsworth, M. D., and Wittig, B. A. "Attachment and Exploratory Behavior of One-Year-Olds in a Strange Situation." In *Determinants of Infant Behavior*, vol. 4, edited by B. M. Foss. New York: Barnes and Noble, 1969.

Bowlby, J. *Attachment and Loss, Vol. I: Attachment*. London: Hogarth, 1969.

Bretherton, I., and Waters, E. *Growing Points of Attachment Theory and Research*. Monographs of the Society for Research in Child Development 50 (1–2, Serial No. 209), 1986.

Caldwell, B. M., Wright, C. M., Honig, A. S., and Tannenbaum, J. "Infant Care and Attachment." *American Journal of Orthopsychiatry* 40, 1970, pp. 397–412.

Farran, D., and Ramey, C. T. "Infant Day Care and Attachment Behaviors Toward Mothers and Teachers." *Child Development* 48, 1977, pp. 1112–1116.

Harlow, H. "The Nature of Love." *American Psychology* 13, 1958, pp. 59–60.

Kagan, J., Kearsley, R. B., and Zelazo, P. R. "The Effects of Infant Day Care on Psychological Development." *Evaluation Quarterly* 1(1), February 1977, pp. 109–142.

Portnoy, F. C., and Simmons, C. H. "Day Care and Attachment." *Child Development* 49, 1978, pp. 239–242.

Rubenstein, J. "Caregiving and Infant Behavior in Day Care and in Homes." *Developmental Psychology* 15(1), 1979, pp. 1–24.

Stern, D. *The Interpersonal World of the Infant*. New York: Basic Books, 1985.

Chapter 6

Bower, T. G. R. *A Primer of Infant Development*. San Francisco: W. H. Freeman, 1977.

Bower, T. G. R. *Development in Infancy*, 2nd ed. San Francisco: W. H. Freeman, 1982.

Samples, R. *The Metaphoric Mind*. Menlo Park, Calif.: Addison-Wesley, 1976.

Chapter 7

Bower, T. G. R. *A Primer of Infant Development*. San Francisco: W. H. Freeman, 1977.

Bower, T. G. R. *Development in Infancy*, 2nd ed. San Francisco: W. H. Freeman, 1982.

Gonzalez-Mena, J. "Gross Motor Development." *Educaring* 3(1), Winter 1981, pp. 1–2.

Pikler, E. "Data on Gross Motor Development of the Infant." *Early Child Development and Care* 1, 1972, pp. 297–310.

Sullivan, M. *Feeling Strong, Feeling Free: Movement Exploration for Young Children*. Washington, D.C.: National Association for the Education of Young Children, 1982.

Tardos, A. "The Pikler/Loczy Philosophy." *Educaring* 7(2), Spring 1986, pp. 1–3.

Chapter 8

Bower, T. G. R. *A Primer of Infant Development*. San Francisco: W. H. Freeman, 1974.

Bower, T. G. R. *Development in Infancy*. San Francisco: W. H. Freeman, 1982.

Kamii, C., and DeVries, R. *Physical Knowledge in Preschool Education*. Englewood Cliffs, N.J.: Prentice-Hall, 1978.

Marzolla, J. *Supertot: Creative Learning Activities for Children One to Three and Sympathetic Advice for Their Parents*. New York: Harper and Row, 1977.

Phillips, J. L., Jr. *The Origins of Intellect: Piaget's Theory*. San Francisco: W. H. Freeman, 1969.

Samples, R. *The Metaphoric Mind*. Menlo Park, Calif.: Addison-Wesley, 1976.

Chapter 9

Bower, T. G. R. *A Primer of Infant Development*. San Francisco: W. H. Freeman, 1974.

Brown, R. *A First Language: The Early Years*. Cambridge, Mass.: Harvard University Press, 1973.

Cazden, C. B., ed. *Language in Early Childhood Education*. Washington, D.C.: National Association for the Education of Young Children, 1981.

Gerber, M. "Babies Understanding Words." *Educaring* 3(4), Fall 1982, pp. 5–6.

Hakuta, K. *Mirror of Language, the Debate on Bilingualism*. New York: Basic Books, 1986.

Heath, S. B. *Ways with Words: Language, Life, and Work in Communities and Classrooms*. Cambridge: Cambridge University Press, 1983.

Chapter 10

Bower, T. G. R. *Development in Infancy*, 2nd ed. San Francisco: W. H. Freeman, 1982.

Erikson, E. *Childhood and Society*, 2nd ed. New York: W. W. Norton, 1963.

Gonzalez-Mena, J. "Toddlers, What to Expect." *Young Children*, November 1986, pp. 47–51.

Honig, A. S. "Compliance, Control and Discipline." *Young Children*, January 1985, pp. 50–58.

Honig, A. S. "Compliance, Control and Discipline." *Young Children*, March 1985, pp. 47–52.

Kelly, C. "Begin with Children." Unpublished manuscript.

Miller, C. S. "Building Self-Control, Discipline for Young Children." *Young Children*, November 1984, pp. 15–19.

Roopnarine, J. L., and Honig, A. S. "The Unpopular Child." *Young Children*, September 1985, p. 61.

Chapter 11

Gerber, M. "Helping Baby Feel Secure, Self-Confident and Relaxed." *Educaring* 1(4), Fall 1980, p. 4.

Gibran, K. *The Prophet*. New York: Alfred A. Knopf, 1965.

Leboyer, F. *Birth Without Violence*. New York: Random House, 1978.

Lee, D. *Valuing the Self*. Englewood Cliffs, N.J.: Prentice-Hall, 1976.

Maslow, A. *Toward a Psychology of Being*, 2nd ed. New York: D. van Nostrand, 1968.

Sternad, R. "Separation." *Educaring* 1(3), Summer 1980, pp. 1–2.

von Franz, M. L. "The Process of Individuation." In *Man and His Symbols*, edited by C. G. Jung and others. New York: Doubleday, 1964.

Chapter 12

Barker, R. C. *Ecological Psychology: Concepts and Methods for Studying the Environment of Human Behavior*. Stanford, Calif.: Stanford University Press, 1968.

Ferguson, J. "Creating Growth-Producing Environments for Infants and Toddlers." In *Supporting the Growth of Infants, Toddlers and Parents*, edited by E. Jones. Pasadena, Calif.: Pacific Oaks, 1979.

Gerber, M., and King, A. "Modifying the Environment to Respond to the Changing Needs of the Child." *Educaring* 6(1), Winter 1985, pp. 1–2.

Greenman, J. "Designing Infant/Toddler Environments." In *Caring for Infants and Toddlers: What Works, What Doesn't*, vol. 2, edited by R. Lurie and R. Neugebauer. Redmond, Wash.: Child Care Information Exchange, 1982.

Jones, E., and Prescott, E. *Dimensions of Teaching-Learning Environments, II. Focus on Day Care*. Pasadena, Calif.: Pacific Oaks, 1978.

Prescott, E. "The Physical Environment —Powerful Regulator of Experience." *Child Care Information Exchange*, Reprint No. 4, C-44.

West, K., ed. *Family Day-to-Day Care*. Mound, Minn.: Quality Child Care, 1979.

Wolf, D. "An Interview with Jim Greenman." *Child Care Information Exchange*, September 1987, p. 19.

Chapter 13

California State Health and Safety Code, Title 22 Child Care Facility Licensing Subchapter 2. Infant Care Centers. Section 101423.1, Infant Care Discipline.

Clark, J. I. *Self Esteem: A Family Affair*. Minneapolis: Winston Press, 1978.

Hall, E. T. *The Hidden Dimension*. New York: Anchor Books, Doubleday, 1966.

Jones, E. *Teaching Adults: An Active Learning Approach*. Washington, D.C.: National Association for the Education of Young Children, 1986.

Lee, D. *Freedom and Culture*. Englewood Cliffs, N.J.: Prentice-Hall, 1959.

Lee, D. *Valuing the Self*. Englewood Cliffs, N.J.: Prentice-Hall, 1976.

Leipzig, J. "Helping Whole Children Grow: Non-Sexist Childrearing for Infants and Toddlers." In *Alike and Different: Exploring Our Humanity with Young Children*, edited by B. Neugebauer. Redmond, Wash.: Exchange Press, 1987.

Pogrebin, L. C. *Growing up Free: Raising Your Kids in the 80's*. New York: McGraw-Hill, 1980.

Samuels, M., and Samuels, N. *Seeing with the Mind's Eye*. New York: Random House, 1975.

Samuels, M., and Samuels, N. *The Well Baby Book*. New York: Summit Books, 1979.

Chapter 14

Bjorklund, G., and Burger, C. "Making Conferences Work for Parents, Teachers and Children." *Young Children*, January 1987, pp. 26–31.

California State Health and Safety Code, Title 22 Child Care Facility Licensing Subchapter 2. Infant Care Centers. Section 101423.1, Infant Care Discipline.

Gonzalez-Mena, J. "Mrs. Godzilla Takes on the Child Development Experts: Perspectives on Parent Education." *Child Care Information Exchange,* September 1987, pp. 25–26.

Gordon, J. "Childcare Professionalism and the Family." *Child Care Information Exchange,* July 1986, pp. 19–23.

Gordon, J. "Separation Anxiety: How to Ask a Family to Leave Your Center." *Child Care Information Exchange,* January 1988, pp. 13–15.

Jones, E., ed. *Supporting the Growth of Infants, Toddlers and Parents.* Pasadena, Calif.: Pacific Oaks, 1979.

Jones, E. *Teaching Adults: An Active Learning Approach.* Washington, D.C.: National Association for the Education of Young Children, 1986.

O'Connell, J. C. "Children of Working Mothers: What the Research Tells Us." *Young Children,* January 1983, pp. 63–70.

Conclusion

Gunzenhauser, N., and Caldwell, B., eds. *Group Care for Young Children.* Johnson and Johnson Baby Products Company pediatric round table series, no. 12, 1986.

Lurie, R., and Neugebauer, R., eds. *Caring for Infants and Toddlers: What Works, What Doesn't,* vol. 2. Redmond, Wash.: Child Care Information Exchange, 1982.

Ruopp, R., Travers, J., Glantz, F., and Coelen, C. *Children at the Center.* Final report of the National Day Care Study, vol. 1. Washington, D.C.: Office of Human Development, Department of Health, Education and Welfare, 1979.

Index

Absorption, in play, 59, 61
Accreditation, of child care
  programs, 208
Acoustics
  of environment, 174
  See also Noise levels
Active adult role, 28–29, 38, 40
"Activity book," 4–5
Additives, food, 166
Adult relations
  caregiver–caregiver, 202–204
  caregiver–caregiver's family, 202
  with children, 44–49
  parent–caregiver, 193–202, 210
  See also Communication;
    Interactions; Parents
Adult role
  active, 28–29, 38, 40
  in infant–toddler education, 28–35,
    38, 40
  in play, 61–69, 190
  receptive, 12–13, 28–29, 38, 40
  See also Adult relations; Facilitation
Aesthetics, in environment, 91, 174
Age appropriateness

for discipline, 187
  of environment, 168–172, 213–229
  in problem-solving approach, 27
Age mix, in play, 64
Aggression, 18–19, 141, 142–143
Allergies, infants and, 166
Alone time, 13, 172, 188
Anger
  attention-getting, 17
  biting expressing, 140
  of caregivers, 17–18, 34, 187, 189,
    195–196
  in discipline, 17–18, 187
  learning to cope with, 34, 150–153
  of parents, 196
  with parents, 195–196
  and separation, 136
Anxieties. *See* Fears
Arrivals, place for, 166
Art experiences, 109
Asking directly, to determine needs, 46
Asking questions, in language
  development, 123
Assertiveness, of caregivers, 189
Attachment, 14, 73–81